A New Introduction to Lega

A New Introduction to Legal Method provides a comprehensive overview of legal science and the scientific character of legal knowledge.

In five chapters, the book analyses and explores: (i) legal methodology in general, the main features of different schools of thought, and the nature of science in general; (ii) American realism, which offers an ideal starting point for law students to reflect on the material they are about to study critically; (iii) rationalism, empiricism, and logical positivism, in particular the work of Karl Popper; (iv) criticisms of essentialism; and (v) the ideological and philosophical background of contemporary liberal interpretation. The inclusion of Dutch, French, and German literature sources makes this law title different from previous writings on legal science.

This textbook is ideal for students of legal method and will be of great interest to those studying legal science, jurisprudence, legal research, and legal skills.

Paul Cliteur is Professor of Jurisprudence at Leiden University, the Netherlands. He is the author of *The Secular Outlook* (2010), *Populist and Islamist Challenges for International Law* (2019, together with Amos N. Guiora), and *Theoterrorism v. Freedom of Speech* (2019).

Afshin Ellian is Professor of Jurisprudence at Leiden University, the Netherlands. He edited *The State of Exception and Militant Democracy in a Time of Terror* (2012), *Counterterrorism after the IS-Caliphate* (2020), and *The Open Society and Its Closed Communities* (2021, together with Paul Cliteur).

A New Introduction to Legal Method

Paul Cliteur & Afshin Ellian

Routledge
Taylor & Francis Group

LONDON AND NEW YORK

Cover image: Photos.com (Getty Images)

First published 2022
by Routledge
4 Park Square, Milton Park, Abingdon, Oxon OX14 4RN

and by Routledge
605 Third Avenue, New York, NY 10158

Routledge is an imprint of the Taylor & Francis Group, an informa business

British Library Cataloguing-in-Publication Data
A catalogue record for this book is available from the British Library

Library of Congress Cataloging-in-Publication Data
A catalog record has been requested for this book

ISBN: 978-1-032-25296-4 (hbk)
ISBN: 978-1-032-25295-7 (pbk)
ISBN: 978-1-003-28257-0 (ebk)

DOI: 10.4324/9781003282570

Typeset in Sabon
by Deanta Global Publishing Services, Chennai, India

Printed and bound by CPI Group (UK) Ltd, Croydon, CR0 4YY

Contents

Introduction

A New Introduction to Legal Method (2022) aims to be a contribution to what the prominent Dutch philosopher Herman Dooyeweerd (1894–1977) called the *Encyclopedia of the Science of the Law*. In the Anglo-Saxon world, this is generally characterized as "jurisprudence." The present volume is a companion volume to *A New Introduction to Jurisprudence* (2019). That book focuses on some normative questions around the foundations of the law, while *A New Introduction to Legal Method* is dedicated to the method of legal reasoning.

At the University of Leiden, where *A New Introduction to Legal Method* is compulsory reading for first-year students, it is used in combination with some classical texts, viz. Bertrand Russell's *The Scientific Outlook* (1931), H.L.A. Hart's *Positivism and the Separation of Law and Morals* (1958), some articles by Ronald Dworkin, and G.J. Wiarda's *Three Types of Legal Reasoning* (1963). It tries to give an idea of the method of science in general and legal science in particular. It defends the idea that legal science is a science, and that the knowledge it tries to acquire is in no way inferior to the knowledge of other sciences.

Chapter 1, "Is legal science a real science?", focuses on the complaint that legal science is *not* "real science." It tries to show that this complaint is unjustified, that it all depends on what you mean by "science." Chapter 1 also explains one of the recent developments in legal science, i.e., the new orientation toward empirical legal studies.

Chapter 2, "American realism," provides an elaborate discussion of American realism as an important movement in legal thought that was highly skeptical about the idea of legal knowledge and the predictability of the judge's behavior. Therefore, it is an ideal starting point for law students to begin reflecting on the material they are about to study critically. This chapter also gives an idea of the main features of the work of prominent American realists such as Oliver Wendell Holmes, Jerome Frank, Karl Llewellyn, and Richard Taylor.

Chapter 3, "Rationalism, empiricism, and logical positivism: a methodological journey through a permanent reversal of doubt and certainty,"

DOI: 10.4324/9781003282570-1

gives an idea of the work of one of the most important twentieth-century philosophers of science: Karl Popper. It also reflects on the rationalist and the empiricist traditions of knowledge acquisition—two traditions in scientific methodology that play an essential role in Popper's work. The work of Descartes, Locke, Berkeley, Hume, and other representatives of the rationalist and empirical traditions is also discussed, as is their contribution to a critical reflection on the foundations of our knowledge.

Chapter 4, "Popper's critique of essentialism and the scientific outlook," critically reflects on the widespread rejection of essentialism as one of the scientific community's original sins. It tries to refute the claim that essentialism is a critical mistake and shows that science and scholarship cannot do without it.

The last chapter, Chapter 5, "Three types of legal interpretation," deals with legal argumentation. It focuses on one of the most successful short accounts of legal argumentation, viz. G.J. Wiarda's *Three Types of Legal Argumentation*. This chapter tries to substantiate the thesis that liberal interpretation has gone too far in contemporary legal practice. We should mind the warnings of Montesquieu that legal certainty and legality are the most precious ideals to which legal scholars and judges can aspire.

Leiden, 26 July 2021
Paul Cliteur and Afshin Ellian

Chapter 1

Is legal science a real science?

> For the rational study of the law the blackletter man may be the man of the present, but the man of the future is the man of statistics and the master of economics.[1]

Every law student has, at one point during their studies, been asked the uncomfortable question by uncles, aunts, or cousins: "Law? Isn't that boring?" Usually, it quickly becomes clear that the questioner believes the study of the law consists of "memorizing legal texts." At first, your response is somewhat awkward, but after some time, fueled by mild irritation at the frequency with which the question is asked, you form a standard answer. Of course the study of the law requires learning some things by heart, but is that not true of every science? Does a chemist not know various formulas? Does a medical professional not know his Latin terminology? Does a historian not know that the French Revolution took place in 1789?

But it does not end; not long after, the law student has to justify himself again. This time, he faces students of other disciplines that he meets in the fraternities, the student houses, and the cafeteria. Here, the objection acquires a more principled character. It is no longer about how "boring" his discipline is, but about how "scientific." Fellow students who practice a "real" science now ask (in a way, a more advanced incarnation of the earlier question, posed by uncles and aunts): "Law? That's not really a science, is it?" One thing seems clear to them: there can be no research in this field. The law is "finished." It is written in the law books. So what is left to discover? It can be read and, if need be, memorized. Or it can be applied, as judges do. But research? Science? No, law has nothing to do with that.

---

1 O.W. Holmes, "The Path of the Law," in: 10 *Harvard Law Review*, 8 (1897), pp. 457–478, p. 469

DOI: 10.4324/9781003282570-2

However, when the uncles and brothers (aunts and sisters would not do such a thing) and the joshing fellow students discover that jurists view the writing of books and articles about their subject as an intellectually demanding activity, they show some surprise. What can a "legal scholar," insofar as it is possible to speak of such a creature, do but *repeat* what has been said before by the legislator or the judge?

A possible answer could be that sometimes a jurist proposes improvements to current law, perhaps comparing various advantages of different provisions within the framework of such an improvement proposal. But, it could be asked, is that the work of a legal scholar? Does a politician not do the same thing? In fact: is this not really the job of the politician, rather than of the legal scholar?

Anyone who has worked with the law for some time comes to see that this far too simple view of the nature of the law and legal science ought to be cast aside. In it, the law is equated with what are believed to be the literal rules found in the written sources, the "black-letter-rules," as the American judge Oliver Wendell Holmes says.[2] The law is much more than that though, and the adaptation and study of the law require more than reporting on these "black-letter rules."[3]

But before we can speak fruitfully about the specific nature of legal science as an autonomous discipline, it is illuminating to first say a few things about science in general. What is science? Van Schilfgaarde writes: "Science is (...) every coherent body of exceptional and justifiable knowledge."[4] About justifiable knowledge he adds that it is a knowing based on evidence. Characteristic of science also are an established method and a body of systematized knowledge. Furthermore, science is associated with knowledge that is *proven*: "Scientific knowledge is proven knowledge."[5] Elements such as objectivity, replicability, falsifiability, consensus, experiment, and predictability also regularly feature in descriptions of science.

Before we discuss the scientific nature of legal science, we will first take a "phenomenological tour" of some characteristics of science. We will not go so far as to attempt a definition of science, but we will, in a random order,

---

2 See also by him: Oliver Wendell Holmes, *The Essential Holmes. Selections from Letters, Speeches, Judicial Opinions, and Other Writings of Oliver Wendell Holmes, Jr.*, edited and with an introduction by Richard A. Posner, Chicago, London: The University of Chicago Press 1992 and Oliver Wendell Holmes, *Collected Legal Papers*, New York: Peter Smith 1952 (1920).

3 See on this: N.E. Simmonds, *The Decline of Juridical Reason. Doctrine and Theory in the Legal Order*, Manchester: Manchester University Press 1984 and N.E. Simmonds, "Law as a Rational Science," in: *Archiv für Rechts- und Sozialphilosophie*, 66 (1980), pp. 535–556.

4 P. van Schilfgaarde, *Klein wijsgerig woordenboek*, Wassenaar: Servire, 1968, p. 175.

5 A.F. Chalmers, *Wat heet wetenschap: Over aard en status van de wetenschap en haar methoden*, fourth edition, Meppel, Amsterdam: Boom, 1987, p. 187.

discuss a number of features with which science is commonly associated. Then we will judge whether, and in what sense, legal science can be said to possess the characteristic in question. From this, a picture of the work of legal science as an idiosyncratic but nevertheless scientific approach will naturally arise. (That is to say, it is not an overextension to qualify the work of the legal scholar as such.)

The first characteristic of science: consensus on a few basic facts

Let us begin with something with which science, at least in the popular imagination, is commonly associated: established, unassailable knowledge on a subject. Can legal science boast of facts about which there is more or less universal consensus?

The Dutch historian H.W. von der Dunk (1928–2018) offers some examples of things that are not disputed by any historian.[6] Historians, he says, can disagree on any number of issues, but no one disputes that Hannibal defeated the Roman legions in the third century BCE, or that there were iconoclastic riots in Flanders in 1566. New research can reopen debate on a previously established historical fact, of course—perhaps Van der Lubbe set fire to the Reichstag after all!—but even when that happens, a new consensus about the new historical fact forms fairly quickly. One may wonder why that is. Probably, it has something to do with the fact that (1) the sources are relatively easy to verify and (2) there is a consensus on which arguments are relevant in supporting the new fact. In the case of the first: certain new documents from archives can constitute convincing proof to the practitioners of the historical sciences. These are empirically provable facts. Also—and this would constitute a second point, one closely related to the first—there is broad consensus on which arguments in support of a certain historical claim are valid. No historian will be able to ignore a newly discovered letter by Spinoza—once its authenticity has been verified—as an irrelevant datum.

But what of legal science? Do we have unassailable certainties in the order of "The Battle of Nieuwpoort took place in 1600"? Of course, in the popular imagination, legal science might be thought to consist of *nothing but* certainties. Not only do contracts always have to be "legally airtight," but legal science itself is also always associated with certainty, stability, irrefutability, and not being open to argument. Perhaps, however, this is an image that legal science itself propagates, but that, all things considered, does have

---

6 H.W. von der Dunk, "Geschiedenis en wetenschap," in: P.B. Cliteur, H.D. Papma, and R.T.P. Wiche, eds., *Overtuigend bewijs. Over het wetenschappelijke van de niet-exacte wetenschappen*, Meppel, Amsterdam: Boom 1994, pp. 38–65.

some strongly ideological features.[7] What facts has legal science produced that approach the unassailability of the previously mentioned "Battle of Nieuwpoort"? Many seemingly obvious answers turn out, upon closer inspection, not to suffice. For instance, the claim that the law is to be found in legal statutes is not entirely undisputed, as we will see in Chapter 5 of this book. Sometimes, the law is a dead letter. The thesis that the law is always geared toward justice, as natural law proponents argue, is also disputed, primarily by legal positivists[8]—who, as we will see, claim to be able to construct a value-neutral concept of the law—but also by the classical and modern Marxists of the Critical Legal Studies movement (CLS), who believe that the law always protects the interests of a particular social class, or is at least politically determined.[9] Claims that judges ought to follow the letter of the law or keep out of politics are also contested.

So it turns out that, at least in areas where the popular conception of legal science assumes certainty and consensus, among legal scholars themselves, this consensus does not exist. Still, within legal science, statements can be made that approach a "Battle of Nieuwpoort" status. The remarkable thing is that these are statements about the nature of the law itself, so fairly "philosophical" claims. For instance, that legal rules have a general nature, or that they should not, in principle, have retroactive force. Similarly, the claim that the law must be knowable by the public (no "Draconian laws" that were posted so high that no one could read them) is also generally accepted. It is legal scholars like Anselm von Feuerbach, Beccaria, the authors of the Federalist Papers (Hamilton, Madison, and Jay),[10] and others who for-

---

7 See on this: Thurman W. Arnold, *The Symbols of Government*, New Haven: Yale University Press 1935; Thurman W. Arnold, "Institute Priests and Yale Observers," in: *University of Pennsylvania Law Review*, 84 (1936), pp. 811–824; Neil Duxbury, "Some Radicalism about Realism? Thurman Arnold and the Politics of Modern Jurisprudence," in: *Oxford Journal of Legal Studies*, 10 (1990), pp. 11–41 and Neil Duxbury, *Patterns of American Jurisprudence*, Oxford: Clarendon Press 1995, pp. 179–180.

8 Such as: H.L.A. Hart, "Positivism and the Separation of Law and Moral," in: *Harvard Law Review*, 71 (1958), cited here in: H.L.A. Hart, ed., *Essays in Jurisprudence and Philosophy*, Oxford: Clarendon Press 1983, pp. 49–87; H.L.A. Hart, "Lon L. Fuller: The Morality of Law," in: *Harvard Law Review*, 78 (1965), pp. 1281–1296, cited here in: Hart, *Essays in Jurisprudence and Philosophy*, pp. 343–365.

9 See for a compiled work by CLS proponents themselves: David Kairys, ed., *The Politics of Law. A Progressive Critique*, New York: Pantheon Books 1990 (1982). About CLS: Andrew Altman, *Critical Legal Studies. A Liberal Critique*, Princeton, NJ: Princeton University Press, 1990; Joseph William Singer, "The Player and the Cards: Nihilism and Legal Theory," in: *Yale Law Journal*, 94 (1984), pp. 1–70; Mark Kelman, *A Guide to Critical Legal Studies*, Cambridge, MA, London: Harvard University Press, 1987. An engagingly written critique is: Louis B. Schwartz, "With Gun and Camera Through Darkest CLS-Land," in: *Stanford Law Review*, 36 (1984), pp. 423–464.

10 See: James Madison, Alexander Hamilton, and John Jay, *Federalist Papers*, Isaac Kramnick, ed., Harmondsworth: Penguin Books 1987, No. 78.

mulated a number of important principles in this area. The principle that law should not have retroactive power is not originally the product of the legislator or the judge, but of the legal scholar. At least, by means of an abstract analysis of the concept of "law," legal scientists have attempted to elucidate how the nature of law resists such a practice.[11] The American legal philosopher Lon Fuller (1902–1978) delineated the following eight features that are prerequisites of law: (1) justice must take the shape of general rules, not of decisions in individual cases; (2) people must be able to acquaint themselves with the content of the rules; (3) laws must only apply to future cases; (4) legal rules must be intelligible; (5) legal rules may not contradict one another; (6) legal rules must not make requirements that people are unable to meet; (7) legal rules must not change too often; (8) the rules must be imposed by the government.[12]

Who will deny that these are central requirements that must be met in order to say that we are speaking of law? That does not mean, incidentally, that all further conclusions Fuller attached to this list are blindly accepted. On the contrary: in legal science literature, great discussion has arisen on the following questions.

First of all: are Fuller's eight prerequisites also norms that the legislator ought to respect on penalty of nullity? In other words: is it the case that if a legislator does not abide by these norms, he is not producing law? Fuller answered this question in the affirmative. In so doing, he subscribed to an old natural law tradition in legal science in which the violation of certain normative requirements the law must adhere to produces "non-law" ("*lex iniusta non est lex*").

Others, however, have dismissed such natural law terminology as rhetorical frippery. Though it may be *bad law* the legislator is producing, it *is* law. It is enforced by judges. The defendant may complain that there is something wrong with the law, but he will still end up on the gallows. The natural law proponent with the noose around his neck is asked: will you still say now that *it is not law* on the basis of which you are about to hang?[13]

It is a confusing discussion. Under its surface, of course, lies the question of what ought to be viewed as characteristic of law. Does one see the law as a system of coercion whose main identifying feature is that it can be upheld by the strong arm? In that case, there is much to be said for what the *critic*

---

11 See on this: Volker Krey, *Keine Strafe ohne Gesetz. Einführung in die Dogmengeschichte des Satzes "nullum crimen, nulla poena sine lege,"* Berlin, New York: Walter de Gruyter 1983.

12 See also: Lon L. Fuller, *The Morality of Law*, New Haven, London: Yale University Press 1978 (1964), p. 33ff. See also: Chapter 1 of Paul Cliteur and Afshin Ellian, *A New Introduction to Jurisprudence*, London, New York: Routledge 2019, pp. 1–36.

13 Austin cited in: H.L.A. Hart, "Positivism and the Separation of Law and Morals," cited here in: Hart, *Essays in Jurisprudence and Philosophy*, pp. 49–87, p. 73.

of natural law thinking puts forward. It is a different matter for those who consider the ethical content of the law, the question of whether the law is just, to be its most important feature. In this case, the condemned will answer: "It is not the *law* that is the basis for my conviction, but the blatant *capitulation of the law* to brute power."

Another issue that garnered a great deal of attention is the question of what to *call* the body of principles that Fuller considers prerequisites to the law. Fuller himself spoke of a "*morality of law.*"

This exposed him to criticism from the British legal philosopher H.L.A. Hart (1907–1992), who believed the principles to be nothing more than effectiveness criteria, not a "morality" of law. If one were to call Fuller's principles moral principles, one might as well call the rules a poisoner follows for the running of a smooth mixing process the morality of her trade. "The morality of poisoning"; the thought alone![14]

Here too, we see that this was not a terribly fruitful discussion, in which "morality" as it was understood by both sides was not well defined. If we are talking about a modern conception of morality, then there is indeed something to be said for not calling Fuller's principles *moral* principles. However, in the ancient conception of morality, the idea of "human excellence" is central, as the philosopher Richard Taylor (1919–2003) expounded in an interesting book on modern and ancient conceptions of morality.[15] In the ancient conception, morality is related to the optimal state of a particular person, process, and so on. And who would deny that a legal system in which Fuller's principles are respected constitutes law in its optimal state?

A third and final controversy with regard to Fuller's principles is whether they are a sufficient or a necessary precondition for good law.

This brings us to the heart of the discussion on constitutionalism, democracy, and human rights. In a country where Fuller's principles are not violated, is terror imaginable? The English are more optimistic on this point than the Americans. The Americans believe that, in addition to the rule of law (the body of Fuller's principles could be described as "the rule of law"), "constitutionalism" (often referred to as the *Rechtsstaat* in Europe) also needs to be realized as an ideal.[16] The latter is about formulating a number

---

14 H.L.A. Hart, "Lon L. Fuller: The Morality of Law," pp. 1281–1296, cited here in: Hart, *Essays in Jurisprudence and Philosophy*, pp. 343–365, p. 350.

15 Richard Taylor, *Ethics, Faith, and Reason*, Englewood Cliffs, NJ: Prentice-Hall, Inc. 1985. See more extensively on this matter: P.B. Cliteur, "Fuller's Faith," in: Willem J. Witteveen and Wibren van der Burg, eds., *Rediscovering Fuller. Essays on Implicit Law and Institutional Design*, Amsterdam: Amsterdam University Press 1999, pp. 100–124.

16 See on the relationship between the terms "constitutionalism," "rule of law," and "morality of law": C.M. Zoethout, *Constitutionalisme. Een vergelijkend onderzoek naar het beperken van overheidsmacht door het recht*, Arnhem: Gouda Quint 1995, pp. 218–223; Scott Gordon, *Controlling the State. Constitutionalism from Ancient Athens to Today*,

of values, usually in the form of fundamental rights or human rights, that the state is not allowed to violate under any circumstances.

When we are talking about established values or facts of legal science, it seems that the least controversy exists about the rule of law and constitutionalism. Different legal scholars will delineate these concepts somewhat differently, but a great deal of consensus does exist on them, as well as on the desirability of realizing them in practice. These are central organizing principles in Western legal science.[17]

Historically, this is an extraordinary state of affairs. It is a unique achievement that, for such a long time, there has been a broad consensus about such fundamental organizing principles of Western constitutional law, and with it, also about the legal science that is focused on a coherent presentation and analysis of Western constitutional law.

The second characteristic of science: the experiment

Besides a consensus about some basic facts as a hallmark of science, another characteristic of science that is often identified is the importance of the experiment. What makes a claim scientific? That it can be "tested." An experiment can be run in which the validity (or invalidity) of the claim can be established. Bertrand Russell (1872–1970) writes:

> Science is the attempt to discover, by means of observation, and reasoning based upon it, first particular facts about the world, and then laws connecting facts with one another and (in fortunate cases) making it possible to predict occurrences.[18]

The word "experiment" comes from the Latin *experiri* (= to test, to try, to prove, to experience). It represents a conscious and active intervention in the state of things in order to produce measurable results. Preferably, an experiment is set up in such a way that it is repeatable, as well as that the experimenter has control over the conditions under which the experiment is run. Most experiments involve the creation of artificial situations that do not occur in nature.[19]

Cambridge, MA, London, Harvard University Press 1999; and Chapter 2 and 3 of Paul Cliteur and Afshin Ellian, *A New Introduction to Jurisprudence*.

17 See on the consensus in this area: Francis Fukuyama, "The End of History?" in: *The National Interest*, 16 (Summer 1989), pp. 3–18, also in: Paul Schumaker, Dwight C. Kiel, and Thomas W. Heilke, eds., *Ideological Voices. An Anthology in Modern Political Ideas*, New York: The McGraw-Hill Companies, Inc. 1997, pp. 409–417; Francis Fukuyama, *The End of History and the Last Man*, New York: The Free Press/Macmillan 1992.

18 Bertrand Russell, *Religion and Science*, London, New York, Toronto: Oxford University Press, 1935, p. 8.

19 D.W. Raven, "Experiment," in: Harry Willemsen, ed., *Woordenboek Filosofie*, Assen, Maastricht: Van Gorcum 1992, p. 145.

Von der Dunk speaks of the fact that the experiment is absent from the study of history. And indeed, the option of running experiments is always viewed as characteristic of the natural sciences, as opposed to the humanities. But what about legal science? In a certain sense, legal science is also unable to experiment the way the natural sciences are. A claim, a newly devised principle, a certain solution to a legal problem cannot be "tested." At least not in the sense that legal science does not fabricate a simulation of reality in which the claim, principle, or solution can be made to function. There are several reasons for this. First, ethics. We are allowed, according to Francis Bacon, to rake nature across the coals, and René Descartes believed us free to do the same with animals.[20] The latter faces severe criticism these days (see chapter 9 on this), and the objections raised in that case are even stronger when experiments are done on people.

We do not know experiments *in this direct sense* in legal science. Still, in another, broader sense, there is some experimentation in legal science as well. Not on the human body, but we do experiment on the organization of society.[21] The American President Franklin D. Roosevelt (1882–1945) once said, while presenting a policy program that was supposed to rescue the American economy, that he was not relying on one theory or another. He stated openly that he would try different things until he found a solution to the country's problems: "The country demands bold, persistent experimentation. It is common sense to take a method and try it: if it fails, admit it frankly and try another."[22] This experimental attitude is not only characteristic of American[23] and British *politics*, but also of *legal thought* in the Anglo-Saxon world. And as Anglo-Saxon legal thought gains influence on the European continent, the "experimentalist" attitude also acquires a greater foothold there. In summarizing the Anglo-Saxon approach to the law, one could say: justice is not primarily to be found in major codifications but in the practice of jurisprudence.[24] This is not just true of private law, but also of public law. The American founding fathers stressed repeatedly that they were not, as the French revolutionaries did, inventing a constitution out of whole cloth, based on the contract constructions and philosophy of

20 See on this: Thomas Henry Huxley, "Science and Culture" (1880), in: Thomas Henry Huxley, ed., *Science and Culture and Other Essays*, London: Macmillan 1882, pp. 1–23.

21 As Mill argues in: J.S. Mill, *On Liberty*, Harmondsworth: Penguin Books 1977 (1859).

22 Cited in: Daniel Boorstin, *The Genius of American Politics*, Chicago, London: The University of Chicago Press 1953, p. 21.

23 The philosopher who is representative of the American mindset when it comes to this is John Dewey. On his "experimentalism," see: Steven C. Rockefeller, *John Dewey. Religious Faith and Democratic Humanism*, New York: Columbia University Press 1991, pp. 440–444.

24 René David, *Les grands systèmes de droit contemporaines*, 11e dr., Paris: Dalloz 1982, p. 383.

Enlightenment philosophers, but that it was experience that guided them.[25] Hence, we encounter repeated references to the old republics in Greece and especially the Roman Republic, and again and again, we see that lessons are learned from the mistakes and successes of past political experiments.[26]

This is also important for the *methodology* of legal science, which brings us to our real subject. In the Anglo-Saxon methodology, as it is expressed particularly in the English common law system, the legal system is viewed as one big experiment.[27] It functions according to Popperian methodology, which means that through trial and error, step by step, certain modifications are made.[28] Small changes are made, the result is examined, and only if the result is satisfactory is the chosen path resumed.

In that sense, it is possible to say that English law involves *constant* experimentation. Granted, these are not experiments in which an artificial replica of nature is constructed, but the situation does exhibit enough other features of the experiment to be classified as such. The experiment is run when the opportunity for it arises naturally, or rather without conscious human manipulation. After all, a judge has to wait for a case to be brought to him. When that happens, everything else can unfold normally, according to the usual guidelines for scientific experiments. This is even partly true of testing the experiment results.

Of course, there is a major difference with the natural sciences (and also with the study of history, in as far as establishing historical facts is concerned) in that although the experiment can be run, we are on far less steady ground in assessing whether the experiment was successful. In doing so, two criteria traditionally compete for primacy, criteria to which the names Kant (1724–1804) and Bentham (1748–1832) are connected. *Kantian* is putting *justice* first. One legal concept is better than another when it leads to more

---

25 On the difference between the French and the American Revolution, see: Irving Kristol, "The American Revolution as a Successful Revolution," in: *Reflections of a Neoconservative*, New York: Basic Books, Inc. 1983, pp. 78–95.

26 See: P.B. Cliteur, "De Federalist Papers," in: P.B. Cliteur, A.A.M. Kinneging, and G.A. van der List, eds., *Filosofen van het klassiek liberalisme*, Kampen: Kok/Agora 1993, pp. 113–135; Bernard Bailyn, *The Ideological Origins of the American Revolution*, enlarged edition, Cambridge, MA, London: The Belknap Press of Harvard University Press 1992.

27 Beautifully described by: Gerald J., Postema, *Bentham and the Common Law Tradition*, Oxford: Clarendon Press 1989 (1986) and P.S. Atiyah and R.S. Summers, *Form and Substance in Anglo-American Law, A Comparative Study of Legal Reasoning, Legal Theory, and Legal Institutions*, Oxford: Clarendon Press 1991 (1987).

28 Incidentally not just a peculiarity of the Popperian approach but also of pragmatism. See on this a discussion between Dworkin and Rorty: Ronald Dworkin, "Pragmatism, Right Answers, and True Banality," in: Michael Brint and William Weaver, eds., *Pragmatism in Law & Society*, Boulder, San Francisco, Oxford: Westview Press 1991, pp. 359–389; Richard Rorty, "The Banality of Pragmatism and the Poetry of Justice," in: Michael Brint and William Weaver, eds., *Pragmatism in Law & Society*, Boulder, San Francisco, Oxford: Westview Press 1991, pp. 89–99.

just results. *Bentham* approaches the question from the perspective of *utility*. When one criterion leads to more *useful* results than the other, it is better.

Both criteria are used in legal science, not only in assessing whether one solution is "better" than another but even in such general evaluations as "is one system better than the other?" In all these cases, the utility perspective and the justice perspective compete.

All things considered, it can be said that if we consider the experiment to be an important criterion in order to call something "scientific," then legal science does not have to fall short.

The third characteristic of science: accumulation of knowledge

The latter brings us to an interesting question: does legal science feature accumulation of knowledge, the third hallmark of science? "Real" science makes progress; pseudoscience goes around in circles.[29] In real science, later generations of scientists can see further because, in Bernard of Chartres' († *c*. 1130) famous words, they are dwarves standing on the shoulders of giants.[30] Oftentimes, a lack of progress and accumulation of knowledge was also an important argument to question the scientific rigor of a certain discipline. Critics of philosophy (among whom some philosophers themselves) have triumphantly remarked that philosophy cannot be a real science. After all, not once has philosophy been able to solve a single one of its problems. Those areas of philosophy that *do* seem to admit of some progress, such as logic, have quickly split off from the mother science to set out their own paths. For the study of history, too, progress (or the lack of it) seems a thorny problem. Is Peter Gay (1923–2015) further ahead than Thucydides (*c*. 460–400)? When it comes to modern narrativism, one can wonder if Herodotus (*c*. 485–425) was not actually just as good a storyteller as Barbara Tuchman (1912–1989).

What about legal science? Has legal science progressed since the time of Hugo de Groot (1583–1645)? The notion of progress in science, like that of progress in general, is not very popular these days. It is even rather chic to speak of it with some disdain. Progress was an uncritical and naïve belief of nineteenth-century thinkers. It was the belief of—staying within legal science circles—Henry Sumner Maine (1822–1888), the first professor of "Jurisprudence" at Oxford, who believed that the "movement from

---

29 Peter Ziegler, "A General Theory of Law as a Paradigm for Legal Research," in: *Modern Law Review*, 51 (1988), pp. 569–592, p. 571.
30 Anne Fremantle, *The Age of Belief, The Medieval Philosophers*, New York: New American Library 1954, p. ix.

progressive societies" would be one from "status" to "contract," from despotism to freedom, from communal property to private property. Maine
became famous for his book *Ancient Law* (1861). He claimed that in early
societies, the law gradually crystallized, starting as decisions, then growing
into habits, and finally becoming the first codifications, of which the Greek
laws of Solon, the Hindu Laws of Manu, and the Roman Law of the Twelve
Tables are examples. Static societies would not move far beyond this stage,
but "progressive" societies, such as the Roman and the English, would.
With the famous line "status to contract," he meant that the first legal relationships between people were determined by their role within the family
and the tribe, but that the individual gradually freed himself from these
bindings and could then decide his own legal rights by means of contracts.[31]

When we read the stories of Maine and other legal scholars from previous centuries, we are struck by their considerable self-confidence. Equally
famous for this is William Blackstone (1723–1780), whose self-congratula-
tory attitude with regard to the English law of his time, as expounded in his
Commentaries on the Laws of England (1765–1769),[32] evoked Bentham's
ire.[33] Blackstone greatly admired English law: not so much the law made by
the legislator, but the common law, the law that, partly developed by doctrine, lives in the traditions and habits that arise from everyday practice in
court decisions. Like Edward Coke (1552–1634) in the seventeenth century,
he approached this law with a near-religious dedication.[34] He was irked
by the lack of interest in the law among his contemporaries. "It has been
the peculiar lot of our admirable system of laws, to be neglected, and even
unknown, by all but one practical profession; though built upon the sound-
est foundations, and approved by the experience of ages."[35]

---

31 Henry Sumner Maine, *Ancient Law. (1861) Its Connection with the Early History of Society, and Its Relation to Modern Ideas*, Foreword by Lawrence Rosen, Tucson: University
of Arizona Press 1986 and Henry Sumner Maine, *Popular Government*, Indianapolis: Liberty Classics 1976 (1885). See on him: Stephen G. Utz, "Maine's *Ancient Law* and Legal
Theory," in: *Connecticut Law Review*, 16 (1984), pp. 821–852.

32 For a modern selection, see: William Blackstone, *The Sovereignty of the Law. Selections
from Blackstone's Commentaries on the Laws of England*, edited with an introduction by
Gareth Jones, London, Basingstoke: Macmillan 1973.

33 See: Ernest Barker, "Blackstone on the British Constitution," in: *Essays on Govern-
ment*, Oxford: Clarendon Press 1965 (1945), pp. 120–154; William Seagle, "Sir William
Blackstone: Law and Popularization," in: William Seagle, ed., *Men of Law*, New York:
Macmillan 1947, pp. 188–212; John W. Cairns, "Blackstone, An English Institutist: Legal
Literature and the Rise of the Nation State," in: *Oxford Journal of Legal Studies*, 4 (1984),
pp. 318–360 and Daniel J. Boorstin, *The Mysterious Science of the Law. An Essay on
Blackstone's Commentaries. With a new Foreword*, Chicago, London: The University of
Chicago Press 1996 (1941).

34 Catherine Drinker Bowen, *The Lion under the Throne: The Life and Times of Sir Edward
Coke*, Boston: Little, Brown and Company 1984 (1956).

35 Blackstone, *The Sovereignty of Law*, p. 3.

This is an interesting passage for us. Blackstone observes progress: the law of his time is better than it was. To this, legal science, of which he is a practitioner, makes a significant contribution. The scientist does not only *describe* the law, but he permeates it, systematizes it, and presents it in a coherent fashion, such that he improves the legal system. As such, much of the common law's progress is due to the doctrine.

Here too, we have identified another important difference between legal science and other sciences: it is a highly practical affair. The natural scientist does not improve nature but comes to know it. The geologist does not alter the Earth's crust but researches it. The legal scholar, however, modifies and even creates the object of his study. As such, the legal scholar makes an important contribution to the perfecting of his research subject. Blackstone's love of the law of his time is therefore largely love of the product of his own creation. (At least, partly.) He said:

> For I think it an undeniable position that a competent knowledge of the laws of that society, in which we live, is the proper accomplishment of every gentleman and scholar; and highly useful, I had almost said essential, part of liberal and polite education. And in this I am warranted by the example of ancient Rome; where as Cicero informs us, the very boys were obliged to learn the twelve tables by heart, as a *carmen necessarium* or indispensable lesson, to imprint on their tender minds an early knowledge of the laws and constitution of their country.[36]

This view would be considered theatrical these days. This kind of grandiosity is practically begging for postmodern deconstruction.[37] We have learned the ways of the world, at least we think we have. We say—loosely following Ranke—that all legal systems are equal in God's eyes. But do we really believe it? Do we really believe that, for instance, a constitutional system with a written constitution, securely established fundamental rights, an independent judiciary, and separation and balance of powers, a system that is constantly pruned, improved, tested for consistency, and further developed by a specially trained legal class (staying in the spirit of Blackstone), is truly equal to a primitive legal system?

Gradually, we are moving from an evaluation of legal science to its *object*, the legal system. This is because they are inseparable. It is an important

36 Ibid., p. 4.
37 Just as: Mark Tushnet, "Critical Legal Studies and Constitutional Law: An Essay in Deconstruction," in: *Stanford Law Review*, 36 (1984), pp. 623–647. See on this: Helen Pluckrose and James Lindsay, *Cynical Theories: How Universities Made Everything about Race, Gender and Identity, and Why This Harms Everybody*, London: Swift Press 2020; Peter Barry, *Beginning Theory: An Introduction to Literary and Cultural Theory*, Manchester: Manchester University Press, 2009 (1995).

contribution that legal scholars such as Blackstone have made us aware of this, a contribution that even the worst critics of Blackstone and his bourgeois legal science do not deny.[38] Legal scholars such as James Bryce (1838–1922) and A.V. Dicey (1838–1922) have continued Blackstone's classical tradition.[39]

The fourth characteristic of science: making predictions

Consensus, experiment, progress in the sense of accumulation of knowledge. Something is still missing here. Let us listen to Auguste Comte (1798–1857), the great prophet of science: "*Savoir pour prévoir, prévoir pour prédire.*" In the natural sciences, prediction, a fourth hallmark of science, plays an important role. A science that can predict proves itself as a practically useful science—an influential science. Prediction allows us to control reality. With the latter, the humanist ideal of knowledge also connects to the ideal of dominion, once the pride of science, now the point on which it is criticized most. The procedure goes as follows. The scientist discovers natural laws. These natural laws allow him to predict certain events. Thales (*c.* 624–545), the continent's first philosopher and astronomer, had not only seen how the heavenly bodies behaved, but he formulated expectations for the future on the basis of those movements, which is how he was able to predict a solar eclipse.[40] Prediction—not on the basis of chance but on the basis of insight into the natural laws that regulate the natural world—has always been viewed as a central feature of science.

Can legal science make predictions? And if so, what can it predict? Unsurprisingly, before Comte, Francis Bacon (1561–1626), the other great prophet of science, also reflected on this question. After all, Bacon was not just an important methodologist of the natural sciences, but also an influential jurist. And just as he tried to free the natural sciences from what he saw as the cobwebs of Aristotelianism, so he also sought to unshackle legal science from the medieval influences on which it had been exposed for so long. In *Maxims of the Law,* a legal tract from 1630, he explains his view.

The "uncertainty of law" ought to be corrected. This he sees as the "most just challenge that is made to the laws of our nation at this time."[41] What he

---

38 See also: Boorstin, *The Mysterious Science of the Law.*
39 See also: A.V. Dicey, *Introduction to the Law of the Constitution*, tenth edition, with an introduction by E.C.S. Wade, London: Macmillan Education 1987 (1885) and James Bryce, *Modern Democracies*, in two volumes, London: Macmillan 1921; James Bryce, *The American Commonwealth*, two volumes, London: Macmillan 1926 (1893).
40 About 28 May, 585 BCE see: Theodor Gomperz, *Griechische Denker. Eine Geschichte der Antiken Philosophie*, I/III, Leipzig: Veit & Comp. 1896, I, p. 39; W.T. Stace, *A Critical History of Greek Philosophy*, London, New York: Macmillan 1960 (1920), pp. 20–24.
41 Cited in: Paul H. Kocher, "Francis Bacon on the Science of Jurisprudence," in: *Journal of the History of Ideas*, 43 (1957), pp. 3–26, p. 5. See also: Daphne Du Maurier, *The Winding*

aspires to is strengthening legal certainty by finding the roots of the law and the foundations of science. Even when the law is interpreted along official lines, the scientist still has an important role to play. The legal scholar, he says, "(can) see more profoundly into the reason of such judgments and ruled cases, and thereby make more use of them for the decision of other cases more doubtful."

The idea appears to be that when one knows the foundations of the law—the principles upon which it rests, the maxims that underpin the many rules—it is possible to apply that knowledge pragmatically: one can predict future developments, both in the short term and long term.

With this, Bacon provides an early justification for an important ideal that will be taken up by a group of early twentieth-century American legal scholars: the American realists.[42] The American realists, as we will see in Chapter 2 of this book, play an important role in the history of legal science in the United States and—to a lesser extent—in Europe. Their position with regard to the subject under discussion here, the status of legal science as a science, is, in a certain sense, ambivalent. On the one hand, they represent a radical break with the past. Their effect seems more destructive than constructive. They leveled severe criticism at a number of classical pretensions of legal science, among which are the traditional ideals of justice and legal certainty. But, in a way, they also demonstrated an optimistic, almost naïve faith in the future prospects of legal science, as long as it could be rooted in a sound social-science foundation.

It is especially the first element with which American realism is associated these days and to which the movement owes its name. They were called "realists" due to their unusual analysis of the law, something that is quickly revealed when reading an essay by the movement's biggest name.[43] According to Oliver Wendell Holmes (1841–1935), we ought to perceive the law the way the "bad man" does. If we ask him what is law, he will not be interested in fancy theories, or even in what the written law says, but only in *the odds that he will be convicted*. Viewed from the bad man's perspective, the law is nothing but the *chance* of being convicted, and it

---

Stair: Francis Bacon, His Rise and Fall, with an introduction by Francis King, London: Virago 2006 (1976), p. 120 and Jean Overton Fuller, *Sir Francis Bacon: A Biography*, London, The Hague: East-West Publications 1981.

42 See on them: P.B. Cliteur, "Amerikaans realisme," in: P.B. Cliteur, B.C. Labuschagne, and C.E. Smith, eds., *Rechtsfilosofische stromingen van de twintigste eeuw*, Arnhem: Gouda Quint 1997, pp. 41–109; J.B. Crozier, "Legal Realism and a Science of Law," in: *The American Journal of Jurisprudence*, 29 (1984), pp. 151–167; Wilfrid E. Rumble, Jr., *American Legal Realism, Scepticism, Reform, and the Judicial Process*, Ithaca, NY: Cornell University Press 1968.

43 See also: Brian Leiter, "Legal Realism," in: Dennis Patterson, ed., *A Companion to the Philosophy of Law and Legal Theory*, Cambridge, MA, Oxford: Blackwell 1996, pp. 261–280.

ought to be the legal advisor's job to *predict* the odds of that happening. With this, Holmes was the first to make an argument for the "prediction theory of law." In a famous passage, he writes that what people want to know, essentially, is how far they can go within a system that is so much stronger than they are. What risk do we take when we do something that we know the legislator has forbidden? Jurists can help the calculating citizens to make these predictions. As such, the jurist's object of study is the prediction, Holmes writes.[44]

Once it has been established that one holds this view of the law, it makes sense for one to become entirely committed to predicting judicial behavior. The crucial question then becomes on what basis the most reliable predictions can be devised. On this, Holmes held fairly traditional views. In his opinion, the "law in the books" was an important tool. Moral notions, however, he saw as an unreliable touchstone.[45] Later realists directed their attention toward other factors, such as the factual behavior of judges in the past ("law in action"). And why should they not also examine the political ideologies and social backgrounds of judges?

Many of the realist attempts to identify the true determinants of judicial behavior proceed like this: "you are saying A, but really it is B." Fred Rodell (1907–1980) believed that we should look at what the judge *actually* chooses, regardless of the *reasons* he gives for doing so. Rodell examined the decisions of Justices Hugo Black (1886–1971) and Felix Frankfurter (1882–1965), two members of the American Supreme Court who had very different ideas about the way judges should operate. Oftentimes, however, they would come to the same decision, and it is impossible to deduce their decision patterns from their beliefs about how judges should function. In one case, Black would hold to the literal wording of the Constitution,[46] and in another, he would read things into the Constitution that could only be found with considerable motivation. In other words: the principles judges *say* rule their thinking often obscure their real reasons rather than explaining them. Rodell writes that Black's "votes on the Court (...) have been and remain predictable with far greater accuracy from his many-faceted evangelical yet practical humanitarianism, than from any complex of abstract jurisprudential principles." The same was true of Frankfurter.

---

44 Holmes, "The Path of the Law," cited here in: Holmes, *Collected Legal Papers*, pp. 167–202, p. 167.

45 He was also one of the most harnessed opponents of natural law. See: Oliver Wendell Holmes, "Natural Law," in: *Collected Legal Papers*, pp. 310–316. See also: James Herget, *American Jurisprudence, 1870–1970*, Houston, TX: Rice University Press 1990, pp. 8–12, 157–158.

46 As he believed ought to be the case; he was, after all, a proponent of "originalism." See: Hugo LaFayette Black, *A Constitutional Faith*, New York: Alfred Knopf 1969.

The rule-skepticism of the American realists

To a layman, it may seem strange for so much attention to be paid to the need for prediction and how it may be realized, when this is supposedly easy when it comes to the law. In the popular imagination, we find the law in the penal code, and the judge applies this according to the letter of the law. However, the realists believed this description to be overly simplistic; they pointed out that the rules were not as clear as they were being made out to be. This element of their thinking is called "rule-skepticism," and in supplying reasons to doubt the rules, the realists have presented us with impressive insights. What were the reasons for rule-skepticism? Rumble, the author of an interesting book about this movement, distinguishes a number of factors that motivated rule-skepticism:[47]

(1) The *multitude of precedents*. It is common to refer to precedents as one of the factors that ought to bring stability to the law. Precedents are decisions by judges in earlier cases that are similar in relevant ways to the case under consideration. If a judge is presented with a case that is indeed highly similar to the case he is called upon to adjudicate, then he is expected to decide the current case *in the same way*. This serves both legal equality and legal certainty. The realists undermined such an optimistic notion. Jurists apparently believe that precedents point in a certain direction, but is that really true? The realists were of the opinion that the sheer number of precedents meant that a line of precedents could be found to support any position. One of the most radical members of the movement, Felix S. Cohen (1909–1953), wrote that "no judge could possibly hand down a decision in any case for which a commentator could not find a precedent, even if the judge himself failed to find one."[48] The pretension that judges follow precedents is contested by realists the same way some atheists contest Christians' claim that they follow the Bible: for every act, some Biblical justification can be found, they say.[49] If the Christian seeks war and aggression, he will say that God is vengeful. If the Christian is after peace, he will quote the Sermon on the Mount. The same is true of books of law and the even more vague reach of legal history; that too points not in one, but many directions. The law and tradition are a grab bag.

---

47 Wilfrid E. Rumble, Jr., *American Legal Realism, Skepticism, Reform, and the Judicial Process*, Ithaca, NY: Cornell University Press 1968, p. 57.
48 See also: Felix Cohen, "Transcendental Nonsense and the Functional Approach," in: *Columbia Law Review,* 35 (1935), pp. 809–849.
49 See on this: Jim Hill and Rand Cheadle, *The Bible Tells Me So. Uses and Abuses of Holy Scripture*, New York: Anchor Books, Doubleday 1996.

(2) Karl Llewellyn (1893–1962), poet, legal scholar, and legal anthropologist, known as a more moderate realist of the second generation, further pointed out that the *techniques for interpreting precedents* also existed in great numbers. Much has been written about precedents, he remarks in *Bramble Bush* (1930), a textbook for beginning law students that aptly expresses the realist mindset.[50] One of the shortcomings of these theories about precedents is that they are not centered on what judges actually *do* with precedents, but on what they *say* they do, so Llewellyn argues (the difference between words and actions had also been analyzed by Rodell, who examined it in judges of the Supreme Court, as we have seen).

(3) Realists also believed that *no rules can be deduced* even from the factual decisions of judges. In his article *A Return to Stare Decisis*, Herman Oliphant (1884–1939) presents us with the following example.[51] A is convinced by her father not to marry B, although she had promised B she would. B sues A's father for damages. However, the judge does not consider the father to be liable. Oliphant now demonstrates how an endless number of rules can be extrapolated from such a decision. The following rules are imaginable: (a) the rule that fathers are entitled to have their daughters break promises; (b) that parents are entitled to this; (c) that parents are entitled to this with regard to both daughters and sons; (d) that everyone is entitled to this in the case of wedding promises; (e) that parents are entitled to do this with regard to any and all promises their children make; (f) that everyone is entitled to do this with regard to promises anyone else makes. None of these rules is a logical consequence of the decision, according to Oliphant.

So, time and time again, we see realists questioning the pretensions of traditional legal science. They could be referred to as "ideology critics." In the legal system and in the legal science that studies and alters this legal system, there is an implicit ideology that holds up certainty, justice, stability, distinction, and other values that do not actually play a very important role in reality. It is the legal scholar who has been schooled in social-science methodologies and enriched by psychological skepticism who can question these pretensions.[52]

The realists have been criticized for their exaggeration. They were really *disappointed absolutists*, it was once noted with considerable psychological

---

50 K.N. Llewellyn, *The Bramble Bush, On our Law and Its Study*, New York, London, Rome: Oceana Publications, Inc. 1960 (1930).

51 Herman Oliphant, "A Return to Stare Decisis," in: *American Bar Association Jnl.*, 14 (1928) and Duxbury, *Patterns of American Jurisprudence*, p. 142.

52 See also: Duxbury, "Some Radicalism about Realism?" pp. 11–41.

insight. They first make impossible demands of the law and legal science (absolute certainty), and when those demands are not met, they conclude that there is no certainty *at all* and that any kind of systematized knowledge of the law, as legal science claims to possess, is an illusion.

One of the peculiar paradoxes of realism is that, on the one hand, the realists criticized traditional science for setting the bar too high, but that, on the other, the science of the law they juxtaposed with it also sank under the weight of impossible demands. Predicting the behavior of judges has turned out to be a lot more problematic than Holmes could have suspected when, in 1897, he wrote that "the prophecies of what the courts will do and nothing more pretentious are what I mean by law."[53] In actuality, these "prophecies of what the courts will do" were at least as ambitious as the old ideals of law and justice that the realists somewhat condescendingly dismissed as the grandiose ambitions of natural law. Predicting judicial behavior, it turns out, is simply not possible.

Here, we are dealing with a critique of the realists' pretensions. Their scientistic view of science has made a significant impact. These days, people seem convinced of the notion that every form of science is always practiced from within a certain framework. The realists sought to study the law as the behavior patterns of judges. However, as was often leveled against them, there is no such thing as judicial behavior as a purely objective datum, without reference to the law. Without taking into account the legal system of rules, the behavior of judges cannot even be identified as being the behavior of a judge acting in his official capacity.[54]

The sharpest criticism of realism from this perspective came from van Hermann Kantorowicz (1877–1940), the founding father of the *Freie Rechtslehre*[55] and not at all a representative of orthodox legal science, quick to dismiss a judge-focused, rather than a legislator-focused legal science. The most serious shortcoming of predictivism, as Kantorowicz noted, was that the concept is confused with one of its elements.[56] Say, we agree with Holmes and his followers, Kantorowicz posited, and we concede that the law is what courts do. It would be the same as saying: "religion" is what the churches preach, "science" is what the universities teach, "medicine" is what the doctor prescribes, a "shoe" is what the cobbler makes. It is putting the horse behind the cart. After all, "church" cannot be defined

---

53 Holmes, "The Path of the Law," cited here in: Oliver Wendell Holmes, *Collected Legal Papers*, pp. 167–202, p. 167.

54 In that sense already: L.L. Fuller, "American Legal Realism," in: *University of Pennsylvania Law Review*, 82 (1934), pp. 429–462.

55 See also: Hermann Kantorowicz, *Rechtswissenschaft und Soziologie, Ausgewählte Schriften zur Wissenschafts-lehre*, Karlsruhe: Verlag C.F. Müller 1962.

56 H. Kantorowicz, "Some Rationalism about Realism," in: *Yale Law Journal*, 43 (1934), pp. 1240–1253.

without "religion," "university" not without "science," "doctor" not without "medicine," "cobbler" not without "shoe." The law is not what courts apply; courts are institutions that apply the law.[57]

From American realism to Critical Legal Studies and law and economics

From what we have seen until now, it appears that legal science conforms to some characteristics ascribed to science, but not with others. We have noted that, especially on the abstract level, namely the question of what law is, legal science has produced certain insights that enjoy great consensus among scientists. In addition, we have seen that legal science even features experiments, at least if one is willing to accept a somewhat broader interpretation of the concept of an "experiment" than is usual in the natural sciences. With regard to the question of progress in science, we have concluded that the optimism of classical authors like Blackstone is not widely supported these days, but that it is equally difficult to consistently deny that there has been any progress at all. When it comes to predictions, legal science has not progressed much since Holmes posited this as a desirable trait, and so it is only on this point that we could say that the scientific rigor of legal science is seriously lacking. The scientistic ideal of the realists is just as controversial today as it was in the time they were writing.[58] It is remarkable, incidentally, that the two strands of realism are still visible in modern-day legal science. Two modern movements within American legal science have continued particular strands of realism: CLS and EAL.

Critical Legal Studies continues the critical line. For CLS scholars, legal science is a form of ideology critique. This is not entirely new. The same sort of comments we hear from Rodell,[59] Jerome Frank (1889–1957),[60] and Thurman W. Arnold (1891–1969) about the indeterminacy of the phenomenon of law, the erratic and unpredictable behavior of judges, and the ideological function of legal values like certainty and stability, we encounter in

---

57 See also: Robert S. Summers, *Het Pragmatisch instrumentalisme, Een kritische studie van de belangrijkste Amerikaanse rechtsfilosofie*, Antwerp, Amsterdam: Standaard Wetenschappelijke Uitgeverij, n.d. (uit het Duits, 1980), p. 144.
58 See on this: "The Neotraditionalist Response," in: Richard A. Posner, *The Problems of Jurisprudence*, Cambridge, MA, London: Harvard University Press 1990, pp. 433–453; Charles Fried, "The Artificial Reason of the Law or: What Lawyers Know," in: *Texas Law Review*, 60 (1981), pp. 35–58; Anthony T. Kronman, "Living in the Law," in: *The University of Chicago Law Review*, 54 (1987), pp. 835–876.
59 Fred Rodell, *Nine Men, A Political History of the Supreme Court from 1790 to 1955*, New York: Random House 1955.
60 Also in: Jerome Frank, *Courts on Trial, Myth and Reality in American Justice*, Princeton: Princeton University Press 1973 (1949).

almost exactly the same words in modern-day protagonists of Critical Legal Studies.

But another side to realism, the attempt to elevate legal science to a higher level by means of social sciences, economics, and statistics (Holmes believed that the future of legal science lay in using the methods of economics and statistics) has also attracted a following.

A second strain (CLS is the first) controlling today's legal science land-scape is that of the *Economic Analysis of Law* (EAL) or *law and econom-ics*.[61] It is said that CLS represents the left-wing of American legal science, and EAL the right.[62]

We will not further address here these attempts to develop a legal science based on social science, which in fact comes down to a reformulation of realism's more positive ideals.[63] Instead, we will follow a third through line in modern legal science, viz., that of those who are inspired by the thought that the law was less easily subjected to a social science approach than had been imagined. In Chapter 5, we will further elaborate on this theme. The following paragraphs may serve as an introduction.

As we said, the law was less easily subjected to a social science approach than had been imagined. One could wonder why that is. If the problem is approached from this vantage point, it can lead to reflection on the specific nature of the law as a social phenomenon, a specific nature that might resist a methodology geared toward the social or natural sciences. Perhaps the law is suited to a methodology *sui generis*. This notion is what guides authors such as Ronald Dworkin (1931–2013) and those who are influenced by hermeneutics. Central to this is the belief that *interpretation* is a core con-cept in legal science. This movement could be called the third main artery in modern reflection on legal science.[64]

A good introduction to this realm of thinking is a passage from the essay by Von der Dunk that was referenced before. Von der Dunk points out that history, by definition, has to do with the past. One of the things with which postmodernism, narrativism, and hermeneutics have reacquainted us is that we can only ever recover a *miniscule fraction* of the past. Also, for

---

61 With as its most active protagonist: Richard A. Posner, *The Problematics of Moral and Legal Theory*, Cambridge, MA, London: The Belknap Press of Harvard University Press, 1999; Richard A. Posner, *Overcoming Law*, Cambridge, MA, London: Harvard University Press 1995; Richard A. Posner, *The Economics of Justice*, Cambridge, MA, London: Har-vard University Press 1981.

62 See also: J.M. Kelly, *A Short History of Western Legal Theory*, Oxford: Clarendon Press 1992, p. 436.

63 See also: H. Franken, "Rechtseconomie en strafrecht," in: E.H. Hondius, ed., *Rechtsecono-mie en recht*, Zwolle: W.E.J. Tjeenk Willink 1991, pp. 163–179.

64 See also: Michael S. Moore, "The Interpretative Turn in Modern Theory: A Turn for The Worse?," in: *Stanford Law Review*, 41 (1989), p. 871ff.

knowledge of that past, we are completely dependent on stories that were passed down. After all, the past itself no longer exists. The only thing we have is *traces* of the past: written and oral traditions.

Here, we see two obstacles that prevent the study of history from going *"den sicheren Gang einer Wissenschaft."* First: the past is so far away; we are no longer immediately familiar with it. Second: we now only know the past through interpretation, so through the filter of others.

For legal science, this picture is rosier at first glance. It seems that we are directly confronted with the law. The law is everywhere. When we buy bread, rent a house, recognize a child; the legal rules are there for the taking. We are all "citizens of Law's Empire," as Dworkin once put it.[65]

On the other hand, the law is also—at least that is what the third movement assumes—a product of scientific construction, just like the past. There may be sources in which we try to find law (legal statutes, habit, and jurisprudence), but based on certain lines of argument, far from everything that seems to emerge as law from these sources is actually accepted as such. Again, the law always reaches us through the filter of interpretation. Let us examine this point further.

With regard to the *law*, we have the phenomenon of the *contra legem* interpretation (an interpretation that contravenes the letter of the law). Sometimes, the law is a dead letter and is no longer enforced. We also know of cases in which certain things are forbidden by law, but in which the prosecution of violations of this type is not a police/political priority. The Dutch soft-drug policy comes to mind: illegal according to the country's Opium Law, but for sale nonetheless. Is it even possible to speak of a legal ban when it is not enforced? The realists made a distinction between what the American jurist Roscoe Pound (1870–1964) called "law in the books" (what is on paper) and "law in action" (what actually happens in society).[66]

When it comes to *custom*, there is even more uncertainty. After all, not all custom is recognized as law. A number of conditions need to be met for this to be the case. Traditionally, the handbooks specify (1) a practice that is

65 Ronald Dworkin, *Law's Empire*, Cambridge, MA, London: The Belknap Press of Harvard University Press 1986.

66 See on this: David Wigdor, *Roscoe Pound, Philosopher of Law*, Westport, CT, London: Greenwood Press 1974, p. x and p. 234; Roscoe Pound, "Mechanical Jurisprudence," in: *Columbia Law Review*, 8 (1908), pp. 605–623; Roscoe Pound, "The Scope and Purpose of Sociological Jurisprudence," I, in: *Harvard Law Review*, XXIV(8) (June 1911), pp. 591–619; Roscoe Pound "The Scope and Purpose of Sociological Jurisprudence," II, in: *Harvard Law Review*, XXV(12) (1911–1912), pp. 140–168; Roscoe Pound, "The Scope and Purpose of Sociological Jurisprudence," III, in: *Harvard Law Review*, XXV(12) (1911–1912), pp. 489–516.

repeated and (2) that those involved are repeating the practice in the belief that they are meeting their legal obligations.[67]

The repetition of the practice is the least problematic, but this too can be questioned. Take, for instance, constitutional law. The parliamentary system consists of a number of rules and conventions that evolved over time between the government and parliament. For example, one rule that is fundamental to the parliamentary system specifies that the government cannot disband parliament over the same issue twice. This is a typical customary constitutional rule. But how did it come about? Really only on the basis of a relatively small number of instances in which there was a conflict between the government and parliament. It is hardly even possible to speak of "a practice that is repeated."

Nevertheless, this state of affairs does not present an insurmountable problem. Perhaps when it comes to the nature of the repeated practice, we ought to make a distinction based on the number of cases that *can* occur. We might conclude then that less stringent demands may be made of constitutional law than private law, in which practices that might constitute customary law are repeated every day.

The second criterion presents bigger problems, however. Clearly, the latter description of the legally relevant custom is wholly circular. As such, custom also does not offer us an unambiguously defined criterion for identifying law.

What of jurisprudence? Are *all* rules formulated by judges' *legal* rules? Again, no. There is no consensus on which criteria judge-made rules must adhere to in order to be considered legal rules. The literature offers the following. First, we have to be dealing with *rules*, meaning the concrete judgment is excluded. For example, a dentist is tapping electricity by placing a small metal rod in the electricity meter, allowing him to keep using electricity without the meter registering it. He is caught and brought before a judge to answer for his crime of "theft." In the penal code, theft is defined as dishonestly *appropriating a good* belonging to another with the intention of permanently depriving the other of it. But the dentist argues: (1) electricity is not a good, and (2) placing a metal rod inside an electricity meter cannot be characterized as appropriating. The Dutch Supreme Court, which sat in judgment of this matter, did not agree with the dentist's defense. Electricity, although immaterial, could be considered as a good; he was convicted of theft.[68] The concrete result of this procedure is that *this* dentist is convicted of theft on the basis of *this* behavior. Now, the central question arises: is this concrete decision law? Yes, people are inclined to say. In a certain sense, it is. It at least *has the force* of law for this dentist. He will, possibly ushered

67 See also: P.W. Kamphuisen, *Gewoonterecht*, The Hague: Martinus Nijhoff 1935.
68 HR 23 May 1921, *NJ* 1921, 564.

by the strong arm, be forced to pay a fine or submit to incarceration. And indeed, in certain radical legal theories, the judge's concrete decision in the concrete case in question is counted as law. This can even be seen as a product of Holmes's position about the bad man. The "bad man" will certainly experience the judge's decision in his case as law. As such, Holmes's radical pupil Frank believed he was speaking entirely in the spirit of the master when he said: what the judge says in actuality is law.[69] However, less radical colleagues of Frank's, even those who sympathized with the American realists' premises, have argued that concrete decisions in concrete cases cannot produce law. Characteristic of the law is that it is about *general rules*, a combination of words that is actually a tautology: the law is about generality, about rules. As such, it is possible to say that the body of *rules* the judge uses to adjudicate conflicts is law, according to John Chipman Gray (1839–1915), a less radical proponent of realism.[70]

Is the study of the law scholarship or science?

So, does the tour we have so far taken paint a picture of legal science as a "scientific" discipline? Or is legal *science* more *scholarship* in the end, as is indeed how it is often referred to in the titles of papers, books, and study programs? And does it matter?

The Dutch philosopher Maarten Van Nierop (1939–2018) writes that when a practitioner of science feels a constant need to reflect on and justify the scientific nature of his science, oftentimes, his science is in trouble.[71] Sometimes, it is even a sign of its approaching end as a scientific institution, as was the case for the science of andragogy in the 1970s.

As things stand, legal science need not worry about the latter. This is not just because of its status as a science, but also due to the social importance of its object of study. Regardless of the difficulties of defining the concept of law, there is general agreement about two things: (1) the law exists, and (2) it ought to be studied.

With regard to the former, legal science has the same luxury as the study of history. It takes a philosopher to say that history does not exist (i.e., that

---

69 See also: Jerome Frank, *Law and the Modern Mind*, Gloucester, MA: Peter Smith 1970 (1930); Jerome Frank, *Courts on Trial, Myth and Reality in American Justice* and Duxbury, "Jerome Frank and the Legacy of Legal Realism," in: *Journal of Law and Society*, 18 (1991), pp. 175–205.

70 John Chipman Gray, *The Nature and the Sources of the Law*, second edition from the author's notes, by Roland Gray, LLB, New York: Macmillan 1948 (1909), who is often viewed as a realist *avant la lettre*.

71 M. van Nierop, "Is filosofie een wetenschap?" in: P.B. Cliteur, H.D. Papma, and R.T.P. Wiche, eds., *Overtuigend bewijs. Over het wetenschappelijke van de niet-exacte wetenschappen*, Meppel, Amsterdam: Boom 1994, pp. 38–65.

the world was created a minute ago, complete with people's memories of a past). That history exists and that it *can* be studied (for now leaving aside the usefulness of this) is clear. But does this work out with, for instance, the object of philosophy? It would be too easy to dwell on the etymology of the word "philosophy" and remark that there is no such thing as *wisdom* or *love of wisdom*, but continuing the reasoning of postmodern theories, the object of philosophy does come close to belletrism or argumentative essay-ism. In fact, the autonomy and irreducibility of the object of philosophy are regularly denied from the discipline itself.

Again: what about the law? Whatever else can be said about it, the law exists. Indeed, legal science is regularly confronted with attempts to deny the autonomy of the law as an independent aspect of reality, but these attempts have not been terribly successful so far. In particular, authors such as Perelman (1912–1984),[72] Fried (*b.* 1935),[73] Kronman (*b.* 1945),[74] Langdell (1826–1906),[75] and others point to the specific and "reductionism-resistant" nature of the law. In his famous *The Path of the Law* (1897), Holmes wrote that the future would belong to the economist and the stat-istician. He predicted that there would be no room in the future for an independent legal methodology. The scientific study of the law would be increasingly left to statisticians and economists. And, indeed, a modern-day discipline such as law and economics does seem to connect with the ideals of Holmes and other realists. Yet, so far, it has not led to the demise of "Law as an autonomous discipline."[76] On the contrary, authors like Fried and Perelman say. Rather than legal science being reconstructed according to the scientistic model of positivism, the specific methodologies of legal science have become a source of inspiration for other sciences.[77]

---

72 Chaïm Perelman, *Droit, Morale et Philosophie*, second edition, Paris: Pichon et R. Durand-Auzias 1976; Chaïm Perelman, *Juridische logica als leer van de argumentatie*, Antwerp, Amsterdam: Standaard Wetenschappelijke Uitgeverij, n.d.

73 Charles Fried, "The Artificial Reason of the Law or: What Lawyers Know," pp. 35–58.

74 Kronman, "Living in the Law," pp. 835–876; Anthony T. Kronman, "Precedent and Tradi-tion," in: *The Yale Law Journal*, 99 (1990), pp. 1029–1068; Anthony T. Kronman, *The Lost Lawyer. Failing Ideals of the Legal Profession*, Cambridge, MA, London: The Belknap Press of Harvard University Press 1993; Anthony Kronman "Alexander Bickel's Philosophy of Prudence," in: *Yale Law Journal*, 94 (1985), p. 1567.

75 See also: J.A. Wightman, "Christopher Columbus Langdell," in: A.W.B. Simpson, ed., *Bio-graphical Dictionary of the Common Law*, London: Butterworths 1984, p. 302; Mary Ann Glendon, *A Nation under Lawyers, How the Crisis in the Legal Profession Is Transforming American Society*, New York: Farrar, Strauss and Giroux 1994, pp. 184–185 and Frank, *Courts on Trial*, pp. 225–246.

76 See also: Richard A. Posner, "The Decline of Law as an Autonomous Discipline: 1962-1987," in: *Harvard Law Review*, 100 (1990), pp. 761–780.

77 See also: Perelman, *Droit, Morale et Philosophie*, p. 193 and Richard A. Posner, *The Prob-lems of Jurisprudence*, Cambridge, MA, London: Harvard University Press, 1990.

Those who defend the autonomous character of legal science in contrast to that of the natural sciences are often inspired by a critique of positivism's *methodological naturalism*. Methodological naturalism denies that there is a difference in methodology between the natural sciences and the humanities.[78] The naturalist believes the following:

- there is a scientific process that is normative for all sciences
- this methodological ideal can be derived from the natural sciences
- the relationship between facts that can be discovered is causal
- natural science explains from causes.[79]

However, the scientist in the field of social studies stands in a very different relationship to his object than a natural scientist, the opponents of methodological naturalism argue. The natural scientist stands *outside of* and *in opposition to* his object. The social scientist, on the other hand, is himself a member of the community or culture he studies. He cannot extricate himself from his own culture: "Er ('Der Forscher'; PC, AE) wächst hervor aus dem Boden, den sein Forschungsobjekt vertritt," Aarnio writes.[80]

Finnish professor of civil law Aulis Aarnio (*b.* 1937) describes the difference between the methodology of the natural sciences and that of the humanities as follows. Nature is governed by *regularities*. It is the natural sciences' job to discover and chart these regularities. In the humanities, however, it is not just about regularities, but about *rules*. Social life is governed by certain rules: moral rules, customary rules, and legal rules. In turn, these rules create institutions, which shape the activities within the society. It is impossible to acquire knowledge and understanding of the society only by studying regularities in the empirical sense. The "raw data," on which the American realists based their claims, are entirely meaningless. Scientific knowledge about society rests on certain "Lesarten der Bedeutungen," not on empirical observation. In other words, it is about how the meanings are to be understood.[81]

Not only does the law *exist* and has it turned out to be fairly "reduction-resistant" in the many centuries legal scholars have studied it, but there has also always been a need for a scientific *study* of the law. Legal science was

---

78 See also: Brian Fay, *Contemporary Philosophy of Social Science. A Multicultural Approach*, Malden, MA: Blackwell 1996.

79 Aulis Aarnio, *Denkweisen der Rechtswissenschaft. Einführung in die Theorie der rechtswissenschaftlichen Forschung*, Wien, New York: Springer Verlag 1979, p. 31.

80 Ibid., p. 27 and J.J.H. Bruggink, "Is rechtswetenschap een wetenschap?," in: J.J.H. Bruggink, *Rechtsreflecties. Grondbegrippen uit de rechtstheorie*, Deventer: Kluwer 1993, pp. 123–147.

81 See also: Aarnio, *Denkweisen der Rechtswissenschaft. Einführung in die Theorie der rechtswissenschaftlichen Forschung*, p. 31.

thought useful. It is not for nothing that legal science is one of the oldest sciences. And it is likely that there will *always* be a need for the systematization of the law and the transference of the legal tradition to new generations of law students. It is possible that these kinds of, from a principled perspective, fairly trivial factors provide an important contribution to the "sicheren Gang einer Wissenschaft." In every society, a need has arisen to develop general legal principles in order to systematize and master the law.

It could be said that the most important task of the legal scholar is to further develop the scheme originally set up by the legislator. In this, of course, the legal scholar is not entirely beholden to the legislator. The scholar can introduce new categories and apply different classifications than those envisioned by the legislator.[82] One of the most important jobs of legal science has always been, however, structuring the legal material in the light of the foundational principles of a legal system. This brings us back to van Schilfgaarde.

At the beginning of this chapter, we offered a definition of science by van Schilfgaarde. Science is about justifiable knowledge, in which van Schilfgaarde defines justifiable knowledge as a knowing based on evidence. How does this ambition stand in relation to legal science? Can there be a legal science interpretation of a "knowing based on evidence"? According to a particular tradition in thought about legal science, that is certainly the case. A systematic and coherent handling of the legal material in the light of a number of foundational principles is the ideal of "classical legal science"; Simmons speaks of "Classical Legal Doctrine" (CLD).

In fact, we have already come across the ideals of classical legal science in our discussion of William Blackstone, one of the most influential minds of this tradition, but we will try to expound further on the ideals of classical legal science and confront them with a number of critiques that are leveled at traditional legal science from relativist movements like CLS. Next, we will focus on the confrontation between CLD and a number of competing traditions, like CLS, in which we are guided to a large extent by the British legal philosopher Nigel Simmonds for our representation of the ideals of the Classical Legal Doctrine.

"Classical Legal Doctrine" versus "Critical Legal Studies"

The first clear description of what was claimed to be a justified study of the law is what Simmonds calls the "classical view." He credits this to Francis Bacon. In his previously cited *Maxims of Law*, Bacon notes that he is out to establish the foundations or maxims of the law that could be extracted and deduced from a "harmony and congruity of cases, and are such as the wisest

---

82 Ibid., p. 52.

and deepest sort of lawyers have in judgement and use," although Bacon does add, tellingly, that these jurists will not have an easy time of formulating these foundational principles.[83]

With this, Bacon pioneered a tradition in legal science that would become highly influential. In the eighteenth century, the aspirations of the classical tradition were described as follows by Sir William Jones in his *Essay on the Law of Bailment* (1781):

> If Law be a *science,* and really deserve so sublime a name, it must be founded on principle and claim and exalted rank in the empire of *reason;* but if it be merely an unconnected series of decrees and ordinances, its use may remain though its dignity be lessened, and he will become the greatest lawyer who has the strongest habitual and artificial memory.[84]

What are the presuppositions and premises of classical theory as we see in Bacon and Jones? Simmonds lists the following three elements.

First and foremost, there is the assumption that the law can be justified in terms of *principles* that undergird that law. Principles, so bacon noted, can be deduced from the "harmony and congruity of cases" and constitute a justification for those cases.

A *second* presupposition of the classical doctrine of legal science is that legal rules can be justified in terms of their *content* and not only by reference to the need to respect the judge's decisions or the democratically elected legislator.

Third is the presupposition that the law incorporates a body of *non-instrumental values.*

This also implies that we cannot *understand* the law without these ideals. Just as the movement of carved wooden pieces on a checkered board is a meaningless and incomprehensible process that only gains meaning when we view it in light of the rules of chess, so it is equally true that the constitutional rules, the "black letter rules" of a constitutional system only acquire meaning in the light of more general values that make up a legal system.

A principle like the "sovereignty of Parliament," the idea that the formal legislator has the final word and that the products of the formal legislator are no longer subject to judicial review based on their congruence with higher constitutional law, can only be understood in light of the English legal system's commitment to a certain conception of democracy. Also, a principle such as the right of constitutional judicial review present in the

---

83 Simmonds, *The Decline of Juridical Reason,* p. 20.
84 Cited in: ibid., p. 21.

American system can only be understood in the light of *another* view of democracy, held there.[85]

These different views of democracy are part of the core structures of American and English constitutional law. Oftentimes, they are not set down as rules in a constitution but are more or less presupposed in the system. They can be gleaned from what legal scholars, commentators, judges, and other parties involved say about their own actions.

It is also clear from this that a conception of legal science that is limited to merely presenting the rules set down in a constitution lacks an essential element.[86]

Great classical exposés of legal fields in the spirit of the Classical Legal Doctrine are A.V. Dicey's *An Introduction into the Study of the Law of the Constitution*, the *Commentaries* by Blackstone, or Bryce's *The American Commonwealth*. Those who have read Bryce or Dicey understand that a chaotic multitude of rules can be transformed into a coherent idea; they have learned to understand the law as a system, a unified body anchored to an idea or a set of ideals.

Such a conception of science is ambitious and asks much of the researcher. Especially in English law, considerable demands are placed on the practitioner of the classical doctrine because the sources offer scant footing. The English system may be coherent, but it is a coherence that is hidden within the system and will have to be extracted and made explicit.

The (un)popularity of CLD

The ideals of the Classical Legal Doctrine are exposed to severe criticism these days. Although CLD is not buckling under the weight, it would still be irresponsibly optimistic to say that the classical tradition is uncontested. The criticism can be placed into four categories.

First, positivism's critique. Positivist writers, both older ones like Austin and Bentham, but also more modern ones, like Hart and Kelsen, criticize CLD on the grounds that it insufficiently respects the separation between the law and morality. (See Chapter 5 on this.)

A *second* category of criticism of CLD is that leveled by scientistic approaches. By this, we mean all those movements that somehow hope to raise legal science's scientific status by regrounding its methodology.

---

85 P.B. Cliteur, "Traditionalism, Democracy, and Judicial Review," in: B. van Roermund, ed., *Constitutional Review, Verfassungsgerichtbarkeit, Constitutionele toetsing*, Deventer, Zwolle: Kluwer/W.E.J. Tjeenk Willink 1993, pp. 55–77.

86 The same is true of article-by-article legal commentaries, as has been customary since: J.T. Buys, *De Grondwet. Toelichting en kritiek, eerste deel*, Arnhem: P. Gouda Quint 1883.

Here, it is no longer the traditional foundation of CLD but that of the social sciences that is the guiding principle. American realism was an early incarnation of this approach, but this line of thought is continued by disciplines such as law and economics (in which the law is studied using methods derived from economics) and jurimetrics (using computers to predict judicial behavior).

A *third* form of criticism is that of those scholars who study what Holmes and Simmonds called the "black letter rules." The "black letter man" does not have a "voice" in the sense that there are no eminent ideologues seeking to achieve convincing legitimacy for his ideal,[87] but in the everyday practice of the law, just as in the study of the law at universities, the influence of the "black letter man" is considerable.

A *fourth* and final form of critique of CLD used to be offered by authors inspired by Marxism and is put forth these days by proponents of the Critical Legal Studies movement. This can be described as ideology critique.

This classification of the different critiques is somewhat artificial because they converge on various points. The "black letter man" makes common cause with the positivist with regard to the ideal of studying the law in a value-neutral way. A positivist like Kelsen will also be able to support much of the ideology critique that CLS levels at CLD. Therefore, we will not take the four movements as our starting point but embark on a thematic approach to the critiques. We identify five points: the distinction between "is" and "ought," the ambition of classical legal science, the problem that not all legal fields are suited to the classical approach, the accusation that the proponent of CLD is a laudator *temporis acti*, and finally, the danger of ideological distortion.

(a) *The separation of "is" and "ought."* One of the classical points of criticism legal positivist authors level against more value-based approaches to law and science (CLD among them) is that "is" and "ought," the law as it "is" and the law as it "ought to be," "law" and "morality," should not be confused. Facts and values are two separate domains of reality.[88] Saying that something is true is very different from saying that

---

87 The work of Scalia is also too "philosophical." See: Antonin Scalia, "Modernity and the Constitution," in: E. Smith, ed., *Constitutional Justice under Old Constitutions*, The Hague, London, Boston: Kluwer Law International 1995, pp. 313–318; Antonin Scalia, *A Matter of Interpretation. Federal Courts and the Law, An Essay by Antonin Scalia with a commentary by Amy Gutmann*, Gordon S. Wood, Laurence H. Tribe, Mary Ann Glendon, and Ronald Dworkin, Princeton, NJ: Princeton University Press 1997.

88 See: Hans Kelsen, *Reine Rechtslehre*, second impression, Vienna: Verlag Franz Deuticke 1960.

something ought to be true. Science describes what is; if scientists start talking about how things ought to be, then they are no longer treading on scientific but on ethical terrain. Those who do not acknowledge this and use scientific prestige to make normative claims are no longer even ethicists but ideologues.

This is a very brief summary of a standard positivistic critique of the kind of scientific practice that we have characterized here as the classical doctrine. To what extent does this critique hold water? Is the classical doctrine indeed guilty of mixing law and morality, and does that render its scientific status null and void? In a certain sense, this both *is* and *is not* the case. For an adequate assessment of this critique, however, we have to distinguish between two kinds of positivism.

The distinction originates with Simmonds. He differentiates between legal positivism and meta-positivism. He defines *legal positivism* as the theory that all law emanates from authoritative sources, in the sense that this was consciously set down or tacitly accepted.[89] The classical doctrine of the law conflicts with legal positivism in that the principles and doctrines central to CLD were never decreed or officially set down.[90] It may even be the case that they were first formulated by a legal scholar. And that legal scholar does not present these doctrines or principles as elements that could enrich the law if they were adopted: he formulates them *as law*.

However, we have to distinguish the legal positivist position that Simmonds calls *meta-positivism*. Characteristic of meta-positivism is the belief that the law is not a kind of moral judgment. Here, he uses the term "moral judgement" as judgments that are made from the perspective of the person who actually sees the morality to which he refers as normative. So, for instance, an assertion that the Catholic Church approves of a certain norm is not a moral judgment in that sense.

CLD rejects legal positivism, Simmonds writes, but not meta-positivism. For making the distinction between the law as it *is* and the law as it *ought to be*, this means the following. The legal scientist who operates according to the tradition of the classical doctrine views the foundational principles as a part of the law. The principles provide an "appropriate justification for the black-letter rules and decisions."[91] The legal rules cannot be separated from the notions of justice that undergird the law: "The doctrinal writer, in so far as he is an heir to the classical tradition, views the law as embodying a coherent conception of justice." The legal scholar arranges the principles

89 Simmonds, *The Decline of Judicial Reason*, p. 22.
90 This point is strongly emphasized by Fuller in: Lon L. Fuller, *The Law in Quest of Itself*, Chicago: The Foundation Press, Inc. 1940 (AMS edition 1978).
91 Simmonds, *The Decline of Judicial Reason*, p. 23.

and rules that are used in the daily practice of the law into more general classifications, thus expressing the "moral perspective of the law." As such, the legal scholar does not just classify the positive law rules in a neutral manner but views them in the light of an "underlying conception of justice."[92]

What does this mean for the separation of law and morality? We *cannot* achieve a full separation of law and morality because the legal rules only acquire meaning in the light of certain principles. These principles form the legal-ethical foundation of the law;[93] they are optimization commands for the law.[94] But when Simmonds speaks of a "suitable justification for the printed rules," he does not mean a justification according to the personal moral standards of the researcher. As such, "suitable" does not mean: "in accordance with the moral principles of the author," but only: "in accordance with the normative foundations of the legal system in question."

Since the personal morality of the researcher still functions as a critical entity that stands in opposition to the legal system, it can be said that the distinction between law and morality is respected.

It can also be described as follows. CLD distinguishes two types of morality: the morality of the legal system itself and the morality of the researcher. With regard to the first, the distinction between law and morality is dismissed as an unfruitful guideline. The second separation, however, is maintained.

Once we have established this, a number of critiques leveled at CLD in this vein are no longer convincing. It has been said, for instance, that CLD stimulates an uncritical attitude with regard to the law. After all, if the distinction between *law* and *good law* is allowed to blur, it can result in the claim that, once a system of norms is considered law, there is also an obligation for people to conform to its demands. This type of criticism does not touch CLD though. After all, the classical legal scholar can argue that he is observing nothing more than that a certain legal system is just according to its own norms. That does not imply, however, that it conforms to the researcher's personal moral convictions.

(b) *The ambition of classical legal science.* A second objection that is made against the classical tradition is that its approach is too ambitious. Here, the "black letter man" is the one doing most of the objecting. His critique is not often sophisticatedly articulated though, since those who support it are not sufficiently interested in philosophy of science

---

92 Ibid., p. 25.
93 In this sense also: Karl Larenz, *Richtiges Recht. Grundzüge einer Rechtsethik*, Munich: Verlag C.H. Beck 1979.
94 K. Raes, "Rechtsbeginselen en de morele eenheid van het recht. Dworkins constructivisme," in: *Ars Aequi*, 40 (1991), pp. 773–785, p. 782. Dworkin could be described as a modern-day proponent of CLD. See: Ronald A. Dworkin, "'Natural' Law Revisited," in: *University of Florida Law Review*, XXXIV(2) (Winter 1982), pp. 165–188.

to express the objection in an intellectually convincing manner. The "black letter man" only *practices* legal science in some way, but any justification requires something that he is not able, nor prepared, to educate himself about: reflection about scientific methodology. The "black letter man" believes that the law should just be written down and only very minimally systematized, certainly without getting into commentary and "sweeping generalizations."

We find this position in several varieties. It is noted, for instance, that the legal scholar is expected to, and was "trained to," *describe* the law. To describe it as it is, not as the scholar thinks it ought to be. On this point, the "black letter man" makes common cause with the positivist. One could, in that sense, call the "black letter man" an "unrefined positivist," "unrefined" meaning that his view contains not even the beginnings of the methodological awareness found in great legal positivists like Hart and Kelsen.

On rare occasions, the "black letter man" is given what we have called "voice." The American judge and scientist Robert Bork regularly condemns the influence of philosophy and the social sciences in legal science.[95] Still, this is fairly rare. Usually, the "black letter man" does not offer his own conception of the practice of science; his is more "water-cooler criticism" of CLD and other approaches to legal science, with which, incidentally, he has acquainted himself only minimally.

(c)   *Not all legal fields are suited to the classical approach.* Another objection to CLD relates to its limited relevance for a large proportion of modern-day law. CLD, so the critic might remark, holds meaning for large legal areas that admit of certain foundational principles. The foundations and premises of *constitutional law*, for instance, can be imagined (rule of law, democracy, legitimacy of government), as can the premises of *criminal law* (the principle of legality, no punishment without culpability) and those of *private law* (freedom of contract). But how can traffic law be viewed in the light of fundamental moral principles? One cannot say that traffic law is less important than contract law, Simmonds writes, but most jurists will still agree with the statement that there are considerable differences when it comes to understanding these legal fields in light of principled foundations.

95 Such as in: Robert H. Bork, *Slouching Towards Gomorrah. Modern Liberalism and American Decline*, New York: HarperCollins 1996; Robert H. Bork, *The Tempting of America, The Political Seduction of the Law*, London: Sinclair-Stevenson 1990. This can also be observed in Antonin Scalia, former judge on the American Supreme Court. See on him: Richard A. Brisbin, *Justice Antonin Scalia and the Conservative Revival*, Baltimore, London: The Johns Hopkins University Press 1997. The same chapter discusses Scalia's view of legal science.

This also gives oxygen to the "black letter man's" criticism. He could argue that CLD was a nice ideal but from a bygone age. All sorts of new legal fields, functional fields, have changed the legal map completely. Modern-day law simply requires a different approach. The older legal fields allow the legal scholar much more room to maneuver. He can outline underlying doctrines. He can extrapolate axioms. He can make constructions. After all, the proponent of the classical doctrine sees the law as "embodying a coherent conception of justice."[96] But the problem is that not every set of rules lends itself to the classical approach. The rules have to be justifiable in terms of a consistent moral theory.[97] If, however, the law cannot be understood in the light of conceptions of justice, but only in the light of practical needs, the issues of the day, the activities of pressure groups, or the interests of those who rank highly in the social hierarchy, the classical doctrine is useless.

(d) *The CLD proponent as laudator* temporis acti. The previous objection contains much that ought to give CLD pause. The next critique is closely related. The classical model, Simmonds writes, is not the legal science of today.[98] These days, the law is increasingly viewed as a body of consciously chosen rules that are meant to serve particular ends. And when the law is *used* as an instrument, people will naturally also start to *see* it as one. Where before, the law was recognized in "Reason and Principle," today, it is viewed as nothing more than a collection of rules meant to be instrumentally utilized. The classical doctrine was primarily the product of the sixteenth and seventeenth centuries. That is why CLD might not be suited to our time, just as it also was not suited to the time before its heyday. Although the classical jurists have predecessors in the Middle Ages, the work of the post-glossators differed significantly from the classical doctrine. In the Middle Ages, glosses were common. Glossing was a matter of adding marginal commentary or explanation with regard to a problematic term to a legal text. Often, this was applied to Roman law.

None of these older forms of legal commentary can be compared to an organized legal argument in which rules and decisions are explained on the basis of their underlying principles.

Nothing is simpler, Simmonds writes, than to declare this medieval handling of the law "unscientific." And indeed, perhaps from our current

---

96 Simmonds, *The Decline of Judicial Reason*, p. 25.
97 See also: Alan Hunt, "The Theory of Critical Legal Studies," in: *Oxford Journal of Legal Studies*, 6 (1986), pp. 1–45; Tushnet, "Critical Legal Studies and Constitutional Law: An Essay in Deconstruction," pp. 623–647.
98 Simmonds, "Law as a Rational Science," in: *Archiv für Rechts- und Sozialphilosophie*, 66 (1980), pp. 535–556, p. 552.

perspective, it is. It is more useful, however, to realize that a certain conception of legal science always correlates with the social and historical context in which it functions. Medieval society was very different from our own. Social immobility and hierarchy set the tone, which points to a conception of rights as inherently unequal privileges enjoyed by the different social classes. The medieval legal order was full of special laws, privileges, and private jurisdictions. There were rules for the clergy, for merchants, and so on. The classical doctrine of legal science would, of course, be helpless in the face of this kind of system.

(e)   *The danger of ideological distortion: CLS versus CLD.* A final charge that is leveled against CLD is an ideology-critical claim. When the law is presented as a coherent body of standards based on a notion of justice, the classical doctrine opens itself up to the charge of ideological distortion. We can imagine different versions of this accusation. For instance, it is said that legal science covers the naked truth of power and coercion with the mantel of justice and impartiality. It has also been argued that the classical doctrine is guilty of presenting what is essentially the product of human whim as an objective fact. In addition, it has been noted that the classical doctrine makes it seem possible that a mess of contradictory principles can be formed into a coherent whole, but can this be achieved without putting too much strain on the material?

It is not possible to discuss and evaluate all points of criticism leveled against the classical doctrine here, so we will limit ourselves to a few remarks.

What does this say about the status of legal science? Is it a science or merely scholarship? We have seen that, measured by the criteria that have historically characterized science, legal science can certainly be called a scientific discipline. But this is only true of what we have here called the classical doctrine (CLD). Merely copying what the law or jurisprudence says cannot rightly be called scientific activity. The "black letter men" can be called scholars and their activities scholarly, but it is no more a science than giving a detailed description of a painstakingly assembled stamp collection.

However, we have also seen that the classical doctrine is under pressure from all sides. Postmodern interpretation theories,[99] American cynical realism, ideology criticism from the CLS movement, and various other movements have seriously undermined faith in a scientific practice based on objectivity, consensus, and reason. Cultural and political developments, such

99 See on this: Terry Eagleton, *Literary Theory. An Introduction*, Cambridge, MA, Oxford: Blackwell 1983; Terry Eagleton, *The Illusions of Postmodernism*, Oxford: Blackwell 1996; Ernest Gellner, *Postmodernism, Reason, and Religion*, London, New York: Routledge 1992.

as the increasing tendency to view the law as a value-neutral instrument in the service of policy aims, have also undercut the ideals of classical legal science.

The position of what the American philosopher Richard Rorty (1931–2007) calls the "ironist" is interesting. According to Rorty, the ironist is constantly trying to historically and naturalistically debunk the pretensions of the philosopher who is in search of objective truths. The ironist resists the stale vocabularies of what has become a scientistic culture, vocabularies which are said to be no more than hurdles in a society that puts free, democratic conversation first. Rorty believes that there should be a poeticized culture in which ideals of freedom and pluralism flourish and in which the utopian fantasist can change the language and start new vocabularies.[100]

These are fine words, and they have clearly had resonance in modern legal science. The ideals of the classical doctrine in legal science, which focus on the detection of the foundations of the law in the form of principles that constitute a justification for the everyday rules, are entirely alien to Rorty's relativism, of course. Several commentaries from CLS circles are strongly inspired by Rorty.[101] Especially with regard to interpretation, Rorty's views carry a great deal of weight these days.[102]

However, one could wonder if the implications of Rorty's ideas for legal science should not necessarily remain limited, considering the specific nature of the law and the interests at stake here. The culture of the utopian fantasist able to start new vocabularies for literature or philosophy might be a real advancement, but whether we should want *judges* to be inspired by these kinds of beliefs is highly doubtful. Surely, not even Rorty himself would applaud a judge interpreting the same legal provision entirely differently for him than for his neighbor. The law is simply not a poem upon which every legal scholar and legal practitioner can unleash his imagination, but a fundamental contract that people have agreed to in order to maintain peace. It has been said that a judge must do that which we all detest: make decisions. And not decisions about his own life, but decisions for other people, decisions that have serious consequences for all those involved. Such a judgment cannot be motivated by the statement that it could also have been different, or that it is possible to see the matter another way. The litigants expect a correct and just decision from the judge.

The problem with law and legal science is that something incredibly prosaic and yet highly consequential is always at stake: the continued existence of an effective and just order. Perhaps then, Rorty's and Nietzsche's

---

100 Richard Rorty, *Contingency, Irony, and Solidarity*, Cambridge: Cambridge University Press 1989, p. 44.
101 Such as: Singer, "The Player and the Cards," pp. 1–70.
102 For a good critique, see: Dworkin, "Pragmatism, Right Answers, and True Banality," pp. 359–389.

Fröhliche Wissenschaft is a slightly less appropriate source of inspiration for the law than it may be for other parts of the culture.

Empirical Legal Studies

Although Classical Legal Doctrine is certainly not dead, we should not be blinded to the fact that legal doctrine has recently gone through a development that may be characterized as a continuation of the direction taken by the American realists. Not in the sense that contemporary scholars take the sometimes sweeping statements of the American realists as their beacon, but in the sense that the American realists advocated empirical elements in their studies. Recently, we can clearly see more attention for what is called "Empirical Legal Studies" (ELS). We will close this chapter with an overview of some recent Empirical Legal Studies and authors advocating more empirical elements in legal scholarship.

Empirical Legal Studies and international law

There are many occasions where empirical research may be a welcome addition to legal scholarship. We will conclude this first chapter of *A New Introduction to Legal Method* with an overview of recent publications inspired by the new orientation toward empirical matters. Let us start with international law. Marlene Wind's *International Courts and Domestic Politics* (2018) presents an interdisciplinary analysis of international law and courts, examining a wide range of courts and judicial bodies, including human rights treaty bodies, and their impacts and shortcomings.[103] This book employs social-science methodology combined with classical case studies. The authors in this collected volume claim that legal dogmatics will not be enough to understand the increasingly complex world in which we live. They advocate empirical legal research as an addition to classical legal scholarship.

We find a similar approach in Schwartz-Shea and Yanow's *Interpretation and Method: Empirical Research Methods and the Interpretive Turn* (2015)[104] with discussions on accessing, generating, and analyzing social-science data, using techniques ranging from reflexive historical analysis to critical ethnography. The authors also reflect on their own research experiences, offering perspectives on how research topics, evidence, and methods intertwine to produce knowledge in the social sciences.

---

103 Marlene Wind, ed., *International Courts and Domestic Politics*, Cambridge: Cambridge University Press 2018.
104 Peregrine Schwartz-Shea and Dvora Yanow, eds., *Interpretation and Method: Empirical Research Methods and the Interpretive Turn*, London, New York: Routledge 2015.

Journal of Empirical Legal Studies

Much of the contemporary research inspired by what might be called "the empirical turn" appears in the *Journal of Empirical Legal Studies* (since 2004),[105] such as Jens Frankenreiter's article investigating the relationship between the behavior of judges at the European Court of Justice (ECJ) and the political preferences of the EU member states. Frankenreiter does this by analyzing the judge's citation behavior. His research shows that ECJ judges will more frequently cite judgments authored by judges who were appointed by member state governments whose preferences regarding European integration are similar. As in the case of US courts, non-random opinion assignment can threaten these results' validity. Frankenreiter concludes that the behavior of the members of the ECJ reflects the political preferences of member state governments.[106]

But other journals also run articles with an empirical element. Arne Niemann, in "EU Refugee Policies and Politics in Times of Crisis: Theoretical and Empirical Perspectives" (2018), advances empirical evidence to deepen our understanding of the crisis around EU refugee policies.[107]

Ilias Kapoutsis, Alexandros Papalexandris, Darren C. Treadway, and Jeffrey Bentley, in "Measuring Political Will in Organizations: Theoretical Construct Development and Empirical Validation" (2017), try to find empirical evidence for a concept like "political will." Does this have any basis in verifiable empirical evidence? Political will is an ambiguous term. It is often used to describe the failings of politicians, governments, and social movements. But can this concept be made operational? Can "will" be measured?[108]

In 2020, a Dutch initiative was launched to publish the Dutch encyclopedia of empirical studies, which presents an overview of Empirical Legal Studies in the Netherlands over the past 25 years.[109]

Some notes on religion

The twentieth century has often been characterized as marked by the return of religion. *God's Century* (2011) tells us that, contrary to predictions of

---

105 Blackwell Publishing, Oxford.
106 Jens Frankenreiter, "The Politics of Citations at the ECJ—Policy Preferences of E.U. Member State Governments and the Citation Behavior of Judges at the European Court of Justice," in: *Journal of Empirical Legal Studies*, 14(4) (December 2017), pp. 813–857.
107 *Journal of Common Market Studies*, 56(1) (2018), pp. 3–22.
108 *Journal of Management*, 43(7) (September 2017), pp. 2252–2280.
109 Catrien C. J. H. Bijleveld, Marijke Malsch, Bert Marseille, Monika Smit, and Arno J. Akkermans, eds., *Nederlandse Encyclopedie Empirical Legal Studies*, The Hauge: Boom Juridisch 2020.

continuing secularization, there is a worldwide increase of religious affili-
ation.[110] Titles such as *God is back* (2009),[111] *Constitutional Theocracy*
(2010),[112] and *American Theocracy* (2006),[113] all testify to this new interest in religion. As one might expect, this has also resulted in much scholarly attention for the relationship between religion and politics, as we can
see in Barry Bussey's *The Legal Revolution Against the Accommodation of
Religion: The Secular Age v. The Sexular Age* (2019),[114] Jasper Doomen's
and Mirjam van Schaik's *Religious Ideas in Liberal Democratic States*
(2021),[115] Hans-Martien ten Napel's *Constitutionalism, Democracy, and
Religious Freedom: To Be Fully Human* (2017),[116] Sophie van Bijsterveld's,
State and Religion: Re-assessing a Mutual Relationship (2018),[117] and
Sohail Wahedi's *The Constitutional Dynamics of Religious Manifestations:
On Abstraction from the Religious Dimension* (2019).[118]

Also, new interesting empirical research has been published on the matters indicated. Brian J. Grim and Roger Finke, in *The Price of Freedom
Denied: Religious Persecution and Conflict in the Twenty-First Century*
(2011), present a wealth of statistical and empirical material on previously
approached subjects as subjects for speculation and conjecture.[119]

Concerning the comparison between religious traditions and tolerance,
new work has been presented by the empirical sociologist of religion Ruud
Koopmans. In "Scriptural Legitimation and the Mobilization of Support for
Religious Violence: Experimental Evidence cross Three Religions and Seven
Countries" (2021), Koopmans, together with his co-authors, aims to give
empirical evidence on what might be called "religious extremism." In their
attempts to mobilize supporters and justify their actions, violent religious

---

110 Monica Toft, Daniel Philpott, and Timothy Samuel Shah, *God's Century: Resurgent Religion and Global Politics*, New York, London: W.W. Norton's Company 2011.
111 John Micklethwait and Adrian Wooldridge, *God Is Back: How the Global Rise of Faith
   Is Changing the World*, London: Allen Lane, Penguin Books 2009.
112 Ran Hirschl, *Constitutional Theocracy*, Cambridge, MA, London: Harvard University
   Press 2010.
113 Kevin Phillips, *American Theocracy: The Peril and Politics of Radical Religion, Oil, and
   Borrowed Money in the 21st Century*, New York: Viking 2006.
114 Barry W. Bussey, *The Legal Revolution Against the Accommodation of Religion: The
   Secular Age v. The Sexular Age*, Leiden: Dissertatie Leiden 2019.
115 Jasper Doomen and Mirjam van Schaik, eds., *Religious Ideas in Liberal Democratic
   States*, Lanham: Rowman & Littlefield 2021.
116 Hans-Martien ten Napel, *Constitutionalism, Democracy and Religious Freedom: To Be
   Fully Human*, London: Routledge 2017.
117 Sophie van Bijsterveld, *State and Religion: Re-assessing a Mutual Relationship*, The
   Hague: Eleven International Publishing 2018.
118 Sohail Wahedi, *The Constitutional Dynamics of Religious Manifestations: On Abstraction from the Religious Dimension*, Rotterdam: Erasmus University Rotterdam 2019.
119 Brian J. Grim and Roger Finke, *The Price of Freedom Denied: Religious Persecution and
   Conflict in the Twenty-First Century*, Cambridge: Cambridge University Press 2011.

extremists often refer to parts of scripture that legitimize violence against supposed enemies of the faith. Koopmans et al. investigate whether references to legitimations of violence in holy scripture can raise support for religious violence by implementing a survey experiment among 8000 Christian, Muslim, and Jewish believers in seven countries across Europe, North America, the Middle East, and Africa. According to the authors, their research shows that religious scripture can be effectively used to mobilize support for violence. They see this as a counterpoint to theoretical arguments that question the causal role of religion. Needless to say, these results have important implications for de-radicalization policies.[120]

Measuring the influence of religious convictions is also the topic of a study into the role of religion in judicial decision-making. Sepehr Shahshahani and Lawrence J. Liu, in "Religion and Judging on the Federal Courts of Appeals" (2017), presented a database of federal appellate cases involving religious liberties decided between 2006 and 2015. These data were used to investigate the role of religion in judicial decision-making. The authors found that Jewish judges are significantly more likely than non-Jewish colleagues to favor claimants in religious liberties. Still, they found no significant effects for other minority religions. The discrepancy between the judicial ruling of judges with a Jewish background and others is that Jewish judges show a more critical concern for the separation of church and state.[121]

Empirical Legal Studies and penal law

The two most influential theories on the legitimation of penal law are the deontological *retributive theory* and the *utilitarian theory of prevention*. For the legitimacy of the act of punishment, the prevention theory looks into the preventive character the penal sanction has or can have on the behavior of actual criminals or future potential criminals. It is clear that, from the perspective of the preventive theory, the legitimacy of punitive sanctions is heavily dependent on the *effectiveness* of the sanctions. Do they have any effect? And if so, are the effects considerable? These questions can be answered empirically.

Other questions regarding punishment also seem to be open to empirical research. For instance, in "Testing the Expressive Theory of Punishment" (2016), Kenworthey Bilz presents empirical support for the argument that the punishment of a wrongdoer affects the social standing of the victim.

---

120 Ruud Koopmans, Eylem Kanol, and Dietlind Stolle, "Scriptural Legitimation and the Mobilisation of Support for Religious Violence: Experimental Evidence across Three Religions and Seven Countries," in: *Journal of Ethnic and Migration Studies*, 47(7) (2021), pp. 1498–1516.
121 *Journal of Empirical Legal Studies*, 14(4) (December 2017), pp. 716–744.

Based on experiments, the author shows that sanctioning a perpetrator increases his victim's social standing in the community. And, conversely, failing to punish diminishes it.[122]

Empirical research is also highly relevant concerning the protracted discussion on the death penalty. The death penalty, abolished in Europe but still practiced in the United States, has always been an intriguing topic for empirical research. Some states in the United States have the death penalty, while others do not. In "The Death Penalty: Should the Judge or the Jury Decide Who Dies?" (2015), Valerie P. Hans, John H. Blume, Theodore Eisenberg, Amelia Courtney Hritz, Sheri Lynn Johnson, Caisa Elizabeth Royer, and Martin T. Wells address the effect of judge versus jury decision-making. They do this by analyzing a database of all capital sentencing phase hearing trials in the State of Delaware from 1977–2007.

It appears that, during the three decades of the study, Delaware shifted responsibility for death-penalty sentencing from the jury to the judge. Currently, Delaware is one of few states that gives the judge the final decision-making authority in capital trials.[123]

And what about the differences between male and female judges? Stephen J. Choi, Mitu Gulati, Mirya Holman, and Eric A. Posner raise a controversial but highly relevant question in "Judging Women" (2011). Their question is this: is there a legitimate ground to believe, as Justice Sonia Sotomayor asserted, that female judges might be better than male judges? Initially, her remarks generated accusations of sexism and potential bias. But what if they were true?

An equally controversial claim, of course, is that *male* judges are better than female judges, for instance, because the latter have benefited from affirmative action. But, again, could this be true?

Usually, these kinds of remarks do not transcend the status of "opinions," based on anecdotal evidence at best. But are they also susceptible to empirical analysis? Using a data set of all the state high court judges in 1998–2000, the authors try to give an empirical underpinning to remarks on these matters.[124]

Of course, due to the contemporary preoccupation with ideals like diversity, these elements—such as the diversity of the jury system—are also apt to be approached by means of empirical methods. Diversity on the jury promotes the perceived fairness of the jury system. In "Achieving Diversity on the Jury: Jury Size and the Peremptory Challenge" (2009), Shari Diamond, Destiny Peey, Francis Dolan, and Emily Dolan examine how the jury-selection process and jury size affect diversity.[125]

122 *Journal of Empirical Legal Studies*, 13(2) (June 2016), pp. 358–392.
123 *Journal of Empirical Legal Studies*, 12(1)(March 2015), pp. 70–99.
124 *Journal of Empirical Legal Studies*, 8(3) (September 2011), pp. 504–532.
125 *Journal of Empirical Legal Studies*, 6(3) (September 2009), pp. 425–449.

Although the concept of "diversity" gets good press nowadays, there is also the shadow side of diversity, viz., polarization. And the phenomenon of polarization gets a much more critical reception. Contemporary society, especially American society, is deemed to be highly polarized. What does that mean for the legitimacy of Supreme Court decisions on controversial matters? Do those ideological divisions affect the legitimacy of American political institutions, the Supreme Court in particular? Based on data from 1987 through 2005, the analysis of James L. Gibson in "The Legitimacy of the U.S. Supreme Court in a Polarized Polity" (2007) reveals that American popular support for the Court has *not* declined.[126]

The articles in journals about empirical matters are proliferating. Also, a good many books have been published on ELS. *The Oxford Handbook of Empirical Legal Research*, Peter Cane and Herbert M. Kritzer, editors, gives a good impression of Empirical Legal Studies in the early years of the first decade of the twenty-first century. It describes the emergence and swift development of the ELS movement and shines a light on methods and research groupings that predate ELS as it is today. "This may be respectively identified as (i) socio-legal/law and society (an interdisciplinary movement with solid roots in sociology but including scholars from a wide range of traditional disciplines including law), (ii) empirically oriented law-and-economics, and (iii) judicial behavior/politics."

Another book to be mentioned in this context is Marijke Malsch's *Law Is Too Important to Leave to Lawyers* (2021).[127] It demonstrates that far-reaching changes are presently occurring in legal systems. As an example, Malsch reflects on the rule of law, which is becoming less self-evident in several countries worldwide. She also highlights new types of crime—like organizational crime, human trafficking, money laundering, and various kinds of online crime—that are on the rise. The new developments can best be approached by a legal method that departs from the traditional legal approach she argues.

A book published with Edward Elgar Publishing has a similar scope: Willem H. van Boom, Pieter Desmet, and Peter Mascini edited *Empirical Legal Research in Action: Reflections on Methods and their Applications* (2018), also to make clear that empirical legal research is a growing field of academic expertise. They emphasize that lawyers are not always familiar with the possibilities and limitations of the available methods. *Empirical Legal Research in Action* presents readers with first-hand experiences of empirical research on law and legal issues.

126 *Journal of Empirical Legal Studies*, 4(3) (November 2007), pp. 507–538.
127 Marijke Malsch, *Law Is Too Important to Leave to Lawyers*, The Hague: Eleven International Publishing 2021.

An important question is how the relationship between ELS and the doctrinal legal doctrine has to be construed. This is the topic treated by Gareth Davies in "The Relationship between Empirical Legal Studies and Doctrinal Legal Research."[128] Davies notes that it has been a trend for American law schools to give due attention to ELS, and this trend is spreading to Europe.

Elaine Mak's inaugural address

New journals and anthologies testify to the vitality of the ELS movement, and new chairs dedicated to this field of research have come to the fore. In the Netherlands, Elaine Mak has taken the Chair of Empirical Study of Public Law, particularly Rule-of-Law Institutions, at the Erasmus University in Rotterdam. She accepted her assignment with *The Possibility of a European Judicial Culture* (2015).[129]

Elaine Mak advocates for the Empirical Study of Public law, in particular concerning the European institutions. She starts with Viviane Reding, former vice-president of the European Commission responsible for Justice, Fundamental Rights and Citizenship. Reding made a plea for European judicial culture. This is necessary, according to Reding, "in order to overcome the problem of diversity between the concepts and legal solutions developed in the EU member states."[130] But, as Mak contends, this can only be successfully done if legal scholars combine legal analysis with the concepts, theories, and methods of other academic disciplines "in order to clarify the current developments regarding European judiciaries and to provide guidance to the future."[131] That Mak does not consider this to be an easy undertaking is clear from her warning that one of the challenges is to "establish the balance between possibly overlapping or conflicting national and European legal rules, and safeguard the fundamental principles of the national legal system."[132]

According to Mak, the empirical approach can also enhance the status of legal scholarship as a real science. Mak refers to an anecdote that is reminiscent of the story that we find at the beginning of this chapter. She references a remark made by the 15-year-old son of a dean of the University of Amsterdam. After the boy had learned that his father was being interviewed for the science supplement of a national newspaper, he said: "What

---

128 *Erasmus Law Review*, 2 (September 2020), pp. 1–12.
129 Elaine Mak, *The Possibility of a European Judicial Culture*, Inaugural Lecture for the Chair of Empirical Study of Public Law, in particular of Rule-of-Law Institutions, at Erasmus School of Law, Erasmus University Rotterdam, delivered on 21 November 2014, The Hague: Eleven International Publishing 2015.
130 Reding, quoted by Mak, ibid., p. 7.
131 Ibid., p. 7.
132 Ibid., p. 11.

are you doing in the science supplement of the newspaper? I thought you were studying law."[133] Mak comments that the son's question reflects "a definition in which 'science' refers to the natural sciences, such a physics and chemistry, and which excludes the humanities and social sciences, such a history, economics, political science, and law."[134] Mak also references the famous words by Oliver Wendell Holmes (1841–1935), but this time not to confront the "black letter man" with the advocates of more judicial discretion, but to confront the black letter bogeyman with the empirical approach of the man of statistics:

> For the rational study of the law the blackletter man may be the man of the present, but the man of the future is the man of statistics and the master of economics.[135]

It is understandable that people who advocate statistics and economics find inspiration in the latter part of this quote. But it is fair to say that correcting the black letter approach to the law is not only possible with statistics and economics but also with methods from the social sciences in the broadest sense of the term. One may think of hermeneutics, techniques, and ways of thinking based on what the Germans call *Geisteswissenschaften*.[136]

What do we mean by "empirical" when we speak of Empirical Legal Studies? Mak gives us the following description: the term refers to "research which, through the use of specific research methods, observes social reality and develops or tests theories."[137] Empirical research is descriptive rather than normative. It uses quantitative empirical approaches, i.e., based on surveys, counting, experiments, and network studies. "Empirical methods represent a relatively new approach in legal research," Mak contends, "in particular in the field of public law."

Mak also gives other empirical legal research a broader dispersion, such as the ideas developed by the American scholar Melissa Waters on what she calls "creeping monism."[138] Her ideas are all the more interesting because she addresses something less widespread in the European context, viz. a critical reflection on the scope and significance of international law. Waters

---

133 Ibid., p. 15
134 Ibid., p. 15.
135 Ibid., p. 16. Holmes, "The Path of the Law," p. 457 and p. 461.
136 Hans-George Gadamer, *Wahrheit und Methode: Grundzüge einer philosophischen Hermeneutik*, fourth edition, Tübingen: J.C.B. Mohr (Paul Siebeck) 1975; Gregory Leyh, ed., *Legal Hermeneutics, History, Theory, and Practice*, Berkeley: University of California Press 1992.
137 Mak, *The Possibility of a European Judicial Culture*, p. 16.
138 Melissa A. Waters, "Creeping Monism: The Judicial Trend Toward Interpretive Incorporation of Human Rights Treaties," in: *Columbia Law Review*, 107 (2007), pp. 628–705.

says: ELS can be an exciting tool to research what has been called "creeping monism." Waters contributes to what in the United States is called the "role of foreign authority in U.S. courts: the use of international human rights treaties in interpreting domestic law." She argues that recent US Supreme Court decisions (including *Roper v. Simmons*) should be viewed

> as part of a transnational trend among common law courts—a trend that she calls creeping monism. Common law judges are increasingly abandoning their traditional dualist orientation to treaties. They are beginning to utilize human rights treaties despite the absence of implementing legislation giving domestic legal effect to the treaties.

Waters says that "by developing various so-called interpretive incorporation techniques, judges are entrenching international treaty obligations into domestic law, thus becoming potent mediators between the domestic and international legal regimes."

Her article

> traces the growing influence of creeping monism and interpretive incorporation to shift the discourse away from the all-or-nothing debate of recent years to a more nuanced understanding of the complexities involved in incorporating international legal sources into the work of domestic courts.

It also "develops a typology of interpretive incorporation techniques that courts are utilizing" and provides—and here ELS comes in—"statistical evidence regarding the use of human rights treaties across jurisdictions."

But, back to Mak. Mak concludes her inaugural address with a plea for a "multidisciplinary, including empirical, research approach."[139] In *A New Introduction to Legal Method*, we support this approach. Empirical Legal Studies can undoubtedly complement traditional, more normative legal research. But it cannot replace it, of course. Especially in a time of great uncertainty, the normative approach remains necessary for future legal scholarship.

The discussion on "crimmigration"

We want to conclude this chapter with some observations on recent work on "crimmigration." This part of legal scholarship can also be seen as a manifestation of Empirical Legal Studies.

---

139 Mak, *The Possibility of a European Judicial Culture*, p. 25.

Two articles are a good introduction to the field, one by the Dutch legal scholars M. van der Woude, J. van der Leun, and J. Nijland titled "Crimmigration in the Netherlands" (2014),[140] and one titled "Deconstructing Crimmigration" (2018) by César Cuauhtémoc Garcia Hernández.[141]

"Crimmigration" is a term introduced in 2006 by the American scholar Juliet Schumpf, the Robert E. Jones Professor of Advocacy and Ethics at Lewis & Clark Law School, denoting the merger of immigration law and criminal law.[142] The point of departure for reflections on this subject is that the American Congress authorized increasingly harsh criminal penalties for immigration offenses. Non-citizens face mandatory deportation and a host of other negative measures. By doing this, the state creates an ever-expanding population of outsiders, the Dutch scholars point out, following Stumpf. Aliens are being made into criminals without the protections that ordinary citizens enjoy.[143]

Hernández formulates the problem as follows: "Born of fears of migrants ferrying drugs into the United States, fueled by concern of foreign terrorists, and concretized by a three-decades long securitization of migration, crimmigration law now occupies a prominent place in the country's legal regime."[144] Unlike for most of the nation's history, Hernández continues, today, immigration poses a "hornet's nest of pitfalls for migrants who encounter the criminal justice system."[145]

The Dutch scholars affirm the importance of the subject as well. Stumpf's analysis also has relevance for the Netherlands and other countries where the same tendencies that are prevalent in the United States can be observed, they claim. Asylum seekers, refugees, and members of ethnic minority groups are subjected to what some scholars call "discourses of criminalization in government policy and legislation." The "unknown and undocumented are not unwanted, but dangerous," as two British scholars note in their analysis of the phenomenon of crimmigration.[146]

---

140 M.A.H. van der Woude, J.P. van der Leun, J.A., Nijland, "Crimmigration in the Netherlands," in: *Law & Social Theory*, 39(3) (Summer 2014), pp. 56–579.

141 César Cuauhtémoc Garcia Hernández, "Deconstructing Crimmigration," in: *University of California Davis Law Review*, 51 (2018), pp. 197–253.

142 Juliet Stumpf, "The Crimmigration Crisis: Immigrants, Crime, and Sovereign Power," in: *American University Law Review*, 56 (2006), pp. 367–419.

143 Van der Woude, van der Leun, and Nijland, "Crimmigration in the Netherlands," p. 562.

144 Hernández, "Deconstructing Crimmigration," p. 197.

145 Ibid., p. 198.

146 Mary Bosworth and Mhairi Guild, "Governing Through Migration Control: Security and Citizenship in Britain," *British Journal of Criminology*, 48 (2008), pp. 703–719, p. 703, quoted by van der Woude, van der Leun, and Nijland, "Crimmigration in the Netherlands," p. 560.

Building on this American and British research, van der Woude, van der Leun, and Nijland issue a warning to the Dutch that the country's reputation as a beacon of tolerance is at stake. "Once internationally seen as a beacon of enlightenment and tolerance concerning migration issues, according to many, the country has now turned into a multicultural disaster."[147]

Van der Woude, van der Leun, and Nijland use crimmigration as a "sensitizing concept." This term was introduced by Blumer in 1954[148] to contrast with so-called "definitive concepts." "Whereas definitive concepts provide prescriptions of what to see, sensitizing concepts merely suggest directions along which to look."[149] Sensitizing concepts can be used as interpretive devices. They can serve as a starting point for a qualitative study.[150] Van der Woude, van der Leun, and Nijland propose the following definition of crimmigration: "the intertwinement of crime control and migration control."[151]

Directly after the Second World War, the Netherlands was a country of emigration. But the situation changed in the early 1960s. With the arrival of guest workers from the Mediterranean, the Netherlands developed into a nation of immigration. Immigration was initially thought to be temporary, but it became permanent because of family reunification, family formation, and asylum migration.

As van der Woude, van der Leun, and Nijland make clear in their contribution, the policy model adopted in the Netherlands to cope with migration was initially *multiculturalism*.[152] That means non-intervention and "special arrangements for migrants, financed by the state."[153] But when linkages between crime and migration became openly discussed, this Dutch consensus evaporated. The politicization of the topic became more intense. Migration and integration of newcomers became a hotly debated issue. Outspoken critics of multiculturalism came to the fore, like the right-wing politician Pim Fortuyn (1948–2002), who was murdered by a "radical-left environmental activist after a radio-interview."[154] These occurrences contributed to the "criminalization of immigration" and the banning of "'undesirable'

147 Ibid., p. 561.
148 Blumer, H., "What Is Wrong with Social Theory," in: *American Sociological Review*, 18 (1954), pp. 3–10.
149 Van der Woude, van der Leun, and Nijland, "Crimmigration in the Netherlands," p. 561.
150 Ibid., p. 561.
151 Ibid., p. 562.
152 See on this: Mathieu Bock-Côté, *Le multi-culturalisme comme religion politique*, Paris: Les éditions du Cerf 2016; Rumy Hasan, *Multiculturalism: Some Inconvenient Truths*, York: Politico's Publishing Ltd 2010; Kenan Malik, *Multiculturalism and Its Discontents*, Calcutta: Seagull Books 2013.
153 Van der Woude, van der Leun, and Nijland, "Crimmigration in the Netherlands," p. 563.
154 Ibid., p. 565.

aliens," as well as the country "criminalizing illegal stay," and embarking on the "immigrationalization of criminal law."[155]

Van der Woude, van der Leun, and Nijland conclude their article with the observation that there are clear indications that crimmigration is occurring in the Netherlands. "Central aspects that we have described in the US literature are also recognizable in the Dutch case." They end their article issuing the following warning:

> Although these developments can be attributed to some extent to panic and generalized fears of change and of outsiders, into which politicians and media have tapped, empirical studies have also shown that crime by young people with a migrant background is a significant problem across Europe (Tonry 1997,[156] Engbersen, van der Leun, and De Boom 2007).[157]

Now, let us end this chapter with a caveat.

The meaning of Empirical Legal Studies

It has been said that the value of Empirical Legal Studies can be compared with Israeli archeology: some of the ideas we deeply cherish about the way reality is structured can nonetheless be false. That can be said about all empirical legal science, of course. Science can present us with facts that we would rather ignore. But presupposed to the "corrective character" of empirical science is that we accept the power of "facts." If we—with Nietzsche—subscribe to the position that there are no facts, only interpretations, all empirical studies are useless. This means that postmodernism and its accompanying relativism are factors that undermine the importance of not only Empirical Legal Studies but all empirical studies.[158] This is a topic we cannot give the attention it deserves within the context of this chapter.

---

155 See the successive paragraphs in ibid., pp. 561–569.
156 Michael Tonry, *Ethnicity, Crime, and Immigration: Comparative and Cross-National Perspectives*, Chicago: University of Chicago Press 1997.
157 Godfried Engbersen, Joanne P. van der Leun, and Jan de Boom, "The Fragmentation of Migration and Crime in the Netherlands," in: Michael Tonry and Catrien J. Bijleveld, eds., *Crime and Justice in the Netherlands*, Chicago: Chicago University Press 2007, pp. 389–452.
158 Alan Sokal and Jean Bricmont, *Impostures Intellectuelles*, Paris: Éditions Odile Jacob 1997.

Chapter 2

American realism

> The law—a body of rules apparently devised for infallibly determining what is right and what is wrong and for deciding who should be punished for misdeeds—inevitably becomes a partial substitute for the Father-as-Infallible-Judge.[1]

Introduction

In the second chapter of *A New Introduction to Legal Method*, we will delve deeper into one of the jurisprudential movements that exerted great influence on contemporary legal thought, viz. American realism, already mentioned in Chapter 1.

In the early twentieth century, a number of writers surfaced in the United States whose work later became known as "American realism." What does "realism" mean here? In philosophy, this term is used to refer to the doctrine of Plato: it is not the concrete things of the here and now that exist in the full sense of the word, but only the "ideas," the general models of the concrete things. The ideas are "res" (Latin for "things"). That is why Plato's doctrine is called "realism."[2] The philosopher ought to devote himself to acquiring knowledge of these ideas.

However, in philosophy, the word "realism" is also used to describe an entirely different theory: the view of reality that presupposes that material things exist independent of the minds of the people perceiving them. For a reader not schooled in philosophy, such a theory will hardly be surprising, because it corresponds entirely with our everyday experience of reality. We assume that the material world will continue to exist even if there are no people to perceive it. In philosophy, however, the position that material

---

1 Jerome Frank, *Law and the Modern Mind*, Gloucester, MA: Peter Smith 1970 (1930), p. 19.
2 A term, incidentally, that only became the common descriptor of Plato's philosophy in the Middle Ages. Before that time, his philosophy was referred to as "idealism" (as it is nowadays).

DOI: 10.4324/9781003282570-3

things have no existence apart from human consciousness has also been defended. The Irish philosopher G. Berkeley (1684–1753) pithily summarized this view with the words "To be is to be perceived." Berkeley argued that his theory, though bizarre at first glance, actually aligns with common sense. How do we know that plants, trees, and houses exist? Is it not only because we can perceive them with our senses? So how can we be certain that things will continue to exist when we do not perceive them?

In contrast with what many see as Berkeley's somewhat bizarre theory, others have defended the "realist" position: the notion that the material world exists independent of human consciousness. For instance, the Russian revolutionary Vladimir Ilyich Ulyanov, better known by the alias Lenin (1870–1924), attempted to substantiate realism in an extensive analysis of Berkeley's views.

Let us return to the subject at hand: American realism. Does realism, in combination with the word "American," have anything to do with the aforementioned forms of realism? The answer is plain: "realism" in combination with the word "American" has little in common with the way the word has traditionally been used in philosophy. In fact, one of the realists, Jerome Frank (1889–1957), even uses the term "Platonism" as a kind of insult. As we will see, Berkeley's realism in particular does have *some* commonality with American realism, but even here, the differences predominate. It seems justified to say that the word "realism," as referring to a school of legal science, most closely resembles realism in the most everyday sense of the word. This "realist" is not impressed with lofty theories and models but focuses on the manifestations of ordinary practice. In a way, the American realists envisioned something similar with regard to the law and legal science. Roscoe Pound (1870–1964) wrote in 1930 that legal realists intended realism to mean: "fidelity to nature, accurate recording of things as they are, as contrasted with things as they are imagined to be, or wished to be, or as one feels they ought to be."[3] Jerome Frank, the realist who coined the term, says that realism means presenting things in a non-romanticized way, as opposed to "fantasying," "prettifying," and "wish-ful thinking."[4] Incidentally, in the foreword of the sixth edition of his book *Law and the Modern Mind* (1930), he expresses regret at having ever used the term "realism."[5] After all, realism already had a specific philosophical meaning, and so it would have been better for him to speak of "constructive skepticism" to refer to the group of legal scholars and practitioners he had classified as realists. (His proposal to

---

3 Roscoe Pound, "The Call for a Realist Jurisprudence," in: *Harvard Law Review*, XLIV (1930–1931), pp. 697–711, p. 697.
4 Jerome Frank, "Are Judges Human?" in: *University of Philadelphia Law Review*, 17 (1931), p. 258.
5 Frank, *Law and the Modern Mind*, pp. viii–xxxi.

speak of skeptics instead had no effect, so we will conform to the standard usage.) According to Frank, realists are characterized by a certain doubt with regard to the traditional ways of looking at the law, as well as by a penchant for reform.

Realism dominated American legal thought for a considerable time. We can distinguish three generations of realists, of which the most important representatives will be presented here.

The first generation consists of O.W. Holmes (1841–1935) and J.C. Gray (1839–1915). Whether this first generation ought to be classified as American realism or as one of its predecessors is, to a certain extent, an arbitrary question. If one believes that the central elements of the later realist movement are clearly present in Holmes and Gray, viewing them as the first generation of realists has merit. Many names are associated with the second generation of realists but usually considered the most famous representatives are J. Frank (1889–1957) and K. Llewellyn (1893–1962).

The most important works of the second-generation realists are *The Bramble Bush* (1930)[6] by Llewellyn and *Law and the Modern Mind* (1930) by Frank.[7] We will primarily speak to Frank's work, not because Llewellyn has not produced interesting ideas, but because Llewellyn often presents a more nuanced adaptation of the realist positions and seems less representative of the movement as a whole.

Some offshoots of realism can also be distinguished. The movement passed its zenith after the second generation, but the work of the American philosopher Richard Taylor (1919–2003) can be considered one of the few offshoots of realism.[8]

A school? A movement? A mindset?

An often-discussed subject in the handbooks is the uniformity of the movement. Is it even really a movement? One thing is certain: there is no common manifesto, no unambiguous creed, and, according to some, not even consensus on a substantial part of the basic principles. Herbert Hart (1907–1992)

---

6 K.N. Llewellyn, *The Bramble Bush, On Our Law and Its Study*, New York, London, Rome: Oceana Publications, Inc. 1960 (1930).

7 William Twining, *Karl Llewellyn and the Realist Movement*, London: Weidenfeld and Nicolson 1973, p. 71. Twining's book is the definitive work on Llewellyn. Julius Paul wrote a monography about Frank's work: *The Legal Realism of Jerome N. Frank, A Study of Fact-skepticism and the Judicial Process*, The Hague: Martinus Nijhoff 1959. See also: Neil Duxbury, "Jerome Frank and the Legacy of Legal Realism," in: *Journal of Law and Society*, 18 (1991), pp. 175–205.

8 For biographical information about him, see John Donnelly's introduction in: Richard Taylor, *Reflective Wisdom, Richard Taylor on Issues That Matter*, Buffalo, New York: Prometheus Books 1989, pp. 11–17.

speaks of "the loosely named 'Realists' of the 1930s."[9] We also hear this from realists themselves. Llewellyn spoke of a "mass of trends in legal work and thinking." There was thought to be no "coherent group." According to Llewellyn, the only characteristics were skepticism, a distancing from traditionalism, and also "curiosity." This shows that the famous representatives of realism do not put a great deal of emphasis on the common factor in their work. There is no realist school, Llewellyn writes.[10] He even adds that it also is not likely that something like a school will ever arise. There is no officially accepted creed that all realists support. "New recruits acquire tools and stimulus, not masters, nor over-mastering ideas."[11] What connects the realists is only what they *deny*. They are more a unified group in their "skepticisms" and in their "curiosity"; classifying the positive content of their thought as unified is much more difficult.

However, one might wonder if they are really that disparate. In a certain sense, Llewellyn sensed this too, because, despite his caution, he still made a list of realism's characteristics, although he presented them as the features of a movement, not of a school. This movement can be distinguished by the common starting point of its different participants. He lists:

(1) The idea that the law is dynamic and that it is made by judges
(2) The idea that the law is a means to an end, not an end in itself
(3) The idea that society is always changing, and more quickly than the law
(4) The temporary separation of "is" and "ought" for study purposes
(5) A certain distrust of traditional legal rules and concepts insofar as these claim to adequately describe what judges and others do
(6) Together with a certain distrust of the traditional rules comes distrust of the claim that it is the rules that determine the judge's decision
(7) The ambition to regroup cases and situations into smaller categories than has been customary in the past
(8) The idea that the law needs to be judged by its effects
(9) The idea that the law needs to be constantly and programmatically criticized.[12]

Here, we try to define realism on the basis of ten characteristics. These features can be ascribed to different realists in different combinations. This

9 H.L.A. Hart, "Positivism and the Separation of Law and Morals," in: *Harvard Law Review*, 71 (1958), p. 593, also in: H.L.A. Hart, *Essays in Jurisprudence and Philosophy*, Oxford: Clarendon Press 1983, pp. 49–87.
10 Karl N. Llewellyn, "Some Realism about Realism," in: *Harvard Law Review*, 44 (1931), p. 1222, also in: *Jurisprudence, Realism in Theory and Practice*, Chicago, London: The University of Chicago Press, pp. 42–77, p. 53. The article was an answer to Pound's critique of the realists in "The Call for a Realist Jurisprudence," p. 697.
11 Llewellyn, "Some Realism," in: *Jurisprudence*, p. 53.
12 Ibid., p. 57.

means that we will not look for a common starting point, like Llewellyn, but will instead attempt to present a number of characteristics that are to be found in various combinations in individual thinkers who are considered part of the movement. So, this is a description of realism in its most common manifestation. That means not every realist will have *all* the characteristics discussed here, and it could even turn out that there is not even a *single* characteristic that they all share.

If one were to demand that there has to be one common characteristic in order to present the movement as a unified whole, it would have to be a very general feature, such as that the realists want to perceive the law "realistically," meaning with a fresh perspective and an eye to what actually happens in legal practice, the latter in contrast to what the handbooks *say* occurs.

A certain preoccupation with the judge as an actor in law formation could also be named as a very general tenet many realists would ascribe to. However, such an approach offers us a too-limited view of realism. We will gain a better understanding of the richness of this movement by examining ten characteristics that can be found in its representatives in different combinations: (i) they resist the tradition of Langdell (more on this in a moment); (ii) they put their trust in the construction of empirical generalizations of judges' behavior; (iii) they are focused mostly on the judge as the competent developer of the law; (iv) realists are rule-skeptics; (v) some realists also embrace fact-skepticism; (vi) they emphasize the role of the judge's decision as a source of law; (vii) they study the determinants of judges' decisions using social science methods; (viii) the law is viewed as an instrument to steer society; (ix) they advocate changes to legal education; and (x) the realists criticize the role of important American institutions, like the Supreme Court.

What they oppose: Langdell's method

But let us begin with what the realists were *against*. Llewellyn and many other commentators have often stressed that realism distinguishes itself from other movements in its rejection of a certain tradition, not so much in its shared positive views about certain principles. So what is it that the realists reject? They reject the "spirit of Langdell."

Frank in particular formulates a critique of the views of the influential legal scholar Langdell that is representative of realism.[13]

13 See on Langdell: Mary Ann Glendon, *A Nation under Lawyers, How the Crisis in the Legal Profession Is Transforming American Society*, New York: Farrar, Strauss and Giroux 1994, pp. 184–185; Anthony T. Kronman, *The Lost Lawyer, Failing Ideals of the Legal Profession*, Cambridge, MA, London: The Belknap Press of Harvard University Press 1993, pp. 170–174.

Christopher Columbus Langdell (1826–1906) graduated from Harvard in 1854, returning to the school as a professor and dean after some time in legal practice. He taught at Harvard for 30 years and introduced the case method for the study of the law in his *Cases on Contracts* (1871). Langdell had an enormous influence on the law program. He turned the position of dean to an office that wielded great power within the university and extended the program to become a jurist to three years. It has been said that he "invented the academic jurist." He appointed young men as teachers without any experience in legal practice.[14]

Incidentally, what Frank writes about Langdell is a somewhat tendentious representation of Langdell's ideals, but that is also how it is so typical of what the realists believed themselves. It is a continuation of the distinction Roscoe Pound introduced between "law in the books" and "law in action." Langdell represented the "book-law" approach.

Langdell was always in the library, Frank writes. He even served as an assistant librarian for a time, and every so often he could be found sleeping at a library table. There is a story about Langdell that one time he woke up and—apparently having dreamed about a bygone era—said: "Oh, if only I could have lived in the time of the Plantagenets!"[15]

The image created of Langdell seems intended to illustrate the contradiction between the practical, experience-driven approach of the realists and the book smarts of the Langdellian style. Admittedly, Langdell worked as a practicing jurist for 16 years. But he rarely argued cases, Frank notes, downplaying Langdell's practical experience again. He did most of his work behind a desk and led a very reclusive life. He also had little to do with the corporate world (also not something that, when pointed out by a realist, is meant as a compliment).

> Is it any wonder that such a man had an almost exclusive interest in books? The raw material that he called 'law', he devoutly believed, was to be discovered in a library and nowhere else; it consisted, as he himself said, solely of what could be found in print.

The relationship between a client and a jurist, the face-to-face confrontation with a jury, the central elements of the business of the law—Langdell actually had very little understanding of these things. "The greater part of the realities of the life of the average lawyer was unreal to him."

---

14 See: J.A. Wightman, "Christopher Columbus Landell," in: A.W.B. Simpson, ed., *Biographical Dictionary of the Common Law*, London: Butterworths 1984, p. 302.

15 Jerome Frank, *Courts on Trial, Myth and Reality in American Justice*, Princeton: Princeton University Press 1973 (1949), p. 225. The Plantagenets were a royal house that originated from the lands of Anjou in France. The final ruler was Richard III of England (1452–1485).

In fact, Langdell turned his limitations into a central part of his legal creed. Jurists ought to close their eyes to any number of factors surrounding the law. The essence of his philosophy of the law is captured in two premises. First, that the law ought to be viewed as a science. Second, that all the available material of that science ought to come from printed sources, from books. He emphatically did not wish to concern himself with the study of the hard realities of legal life, such as what happened in a courtroom. In that sense, he was miles away from the ELS movement that we have treated at the end of Chapter 1. He declared the library to be the jurist's main domain of research. As the chemist has his laboratory, the jurist has a library. Harvard, in particular, ought to distinguish itself from other universities by a strict focus on the library, on book learning. "Without the library the School would lose its most important characteristics, and indeed its identity," Langdell solemnly declared. And, for a long time, these ideas became the ruling orthodoxy at Harvard's Law School. "The neurotic escapist character of Langdell soon stamped itself on the educational programs of our leading law schools," Frank remarks.[16] What qualifies someone to teach law is not experience at a law firm, but legal scholarship.

If these were the beliefs of one of the most respected professors at Harvard, it is not hard to imagine what the law program looked like, according to Frank. Many of the law schools employed people who had never advised a client, drafted a contract, consulted a witness, or argued a case in front of a judge. "The Langdell spirit choked American legal education. It tended to compel even the experienced practitioner, turned teacher, to belittle his experience at the bar."[17]

Studying the law in real life

Langdell developed the so-called "case-system." That means students are expected to study certain cases. In and of itself, this is not something to which the realists object. After all, cases are real-life examples, and can therefore garner realist support. However, the realists did object to the academic way in which these cases were studied. Frank disapprovingly notes, for instance, that only a *part* of the case under consideration was actually analyzed: the legal part, the part that is put before the higher court to be adjudicated. This leaves out the *facts* and what the lower courts (the trial courts) have said about them. We will come back to Frank's critique of this later. Here, the issue only represents a criticism of the way Langdell analyzed cases.

Langdellian legal science studied only a *part* of the law: not a case, but an element of a case. The law students are flower growers who only practice

16 Ibid., p. 227.
17 Ibid., p. 227.

cutting the flowers and pay no mind to the ground in which they grow, Frank writes. They are like dog breeders who have only ever seen stuffed dogs. Frank asked his students who of them had ever seen the inside of a court-room, and only a few raised their hands. Why do students not *directly* study the material they will later be expected to master? The leading institutes of legal education are still "library law schools" or "book-law schools." They are not what they should be: "lawyer-schools."[18]

What can be done to change this? Frank makes four suggestions. First, a considerable number of teachers should have practical legal experience. This does not have to be true of all teachers, but at least some of them should be well-versed in real-life legal practice.

Incidentally, Frank does believe that there should be room in every school for what he calls the "book-teacher," but it should no longer be the case that "library-law" completely dominates the universities, as it does now.[19]

Second, the case-system ought to be changed in that the *entire* case is made the object of study. The textbooks should also be adapted accordingly.

Third, Frank makes a case for what we now call "skills." The idea is that the student learns by *doing*, not just by reading and talking about what can be done.

Finally, Frank calls attention to what we now call an interdisciplinary approach to problems. Other sciences, such as history, economics, political science, psychology, and anthropology, should also be studied by legal scholars, and not as *separate* disciplines, apart from the law, such as when a law program is preceded by introductory courses in these sciences, but in an integrated framework.

Realism's first founding father: Holmes

So, no book smarts, but the gritty reality of real-life legal practice. Out of the library and into the courtroom. This naturally brings us to the person who plays a prominent part in realist philosophy: Oliver Wendell Holmes Jr. (1841–1935), the first founding father of realism.[20] Holmes was a kind of patron saint to the realists. He is revered by all as a kind of infallible exemplar. He embodies the ideal of a scholar with practical experience. His writings are characterized by his cynical vision and the grandiose style in which he presented his thoughts.

---

18 Ibid., p. 230.
19 Ibid., p. 232.
20 See: Robert Goedecke, "Holmes, Brandeis, and Frankfurter: Differences in Pragmatic Juris-prudence," in: *Ethics*, LXXIV (January 1964), pp. 83–96; A.M. Hol, "Oliver Wendell Hol-mes," in: P.B. Cliteur and M.A. Loth, eds., *Rechtsfilosofen van de twintigste eeuw*, Arnhem: Gouda Quint 1992, pp. 11–45.

Holmes was born in Boston, and after the Civil War (1861–1864), in which he fought, he studied at Harvard Law School. After having gained some experience in legal practice, he taught at Harvard from 1870 till 1883, in the final years as a professor. It was in this period that he wrote his only book: *The Common Law* (1880).[21] He did write countless essays, though, and book reviews and letters, as well as giving many lectures.[22] Many of these writings were later published.[23] Those especially reflected his immense erudition. He moves with apparent ease from James's philosophy to the work of Dante and from there to Supreme Court rulings or a recent tome in the field of legal science.

After 1883, Holmes once again devoted himself to legal practice. In 1883, he became a member of the Massachusetts Bench, and in 1899, he became *Chief Justice of the Supreme Judicial Court of Massachusetts*. In 1902, President Theodore Roosevelt made him a member of the national Supreme Court, a position from which he did not step down until as late as 1931.

Holmes is a legendary figure in the American legal tradition. In the sense that he was the source of countless fledgling ideas developed further by others, he can be compared with Socrates. In the famous *Locher*-case, Holmes provided the beginnings of a modern theory of federalism, the idea of judicial self-restraint, and the idea of a living constitution, described by Posner as "the idea that the Constitution should be constructed flexibly, liberally, rather than strictly, narrowly."[24] However, the best way to describe Holmes's views on interpretation is that he believed that the Constitution should not be an instrument of the "dead hand of the past."[25]

Holmes was also a kind of liberal, although it is hard to say what kind of liberal.[26] Not a New Deal liberal, in any case. The interesting thing was that the social experiments he believed the legislator should be free to run did not

21 Oliver Wendell Holmes, *The Common Law*, in: Mark DeWolfe Howe, ed., Boston, Toronto: Little, Brown and Company 1963 (1881).
22 *Holmes-Laski Letters, The Correspondence of Mr. Justice Holmes and Harold J. Laski 1916–1935*, two volumes, Mark de Wolfe Howe, ed., New York: Atheneum 1963; *Holmes-Pollock Letters, The Correspondence of Mr Justice Holmes and Sir Frederick Pollock, 1874–1932*, Mark DeWolfe Howe, ed., two volumes in one second edition, Cambridge, MA: Harvard University Press 1961.
23 Oliver Wendell Holmes, *Collected Legal Papers*, New York: Peter Smith 1952 (1920); *The Essential Holmes, Selections from the Letters, Speeches, Judicial Opinions, and Other Writings of Oliver Wendell Holmes, Jr.*, edited and with an introduction by Richard A. Posner, Chicago, London: The University of Chicago Press, 1992; *The Holmes Reader*, selected and edited by Julius J. Marke, New York: Oceana's Docket Books, Dobbs Ferry 1964.
24 Smith, *The Essential Holmes*, p. xii.
25 Ibid.
26 See: Edward White, *The American Judicial Tradition, Profiles of Leading American Judges*, expanded edition, New York, Oxford: Oxford University Press 1988, the chapter "Holmes, Brandeis, and the Origins of Judicial Liberalism," pp. 150–177.

carry his personal approval. There was also a somewhat cynical side to him, sometimes attributed to his experiences in the Civil war.[27]

Holmes was also—like many influential people—controversial. His exact contribution to American legal science is still a matter of debate. Posner writes that most of Holmes's brilliant written dissenting opinions owe their fame and influence to their author's rhetorical skill, not to the veracity of their arguments.[28]

We think Posner is right. Holmes was a great judge partly *because* he was a great writer. In Posner's anthology, Holmes's wealth of ideas is evident. It also shows that he was much more than a writer about exclusively legal subjects. In his unconnected snippets and thoughts, aphorisms, and essays, he is revealed to be a pragmatist, atheist, liberal, materialist, aesthetic, utilitarian, militarist, skeptic, biologist, Darwinist, Calvinist, positivist, stoic, behaviorist, existentialist, and glorifier of a Nietzschean "will to power" ideology. "Whether the elements of his thought coalesce to form a coherent philosophy of life I doubt," Posner writes, and those who have read the collection will agree. To Posner, Holmes is one of the "anti-philosophers."[29] The curious combination of Calvinism and cynicism could perhaps be characterized as "Calvinism without God."[30]

An abstract analytical presentation of Holmes's thinking is virtually impossible. Those who wish to typify his thinking are best served by referring to the man himself. we will do the same.

Holmes the aphorist

Oftentimes, Holmes expresses a distaste for big and grandiose ideas. "My bet is that we have not the kind of cosmic importance that the parsons and philosophers teach. I doubt if a shudder would go through the spheres if the whole ant heap were kerosened," so Holmes wrote in an oft-quoted passage.[31] He adds an interesting note: "I think the attitude of being a little god, even if the great one has vanished, is the sin against the Holy Ghost."[32]

---

27 See: Edmund Wilson, "Justice Oliver Wendell Holmes," in: *The Portable Edmund Wilson*, edited, with an introduction and notes, by Lewis M. Dabney, Harmondsworth: Penguin Books 1983, pp. 507–555.

28 Smith, *The Essential Holmes*, p. xvii.

29 Ibid., p. xx.

30 A qualification that Posner also considers applicable to Victorians like James Fitzjames Stephen. See: James Fitzjames Stephen, *Liberty, Equality, Fraternity, And Three Brief Essays*, with a new foreword by Richard A. Posner, Chicago, London: The University of Chicago Press 1991.

31 Smith, *The Essential Holmes*, p. xxii.

32 Ibid., p. xxvii.

Perhaps Holmes is best characterized as someone who constantly offers up half-truths that are food for thought. The phrasing stimulates reflection, but the limited perspective of many of his aphorisms also always becomes quickly apparent.

In his assessments of others, he is often surprisingly direct and on point. About Roscoe Pound (1870–1964), one of the most important names in "Sociological Jurisprudence" and a source of inspiration to many realists, Holmes writes that he regularly shares Pound's views, but that he nevertheless feels ambivalent. "I admire and am overwhelmed by his learning, but I rarely find that unexpectedness which as you say is the most attractive thing." He also notes that Pound often presents new facts, but never new theories.[33] Those who have read Pound's endlessly lengthy essays, involving ever more material, authors, and footnotes, can see what he means. Harold Laski (1893–1950), someone with whom Holmes exchanged letters, said about this: "I think he (Pound; PC & AE) believes in the natural right of every German to be quoted." Felix Frankfurter (1882–1965) also made critical remarks about Pound's tendency to support all his findings with endless quotations: "Pound is too damned scholarly for me." Laski wrote that if Pound were to, in an essay on a legal science topic, make the assertion that bathrooms in the United States had undergone an important development, he would support it with references to (a) *Sanitary News* (b) the *Plumbers Journal* (c) a Department of Commerce report on the production of leadless glass, including a footnote referencing a Czech dissertation about the sociological meaning of bathrooms the writer had personally never laid eyes on.[34]

A little snide perhaps, and it does not do justice to the value of Pound's scholarship, but a case can also be made that the superfluity of material constitutes an impediment to unencumbered judgment. That a man like Holmes, with his neat style, but also with his impatient attitude with regard to theorizing, is not enamored of the fairly dry schematisms of Hohfeld (1879–1918)[35] is predictable. About Hohfeld, he writes: "I think all those systematic schematisms rather bores." This remark is also important: "I even doubt the profit of the terminology of rights (the hypostasis of a prophecy)."[36] The latter has great significance to the discussion about whether we should present fundamental interests in the form of rights or if we should leave most of the law in the hands of the regular legislator for

33 Ibid., p. 51.
34 David Wigdor, *Roscoe Pound, Philosopher of Law*, Westport, CT, London: Greenwood Press 1974, p. 285.
35 Wesley Newcomb Hohfeld (1879–1918) taught law at Stanford and Yale. He is famous for his *Fundamental Legal Conceptions as Applied in Judicial Reasoning* (1919), in which he tried to systematize and create clear guidelines for the use of the concepts right and duty.
36 Smith, *The Essential Holmes*, p. 65.

a utilitarian weighing of interests. The realists were utilitarians and instrumentalists, important opponents of the legal theory of those who believe in the primacy of rights.

It is not easy to group Holmes's views into just a few categories, but if we attempt it nonetheless, the following picture emerges. First and foremost, he was a proponent of what could be called a pragmatic conception of truth.

> I assume that I am in the world not in me. Next when I say that a thing is true I only mean that I can't help believing it - but I have no grounds for assuming that my can't helps are cosmic can't helps and some reasons for thinking otherwise. I therefore define the truth as the system of my intellectual limitations.[37]

He also writes: "All I mean by truth is the path I have to travel. Whether that compulsion that draws me to one woman and repels me from another I don't know."[38]

Holmes was in contact with philosophers like William James (1842–1910), John Dewey (1859–1952), and other pragmatically oriented thinkers, which is clearly visible in his statements.

> When I say that a thing is true, I mean that I cannot help believing it. I am stating an experience as to which there is no choice. But as there are many things that I cannot help doing that the universe can, I do not venture to assume that my inabilities in the way of thought are inabilities of the universe. I therefore define the truth as the system of my limitations, and leave absolute truth for those who are better equipped. With absolute truth I leave absolute ideals of conduct equally on one side.[39]

He is also often mentioned as a critic of a too lofty view of mankind and the world. "The eternal demand for the superlative degree—the unwillingness to accept less than being in on the ground floor with God—don't impress me much, except as a fact in psychology."[40] "All 'isms seem to me silly—but this hyperaethereal respect for human life seems perhaps the silliest of all."[41]

He advises his friend Laski not to get involved in politics. It is better to write the big book, Holmes believed (although he never did so himself):

37 Ibid., p. 107.
38 Ibid., p. 112.
39 Ibid., p. 118.
40 Ibid., p. 112.
41 Ibid., p. 113.

"for the present at least, you are in the right place now, and that the big book is better both as a contribution to the world and as a form of self-expression."[42] Those familiar with Laski's wealth of production know he followed Holmes's advice. Although, he probably would have done the same without Holmes's council.

Holmes has an equally down-to-earth view of values. "If, as I think, the values are simply generalizations emotionally expressed, the generalizations are matters for the same science as other observations of fact."[43]

"Our system of morality is a body of imperfect social generalizations expressed in terms of emotion."[44]

He formulated his relativistic attitude with regard to Laski's (socialist) ideals as follows in 1925:

> As you will have expected I don't sympathize very greatly with your dream. You think more nobly of man than I do—and of course, you may be right. But I look at men through Malthus's glasses—as like flies—here swept away by pestilence—there multiplying unduly and paying for it. I think your morals (I am struck by the delicacy of your feeling) are not the last word but only a check for varying intensity upon force, which seems to me likely to remain the ultimate as far as I can look ahead.[45]

Holmes as the founding father of the prediction theory of law

However interesting these views of Holmes the aphorist may be, as the founder of American realism, he is primarily significant for one particular passage. It is the famous paragraph in which he introduces the criminal, the "bad man," who offers us the perspective through which we ought to approach the law. "Take the fundamental question, What constitutes the law," Holmes writes in his famous essay *The Path of the Law*.

> You will find some text writers telling you that it is (...) a system of reason, that it is a deduction of principles of ethics or admitted axioms or what not, which may or may not coincide with the decisions. But if we take the view of our friend the bad man we shall find that he does not care two straws for the axioms or deductions, but that he does want to know what the Massachusetts or English courts are likely to do in fact. I

42 Ibid., p. 115.
43 Ibid., p. 116.
44 Ibid., p. 119.
45 Ibid., p. 140.

am much of his mind. The prophecies of what the courts will do in fact, and nothing more pretentious, are what I mean by the law.[46]

Holmes also tried to approach other legal concepts this way, such as the central term "legal duty." From the perspective of prediction theory, legal duty is "a prediction that if a man does or omits certain things he will be made to suffer in this or that way by the judgment of the court."[47]

At first glance, this approach to the concept of law seems fairly strange. However, with some contemplation, it appears there is at least *something* to be said for it. Say a client goes to his lawyer. What does this client want to know? He wants to know his odds of winning the case (in case of a civil procedure) or his odds of acquittal or dismissal (in a criminal procedure). One might imagine, for instance, that the electricity-tapping dentist asked his lawyer: "what are the odds that the judge will qualify the tapping of electricity as theft?" What will a cautious lawyer (experienced in the realities of legal practice) answer? He will say that this is hard to predict. Theft, on the basis of art. 310 Sr, requires a *good* being *appropriated*. But is electricity a good? And will the judge view placing a metal rod into a meter as appropriation?[48] There are no precedents going one way or the other. As such, there is not much more the lawyer can do than say it depends on the judge.

The client will not be happy to hear this. "But surely there must be legal rules," he will say to his lawyer. "That all depends," the lawyer will reply, "because how these possible rules will be interpreted is so uncertain that there might as well not be any rules at all." The only thing the lawyer can do is conjecture about how the judge will decide the case: "the prophecies of what the courts will do."

Holmes's theory is quite persuasive—especially in cases such as the one above—but it also raises some concerns. For instance, it could be said that large sections of law are not adjudicated in court, thus leaving them outside of Holmes's conception of the law. What about rules that stipulate the court's own jurisdiction, for instance? Also excluded would be administrative and constitutional rules, about which there is no litigation (particularly in a legal system that does not have the power of judicial review). So, one might wonder if this is an ideal definition of law.

However, some commentators have argued that such an approach does not do justice to the realist perspective of the law. With regard to predictivism, two theories are defended. First, the view of those who say that the

---

46 O.W. Holmes, "The Path of the Law," in: *Harvard Law Review*, 10 (1897), p. 457. Also included in the *Collected Legal Papers*.
47 Holmes, *Collected Legal Papers*, p. 169.
48 HR May 1921, NJ 1921, 564 (Elektriciteit).

realists never made these statements about the law in an attempt to present a *definition* of it. This is the position of, for instance, William Twinning (*b.* 1934). The proponents of this first perspective note that the realists only ever intended to give practical guidance and advice that would allow jurists to predict what the law says in a particular case. According to the theorists who defend this notion, it would also be somewhat unjust to take the realists to task for something they never intended. In opposition to this, however, there is Summers's view, arguing that—even though the aforementioned, more modest position is defended by some jurists—prediction theory always tends to expand into highly general theoretical claims that far exceed the context of the concrete.[49] Furthermore, according to Summers, it cannot be denied that most realists were predictivists in the latter, more expansive sense.

The judge at center stage. Realism's second founding father: Gray

If we accept the tradition of Langdell as the first characteristic of realism and the desire to predict the law on social science grounds, as Holmes advocated, as the second, then the third characteristic of American realism could be said to be the central role it accords the judge. We already find that role emphasized in Holmes's words that were quoted before: "the prophecies what the *courts* will do" (italics added; PC). However, we find the most impressive expression of this concept in realism's second founding father: John Chipman Gray (1839–1915).

Gray was born in Brighton, Massachusetts, and graduated from Harvard College in 1859 and from Harvard Law School in 1861. The following year, he was sworn in as a lawyer. Like Holmes, he served during the Civil War. In 1866, he helped found the famous *American Law Review*, and in 1869, he went to work as a lecturer at Harvard Law School. In 1875, he became Story Professor and later Royall Professor (1883–1913) there. He managed to combine an academic career with legal practice. His *Restraints on Alienation* (1883) and *Rule against Perpetuities* (1886) became classic handbooks. Mostly in the area of real estate law, Gray built a serious reputation. His most notable contribution to legal philosophy is the lectures published under the title *The Nature and Sources of the Law* (1909).[50] This

---

49 Robert S. Summers, "Pragmatic Instrumentalism in Twentieth Century American Legal Thought-a Synthesis and Critique of Our Dominant General Theory About Law and Its Use", *Cornell Law Review*, 66 (1981), p. 861.
50 John Chipman Gray, *The Nature and Sources of the Law*, second edition from the author's notes, by Roland Gray, LLB, New York: Macmillan 1948 (1909).

is a series of talks that he had given as the Carpentier Lectures at Columbia University in 1908.

The second edition of *The Nature and Sources* could no longer be completed by Gray himself. In 1921, his son, Roland Gray, published the second edition, for which Gray himself had left notes and collected a wealth of material. Christie describes Gray's particular significance as follows: "His writings exhibit a fascination with the old abstract problems of legal analysis together with a down-to-earth concern with law as it affects the lives of ordinary citizens."[51]

Gray describes the concept of law like this: "The Law of the State or of any organized body of men is composed of the rules which the courts, that is, the judicial organs of that body, lay down for the determination of legal rights and duties."[52] He also writes: "The Law of a country at any time is made up of the rules that its courts are then applying in the decision of cases."[53] Gray believes we should make a sharp distinction between *sources of law* and *law itself*. Legislation, precedent, and custom are the only sources of law. However, the rules the judge uses to decide the cases put before him are law itself. It can also be put like this: legislation is potential law; it becomes actual law when the judge interprets it.

In the handbooks, the realists' theories are also presented as a variation on the positivist philosophy of Austin and his followers. After all, just like positivism, realism views the law as an expression of the will of the state. The only difference is that the realists believe this expression manifests itself through a certain medium: the judge's decision. To the realists, it is not the legislator who is sovereign, but the judge: "for the realist the sovereign is the court."[54]

In his book, Gray also challenges three competing approaches to the law. First, Austin's famous command theory, which views the law as a command by the sovereign; this is the theory to which Gray's realism is a modification. Second, Von Savigny's theory, in which the law is equated with the people's

---

51 See: George C. Christie, *Jurisprudence. Text and Readings on the Philosophy of Law*, St. Paul, MN: West Publishing Co. 1973, p. 602. Christie also gives biographical overviews of Holmes, Herman Oliphant, Joseph C. Hutchenson, Jr., Frank, Llewellyn, and Gray. Interestingly, he counts Gray among the legal positivists, not as belonging to realism "in the strictest sense of the term." He does note that the seeds of legal realism are present in Gray.

52 Gray, *The Nature and Sources of the Law*, p. 84.

53 Ibid., p. 272.

54 P.J. Fitzgerald, *Salmond on Jurisprudence*, twelfth edition, London: Sweet & Maxwell 1966, p. 35. See also: W. Friedmann, *Legal Theory*, fifth edition, London: Stevens & Sons 1967, p. 265, who speaks of the "substantial modification of analytical positivism, of which John Chipman Gray in America and John Salmond in England are the principal representatives." See also the commentary of Lon L. Fuller, *The Law in Quest of Itself*, Chicago: The Foundation Press, Inc. 1940 (AMS edition 1978), p. 48.

shared legal consciousness. And third, the theory in which the law is viewed as a body of principles the judge discovers (J.C. Carter).

The first two theories offer Gray the least difficulties. Austin is wrong, because a command by the sovereign that is not enforced by the judge is a dead letter, and we do not call a dead letter law. Von Savigny's theory, which reduces the law to legal consciousness, also has easily identifiable flaws. The people's legal consciousness is entirely indifferent to most of what we call law. Gray illustrates this by means of what we call the dispatch/receipt rule, which has to do with contracts in private law. According to Massachusetts law, a written offer to enter into an agreement becomes a binding contract the moment the other party's acceptance is *received* by the person who made the offer. This is called the receipt rule. New York, however, uses the so-called dispatch rule. This means that the agreement enters into force the moment the accepting party *sends out* their acceptance. The question here is: can it be said that the *collective legal consciousness* of the people of Massachusetts differs on this point from that of the people of New York?

An affirmative answer to this question would have to be highly contrived, Gray remarks. After all, in reality, no more than one percent of the population of these states are even aware of these rules.

So, Gray rejects Austin and Von Savigny's positions and moves on to a third theory, that of American jurist James Coolidge Carter (1827–1905).[55] Positive in Carter's thinking is that he accords an important role to judicial activity. However, Carter holds fast to one point of tradition the realists cannot stomach: the claim that the judge *finds* the law; he does not *make* it. That is why Gray rejects Carter's theory as well. Carter underestimates judicial creativity. First, Gray argues, a judge often has to render a verdict in cases that contain no legal handholds. Furthermore, the law is often modified by the judge, also when there are definite handholds to be found in it. Gray approvingly quotes Bishop Hoadly (1676–1761):

> whoever hath an *absolute authority* to *interpret* any written or spoken laws, it is *he* who is truly the *Law-giver* to all intents and purposes, and not the person who first wrote or spoke them.[56]

55 An unknown thinker in Europe, Carter (1827–1905) was president of the American Bar Association and proponent of a conception of law related to the Historical School. Like the early Von Savigny, he too fought against codification plans in his pamphlet *The Proposed Codification of Our Common Law* (1883). Posthumously published was: *Law: Its Origin, Growth and Function*, New York, London: G.P. Putnam's Sons 1907.

56 Hoadly Benjamin, Bishop of Bangor. Sermon preached before the King, 1717, p. 12. Gray, *The Nature and Sources of the Law*, p. 125.

Early rule-skepticism. Frank and others

It is a known fact that, within a certain movement, the first generation of thinkers chooses a particular premise, and the second generation commits itself to that premise and radicalizes the philosophy. We see this radicalization of the original ideas in second generations of Enlightenment thinkers both in ancient Greece and in eighteenth-century France. The same is true of the realists. Holmes and Gray are moderates compared with legal science iconoclast Jerome Frank, whose ideas were toned down by a later generation of realists, and even by his own contemporaries because few shared his conclusions.

This mechanism of increasing radicalism is clearly at work in so-called "rule-skepticism." We could classify "rule-skepticism" as a fourth element of realist thought. Both Frank and Llewellyn were rule-skeptics. We will illustrate rule-skepticism mostly by Frank's work because he coined the term and gave the clearest presentation of it.

Jerome Frank was born in the city of New York in 1889, the son of a father who was already a successful jurist.[57] After moving to Chicago, he studied at the University of Chicago, where, besides law, he also majored in literature and political science. He graduated in 1912 and then went into legal practice in Chicago. Incidentally, he had the highest grade point average ever recorded at the Law School. From the start of his education, his interests were varied. He also wrote a novel that was never published, and his friends mostly came from the literary scene. He underwent psychoanalysis and incorporated his knowledge of and interest in Freudianism in his first book *Law and the Modern Mind* (1930), which he had written in his free time.[58] *Law and the Modern Mind* garnered a great deal of attention, in academic circles, but also outside of them. In 1932, he was appointed as a Fellow at Yale Law School, and he later also taught at the New School for Social Research in New York. On the recommendation of his friend Felix Frankfurter, he was named as General Counsel to the Agricultural Adjustment Administration at the Department of Agriculture. However, his interventions led to a long conflict about the powers of the committee, and he was eventually fired. He encountered a great deal of resistance in other positions as well. In 1941, he was appointed to the United States Court of Appeals for the Second Circuit, where until his death in 1957, he would accrue the judicial experience he so engagingly incorporated into his books.

Many consider *Law and the Modern Mind* as his best book, and it is certainly the most well-known. However, the theme of the book is as least

---

57 See for biographical information about Frank: Julius Paul, *The Legal Realism of Jerome N. Frank, A Study of Fact-skepticism and the Judicial Process*, The Hague: Martinus Nijhoff 1959; Christie, *Jurisprudence. Text and Readings on the Philosophy of Law.*

58 Frank, *Law and the Modern Mind.*

as aptly expressed in his later and more mature *Courts on Trial* (1949).[59] Moreover, in the later work, Frank engages in debates with other realists, making it more interesting than the earlier work.

Here, we will not address Frank's views of miscarriages of justice, as presented in *Not Guilty* (1957). We will restrict ourselves to his opinions about legal education and rule-skepticism. Especially in the case of rule-skepticism, which we see in both Frank and Llewellyn, it appears that the second generation of realists distanced themselves from the more moderate position of Holmes and Gray. We have seen that Gray's vision of the law has revolutionary tendencies, but he remains true to a number of traditional notions about the law. What is revolutionary about Gray's doctrine is that judges apply the rules that *they make themselves*. So, it is not the legislator who makes the legal rules, but the judge. But the theory also has a traditional side: according to Gray, the law does consist of *rules*.[60] As such, Gray remains entirely in harmony with the conventional view, as expressed, among others, by Blackstone.

For realists, William Blackstone (1723–1780) largely fulfills the same role as Langdell: target.[61] Just like Langdell, Blackstone represented a certain legal orthodoxy. He had a strong belief in the meaning of rules. Law, Blackstone writes, must always be about a *rule*. This means that, for instance, the legislator's (or the judge's) individual act of confiscating Titius's belongings cannot be called law.[62] After all, "the operation of this act is spent upon Titius only, and has no relation to the community in general."[63]

As said, in the further development of the realist doctrine, there is an increasing skepticism with regard to rules.

Frank posits that if rules existed, they would at least play a far less significant role in the law than has been traditionally assumed. The judge *first* has a sense of the court case's ideal result, and *then* he looks for the arguments and rules that justify his decision, Frank believes. Judges are in no sense *guided* by rules. It is not the legal rules that decide which of the parties wins, but a spontaneous impulse in the mind of the judge about who he thinks *should win*.

---

59 Frank, *Courts on Trial*.
60 See: Theodore M. Benditt, *Law as Rule and Principle, Problems of Legal Philosophy*, Sussex: The Harvester Press 1978, p. 6.
61 Incidentally, Blackstone also received considerable criticism from Bentham. See on this: Ernest Barker, "Blackstone on the British Constitution," in: *Essays on Government*, Oxford: Clarendon Press 1965 (1945), pp. 120–154; Gertrude Himmelfarb, "Bentham Versus Blackstone," in: *Marriage and Morals among the Victorians and Other Essays*, New York: Vintage Books 1986, pp. 94–111.
62 William Blackstone, *The Sovereignty of the Law*, selections from Blackstone's *Commentaries on the Laws of England*, edited with an introduction by Gareth Jones, London. Basingstoke: Macmillan 1973, p. 32.
63 Blackstone, *The Sovereignty of Law*, p. 32.

Frank does realize that his view of the law garners opposition, but he believes himself capable of unmasking this opposition as motivated by a childish desire for certainty. For this, he refers to the theories of the French psychologist Jean Piaget (1898–1980).

Piaget's theory posits the following. Every child is painfully aware of his inability to control the world. He needs help from his parents. And since the child learns to see that his parents do seem able to control the external world, he considers them nearly omnipotent. His mother he will come to view as the embodiment of everything that is protective and tender, while his father personifies all that is certain, infallible, "law-making, law-pronouncing and law-enforcing." As such, every child develops an irresistible desire for an all-knowing, all-powerful father who acts as a mediator between him and the uncertainties of life.

However, the father cannot continue to fulfill that role, so later in life, father-substitutes are found in, for instance, a priest, a pastor, and other leaders. When the person grows up, and these replacement figures are also exposed as fallible, the desire for father-substitutes gradually becomes more subconscious, as well as "more vague and impersonal." And this brings us to the law:

> The law—a body of rules apparently devised for infallibly determining what is right and what is wrong and for deciding who should be punished for misdeeds—inevitably becomes a partial substitute for the Father-as-Infallible-Judge. That is, the desire persists in grown men to recapture, through a rediscovery of a father, a childish, completely controllable universe, and that desire seeks satisfaction in a partial, unconscious, anthropomorphizing of Law, in ascribing to the Law some of the characteristics of the child's Father-Judge.[64]

So, the desire to derive certainty from the law is a "childish desire." It is a substitute for the certainty we used to draw from a father's authority. As such, we should leave it behind. The law is simply not able to provide certainty, and it would also be wise not to expect it to.

So much for the nature of the realist doctrine. But what brought them to breaking with the traditional idea that the law is about general rules? What were the reasons for rule-skepticism?

Six reasons for rule-skepticism

Wilfrid Rumble, an author of a book on American realism, distinguishes six factors that drove rule-skepticism:

64 Frank, *Law and the Modern Mind*, p. 19.

(a)   The *multitude of precedents*.[65] Some jurists believed that precedents pointed in a certain direction. The realists, however, thought that there were so many precedents that a line of precedents could be found to justify any decision. Felix Cohen wrote that

> no judge could possibly hand down a decision in any case for which a commentator could not find a precedent, even if the judge himself failed to find one. To say that a decision is unprecedented is to say either (i) that we do not agree with the use it makes of the precedents, or (ii) that we do not know the precedents that might be cited in its support.[66]

(b)   Llewellyn also pointed out that the *techniques for the interpretation of precedents* were also numerous. In *Bramble Bush*, he remarks that much has been written about precedents. One of the shortcomings of these publications, however, is that they do not focus on what judges actually do with precedents, but what they say they do.[67]

(c)   In addition, the realists believed that it is also impossible to deduce rules from the actual decisions of judges. In his article *A Return to Stare Decisis*, Herman Oliphant offers us the following example. Anja is persuaded by her father not to marry Berend, although she had promised to do so. Berend sues Anja's father for damages. The judge rules that the father is not liable. Now, Oliphant demonstrates how such a decision can generate an endless number of rules. The following rules are imaginable:

(1)   The rule that fathers have a right to have their daughters break promises
(2)   That parents have this right
(3)   That parents can do this with regard to both daughters and sons
(4)   That anyone has a right to do this when it comes to wedding promises
(5)   That parents have a right to do this with regard to all promises their children make
(6)   That everyone has a right to do this with regard to any promise anyone else makes.

65 Wilfrid E. Rumble, Jr., *American Legal Realism, Skepticism, Reform, and the Judicial Process*, Ithaca, NY: Cornell University Press 1968.
66 Felix S., Cohen, *The Legal Conscience: Selected Papers of Felix S. Cohen*, New Haven: Yale University Press 1960, p. 129.
67 Llewellyn, *Bramble Bush*, p. 64. See also: Karl N. Llewellyn, *The Common Law Tradition, Deciding Appeals*, Boston, Toronto: Little, Brown and Company 1960, pp. 522–525.

None of these rules is the logical consequence of the decision, Oliphant says.[68]

(d) Also visible in realists is a keen awareness of the ambiguity of the court-room. Frank points out, for instance, that Leon Green, Walter Cook, Thurman Arnold, and others (all of them inspired by O.W. Holmes) analyzed the courtroom as follows: "We skinned the peel of much legal jargon; many law-words (not all, of course) then proved to be like onions—you peeled and peeled and there was nothing left."[69]
(e) In addition, the realists were highly sensitive to the strong social dynamic that was thought to make it impossible to capture the social reality in a body of rules. Again, it was Frank who eloquently phrased the realist position:

> Even in a relatively static society, men have never been able to construct a comprehensive, eternized set of rules anticipating all possible legal disputes and settling them in advance. Even in such a social order no one can foresee all the future permutations and combinations of events.[70]

Situations that were not foreseen at the moment the rules were created will always present themselves. Even in the past, it was impossible to capture the complex social reality in rigid rules; this is even truer in the rapidly changing social reality of modern times.
(f) Finally, the realists place a certain emphasis on the uniqueness of the factual circumstances of every case.

The fully formed rule-skepticism of Richard Taylor

Rule-skepticism is such an important part of the realist inheritance that it is worth considering for a moment longer. The problem is, however, that we do not find terribly convincing arguments for rule-skepticism in Frank, Llewellyn, or Oliphant. The most interesting reflections on this topic are to be found in a relatively unknown name: the philosopher Richard Taylor (1919–2003).

The introduction of Taylor as a representative of realism requires some justification. What and whom one chooses to consider representative of

68 H. Oliphant, "A Return to Stare Decisis," in: *American Bar Association Journal*, 14 (1928), p. 14, also in: Christie, *Jurisprudence. Text and Readings on the Philosophy of Law*, p. 668.
69 Jerome Frank, "A Lawyer Looks at Language," in: S.I. Hayakawa, ed., *Language in Action*, New York: Harcourt, Brace 1941, p. 329.
70 Frank, *Law and the Modern Mind*, p. 6.

realism is a matter of choice. Certain reasons can be offered for that choice, but in principle, which names represent the movement is not set in stone. In most studies, Jerome Frank is counted among the realists. But anyone familiar with Frank's critical attitude toward a large part of the realist philosophy of, among others, Karl Llewellyn could suggest that he should more appropriately be viewed as one of the most eloquent critics of realism.

Holmes is usually seen as a precursor to the realists but changing the periodization can also render him an early representative of the movement. Roscoe Pound is usually not counted among the realists but connected to "Sociological Jurisprudence." Sociological legal science is viewed as a moderate realism or as a school that is related to realism, but that is different from realism on a number of points. However, if someone were to move the labels just slightly, they would also be able to distinguish a moderate version of Pound's realism and a more radical version of Frank's.

What is true of Pound, Holmes, Frank, and others is also true of Gray. Some put Gray in the category of analytical jurisprudence, others count him as a legal positivist, and yet others present his work as a precursor to realist philosophy. As such, classification follows the varying criteria used by the authors of the handbooks.

It is not common, however, for people writing in the 1960s and 1970s to be counted as realists. An exception to this is Richard Taylor, an American philosopher whom Theodore Benditt presents as a late representative (perhaps the "last" representative) of realism.[71]

Taylor is primarily a general philosopher, but he has written so much about law and politics that it seems justified to give him a place in the history of legal philosophy. His legal philosophical views, as they are put forth in *Law and Morality*,[72] *Freedom, Anarchy, and the Law*,[73] *Good and Evil*,[74] and *Ethics, Faith, and Reason*,[75] show such a resemblance to the ideas of early realists that Benditt's choice to count him among the realists does seem warranted. The temptation only increases when we see that Taylor offers a philosophical justification for realist convictions that is more impressive than those of Frank and Llewellyn.

In a certain sense, Taylor expands rule-skepticism, while also giving it an entirely different twist. He discusses the endeavor to bind people's behavior to moral and legal rules within the framework of a critique of what he calls

---

71 See also the attention paid to Taylor in: J.B. Crozier, "Legal Realism and a Science of Law," in: *American Journal of Jurisprudence*, 29 (1984), pp. 151–167, p. 158.

72 An article in *New York University Law Review*, 43 (1968), pp. 611–650.

73 With the subheading "An Introduction to Political Philosophy," Buffalo, New York: Prometheus Books 1980 (1973).

74 With the subheading "A Forceful Attack on the Rationalistic Tradition in Ethics," Buffalo, New York: Prometheus Books 1984.

75 Published at: Englewood Cliffs, NJ: Prentice-Hall, Inc. 1985.

"casuistry." This is a method used not only in legal interpretation but also in ethics. So, in his sobering treatment of this endeavor, Taylor not only deals with law and legal science but also with our everyday reasoning about morality.

The procedure of casuistry, Taylor writes, is the method most people use when they are thinking about morality. What he tries to show, however, is that this method does not work and that people are actually making moral judgments in an entirely different way, not guided by rules. In our moral judgment, rules do not play the role we are inclined to ascribe to them. "What are appealed to as moral principles are usually rationalizations for courses of action decided on quite independently of any such principle."[76]

Taylor tries to prove this with a line of reasoning that can be summarized like this. (i) First, there is no universal moral principle that tells us how to do the morally right thing under all circumstances. After all, such a principle always allows for exceptions. (ii) Such an exception cannot, of course, be based on the principle itself, and can only be made on the basis of (a) a still higher principle or (b) different grounds. (iii) That it cannot be made on the basis of a higher principle is self-evident, because then *that* principle would also admit certain exceptions (see i). (iv) So, the exception has to be made on the basis of another consideration. Taylor points to the significance of "ordinary human feeling." (v) Finally, he posits that because it is this ordinary human feeling that guides us in these moral decisions, the moral principles are redundant. They contribute nothing to our eventual acceptance or rejection of a certain issue or behavior.

The pretension of Taylor's view of our moral judgment is far-reaching. He wants to claim that the "usual, typical, and moral approach to questions of morality is basically wrong."[77] Taylor illustrates his thesis by giving a number of examples. We will first adopt a general example and then move to one that proves that Taylor's critique is also effective in the area of the law.

How does a draftee justify his refusal to serve in the military?

Say, a draftee decides that he does not want to serve in the armed forces. To avoid this, he would have to go to jail or flee the country. Alternatively, he can appear before a committee that assesses his reasons for refusing to serve. What can he appeal to there? He could say: "Killing is wrong." He would then be appealing to a general rule, a principle that he considers central to his

76 Richard Taylor, *Good and Evil: A New Direction: A Forceful Attack on the Rationalistic Tradition in Ethics*, Buffalo, New York: Prometheus Books 1984, p. 162.
77 Ibid., p. 163.

ethics. But they will then ask him: *every* form of killing? Is killing a fly wrong as well? He will then adjust his principle. He will say: not *every* form of killing is wrong. It is about killing human beings. It is wrong, he could posit as a supposed universal principle after this line of questioning, to kill *people*.

But this does not satisfy the committee. They confront him with the fact that, in that case, he will also no longer be able to drive cars, approve of airplane travel, or stand by as people build bridges—after all, these are all activities that might cause people to lose their lives. What will he say to that? The answer is readily available. He will say that he is talking about the *conscious* or *intentional* killing of people. He does not want to be a part of shooting people with guns, as soldiers do, or blowing up buildings with people inside them. Again, Taylor notes, he has adjusted his principle. But suppose this does not satisfy the committee either. After all, they could ask the draftee what he would do if a psychopath were to attack his wife with a knife, intending to kill her. Say the draftee was standing close by with a gun in his hand. He can only stop the psychopath by killing him. What then? He would shoot, of course, but would that not also be the intentional killing of a human being? In fact, would it not be reprehensible according to his own principle? What happens next is painfully predictable. The principle is adjusted again.

Taylor is out to make two points clear here. First, a formulated principle keeps undergoing adjustments in order to exclude certain cases. In the first adjustment, animals were excluded. In the second, the accidental, unintentional killing of a person was excluded. In the third, knife-wielding attackers were.

Also relevant is the question *why* these elements are excluded from the principle. Apparently not because the principle did not apply to them; it clearly did. What it seems to come down to is that the principle really only had the function of allowing the draftee to avoid military service. This was apparently immutable. Regardless of any principle, the intent was to successfully argue that serving in the military is wrong.

So much for rule-skepticism. Rules do not play the role that some say they do, because they are adjusted every time we do not like their application. Apparently, things are constantly excluded from the principle on the basis of a notion of what is ethically wrong and right *without reference to principles*. "This is the whole course of discussion," Taylor writes.

> Something is just assumed to be wrong and other things not wrong, quite independently of any principles of right and wrong, and then the whole discussion is aimed at finding some principle that will *fit* what is thus already assumed.[78]

78 Ibid., p. 165.

That is not justification, Taylor says. It is at most an exercise in definition and at worst pure rationalization.

So the question we ought to ask ourselves is this: if a person knows what is right and wrong beforehand, *how* does he know this? There is no other possible explanation than that this knowledge is based on "common sense or ordinary human feeling."[79] It means that we always *first* have to know what we ought to do and *then* decide if it aligns with a particular principle. The principle can never tell us what to do. It is the other way around. If we did not know what to do beforehand, we would not know what principles to embrace.

Taylor's vision applied to a legal example

Taylor's view of the importance, or better said, the *non-importance* of rules is, of course, of great relevance to legal science, especially legal interpretation. He is very much aware of this himself, and in a follow-up to the reflections described earlier, he draws the conclusions this has for legal reasoning. "Casuistic reasoning is part of the very essence of juridic thinking," he writes.[80] As such, the system cannot function properly, Taylor goes on, on the grounds described previously. However, the common law tradition has come up with a solution to this by enabling judges to invent new laws if the circumstances call for it. If this were not an option, Taylor believes, then a legal system would be impossible because then there could be no exceptions to rules, something that happens all the time in casuist reasoning. So baked into the system is a kind of systematic hypocrisy that is crucial to a well-ordered social life. Exceptions to rules are constantly made on the basis of considerations that judges invent.

As an example, Taylor points to the famous case of Elmer Palmer, from the *Riggs v. Palmer* decision, about which he philosophizes a little. There is a rule that says that a deceased person can leave his estate to an inheritor. The rule also specifies the circumstances under which a judge can declare a will to be invalid. These circumstances do *not* include the situation in which an inheritor has murdered the deceased person whose estate they stand to inherit. Now, this turns out to be the case. What does the judge do?

The answer is self-evident. The judge does not grant the inheritance on the basis that if this circumstance had occurred to the legislator, he would have included it among the circumstances under which inheritance cannot be granted. This teaches us something about judges and judicial reasoning.

---

79 Ibid., p. 171.
80 Ibid., p. 177.

Judges do not apply a rule when they know that its application will do more harm than good. Like ordinary people, most judges have common sense, and they are especially good at applying it to all kinds of situations. Judges also have a sense of the values most people uphold, and when the application of a law would violate them, they do not apply that law.

Incidentally, this way of working is not only used in not applying laws, but also in defining terms used in the law. Words such as "signing" (has the contract been signed?), "born in..." (a child born on an airplane), "vehicle" (is an old armored truck displayed as a monument a vehicle?), and so on, are defined in such a way as to achieve the result to which common sense directs us.

The construal of these legal terms is called "interpretation," but that is a highly misleading term, Taylor says. "Interpretation" suggests that there is an underlying meaning that is, in essence, waiting to be uncovered by judicial activity. In reality, meaning is not something that is *found* but that is *ascribed* to a term. And this ascription is in no way a neutral process. "It is entirely governed by the conclusion, already arrived at, that the new meaning will tend to support."[81] The meanings of the words are largely invented to support the conclusion that had already been established.

The philosophical background of rule-skepticism

The addition Taylor makes to the realism of the legal scholars Llewellyn, Frank, and others is valuable because, in a certain sense, it draws the most radical conclusions from the realist position. In essence, Taylor's position is an extreme voluntarism and a rejection of the possibility of coming to a rationalist grounding of our ethical values.[82] That Taylor does not shy away from this is apparent in his many publications. It is even in the subtitle of the book in which he offers the examples presented here. Taylor intends to offer a "forceful attack on the rationalistic tradition in ethics." And his attack is certainly powerful. According to Taylor, right or wrong can never be proven or made plausible with an appeal to reasons and rules. "No significant idea of ethics was ever *proved* anyway. That has not stopped men from founding nations on such ideas, and fighting wars and revolutions in their name."[83] Taylor views the history of normative thinking (including both ethics and law) as ruled by a conflict between two types of moral thought. One is rationalism (reason and the ability to use rules is central) and the other is voluntarism (the will and the ability to use feelings are

81 Ibid., p. 183.
82 Voluntarism is also clearly present in: Max Radin, *Law as Logic and Experience*, New Haven: Yale University Press 1940, reprint Archon Books 1971, p. 7.
83 Taylor, *Good and Evil*, p. xi.

central). It will not surprise anyone that Taylor offers a scathing critique of Immanuel Kant, the philosopher who went furthest in the belief that people's ethical conduct could be subjected to rules, not just legal but also ethical rules.

The rationalist tradition was most dominant in the history of ethics. So much so that people are often barely able to imagine the persuasive power of voluntarist thinking: "It hardly occurs to anyone that there might be a kind of moral justification that has nothing whatsoever to do with reason, a kind of justification that rests more upon seeing than thinking, and involves wisdom rather than dialectic."[84] Still, this voluntarist tradition has right on its side, Taylor believes. According to the voluntarists, it is only because human beings have a will—meaning they have desires, feelings, needs, and tendencies—that a distinction between right and wrong can even be made. The original goodness of a thing exists only in that it is desired by someone. The bad, then, is a circumstance that stands in the way of the fulfillment of a desire.

Once this has been recognized, the role of reason changes substantially. Reason can only—within certain parameters—establish what *is* the case, never what *ought to be* the case. It is utterly absurd, therefore, to think that reason can direct or control the will. The fact that this is an age-old ideal does not make it any more acceptable.

The rationalist line was developed by Socrates, Plato, and Kant. Taylor says about this: "I believe that it is a profound philosophy, but I also believe that its presuppositions are profoundly and dangerously wrong."[85] As long as people keep believing—as Socrates did—that there is a natural right and wrong, independent of human needs and feelings, the spirit of Socrates will continue to mislead us.

Characteristic of Socrates's approach is that the good can be *known*, exactly the way we can know other things in nature. He simply assumed that something is good in and of itself and that we can look for it the same way we can look for natural objects.

From that perspective, we can also understand Socrates's belief that someone who knows what is right is incapable of doing wrong. The implications of that view are immense. Knowledge of goodness is a sufficient precondition to guarantee a virtuous life. Philosophy, he believed, was the path to that knowledge, and it is therefore also the path to a virtuous life. Plato seems never to have doubted the existence of something like true justice. In his reflections on the idea, it becomes something that leads a shadowy life in another world. It can only be accessed by reason.

84 Ibid., p. 14.
85 Ibid., p. 47.

Kantians emphasize the fact that when a man tries to help the sick and dying, he should not do this out of compassion or love, because Kantians reject these types of emotions as "pathological." They believe that moral acts should be driven by a rational respect for duty, a respect that should fill the virtuous man with reverence. Moral acts can—in other words—never be based on feelings, but only on respect for the moral law.

> To be genuinely moral, a man must tear himself away from his inclinations as a loving human being, drown the sympathetic promptings of his heart, scorn any fruits of his efforts, think last of all of the feelings, needs, desires, and inclinations either of himself or of his fellows and, perhaps detesting what he has to do, do it anyway - solely from respect for the law.[86]

Taylor rejects this preoccupation with rules and duty. He does so with reference to an empirical fact that is of great importance in ethics. It *is* possible for human beings to act out of love and selflessness. This *happens* in the real world. People turn out to be capable of a form of mutual aid that cannot merely be explained by self-interest.[87] Anyone would pick up a baby bird that has fallen from its nest and return it. Many people yank on the wheel when a dog or cat runs onto the road. We could offer endless examples like these, Taylor writes. They exist, and they are not even rare. It may seem banal at first glance, but these kinds of examples are of great importance. They form the basis for "claiming that human life has a moral dimension."[88] The rationalist tradition in ethics ought to be rejected, and the new lead that should be followed is the actual existence of people's sense of morality.

Differences between the realists

Taylor's philosophy greatly resembles Jerome Frank's. Both are rule-skeptics but in a radical sense. They not only conclude that rules do not provide solid footing, but they also do not attempt to solve this problem. They reject thinking in terms of rules, rejecting the quasi-certainty it is supposed to bring. In this, they go much further than other realists. Mostly, the other realists observed that legal rules did not offer certainty, then went on to advocate replacing them with rules that could be based on empirical generalizations.

---

86 Ibid., p. 113.
87 Taylor bases this approach on Schopenhauer's ethics. See: Richard Taylor, "Schopenhauer," in: D.J. O'Connor, ed., *A Critical History of Western Philosophy*, New York, London: The Free Press 1964, pp. 365–384.
88 Taylor, *Good and Evil*, p. 192.

That is why Frank rightly writes that the group of thinkers categorized as realists is far from homogenous. Its "members" strongly disagree on a variety of subjects. Their only shared idea seems to be a certain skepticism of the traditional way of thinking about the law-finding process. But then a distinction can be made between the group that considers rule-skepticism a stepping stone to other factors that make judicial behavior understandable and the group that says it is perfectly comfortable living with all the uncertainty. Clearly, Frank and Taylor belong to the latter.

It can be said that the most impressive representative of the first group is Karl Llewellyn (1893–1962). Llewellyn, too, is a rule-skeptic, but he is interested in offering ways to reduce the uncertainty. As such, what these moderate realists of Llewellyn's stripe advocate is, like traditional jurists, reducing legal uncertainty. They think it would be good if it were possible to predict, with a great deal of accuracy, what the outcome of certain legal procedures will be. They feel that ordinary citizens cannot derive enough certainty from the law. Moderate rule-skeptics believe that the malaise of the law stems from the fact that the formal rules, the paper rules, do not provide a sufficient basis on which to predict the outcomes of court cases. They try to correct part of this problem by trying to discover "real rules" behind the paper rules. These real rules ought to be able to give insight into judicial behavior. They are meant to be a better prediction instrument than the paper rules.

Frank offers two points of criticism with regard to these rule-skeptics. The first critique is that he does not share their *ideal*. In large part, he explained his reasons for this in his early work *Law and the Modern Mind*. In it, he unmasks the search for certainty as a childish pursuit. His arguments for this have come up before, and so we will not return to them here. It might be useful, however, to say something about the second point on which Frank criticizes the more moderate realists. Not only does he not share their ideal (creating more legal certainty), but he also argues that their ideal can never be realized using the method they employ (discovering rules that are empirical generalizations of judicial behavior). After all, the rules are not the cause of the uncertainty; the establishment of the facts is. In Frank's opinion, Llewellyn and the other realists do not go far enough. They have not, in a sense, exposed the true cause of the uncertainty of the judicial decision. The fact that rules do not offer a good basis for prediction might be one factor contributing to the uncertainty, but it is not the only one, and certainly not the most important one. Here, Frank points to the uncertainty of the facts. This brings us to fact-skepticism as one of the central elements of the realist legacy. We could call fact-skepticism the fifth characteristic of the realists. Some caution is warranted here though, because it is a feature that only applies to some, maybe even only a small number of realists. We will nevertheless use it here because we have made clear at the beginning that the characteristics discussed here are distributed among the population of realists in different combinations. Also, it is such a famous part of the realist legacy that it cannot be ignored.

Fact-skepticism

As said, from the rule-skeptics, Frank distinguishes the "fact-skeptics." These fact-skeptics also try to see behind the paper rules, and they are also rule-skeptics in the sense that they believe elements other than the rules of the legal system ought to be the object of attention. However, the fact-skeptics go much further in their attempt to discover factors that explain judicial behavior. They part with the one-dimensional preoccupation with higher courts and stimulate research into the behavior of the "trial courts," the lower judges who decide on the facts. Frank counts among the fact-skeptics: Leon Green, Max Radin, Thurman Arnold, William O. Douglas, and E.M. Morgan.[89]

Also a rule-skeptic, together with Llewellyn, is Felix Cohen (1907–1953). In his controversial article "Transcendental Nonsense and the Functional Approach," Cohen writes that although there is great uncertainty when it comes to the law as it is set down in the books, it ought to be possible to recognize a "significant body of predictable uniformity in the behavior of the courts."[90] Cohen also rejects the notion that logic alone can predict judicial behavior, but he believes that psychology, economics, and politics can take us a long way. If the scientific arsenal is expanded, Cohen believes it is possible to predict "the motivating forces which mold legal decisions."

Frank rejects this as an illusion. Cohen's argument fails because he, too, only looks toward the rules.[91] Frank expressed fact-skepticism with the formula: R × F = D. When one looks at what a legal rule actually consists of, it turns out to be nothing more than a conditional sentence to which certain facts and conditions are attached. The structure of a legal rule is as follows. *If* certain facts occur, a certain legal consequence will take effect. This can be translated in the following way. A legal rule (R) is applied to certain facts (F), from which a judicial decision (D) follows. R × F = D.

The traditional realists say that because of our dynamic society, the rules (Rs) have become unstable. Certainty about the law is no longer possible, they believe. Usually, they point to the increased number of rules, the conflicts between them, the flexibility of some of the rules, and other

---

89 Frank, *Courts on Trial*, p. 74.
90 Felix Cohen, "Transcendental Nonsense and the Functional Approach," in: *Columbia Law Review*, 35 (1935), pp. 809–849, p. 809.
91 Frank, *Courts on Trial*, p. 149.

characteristics of the rules. "Those thinkers, perceiving the absence of rigidity in some rules, have assumed that the certainty or uncertainty of the D's, in the R × F = D equation, stems principally from the certainty or uncertainty of the R's."[92] But that is a mistake, Frank believes. "That assumption leads to a grave miscomprehension of court-house government and to the neglect by most legal scholars of the more difficult part of the court's undertaking." No matter how certain and solid the rules are; the uncertainty of the result will remain. That is because the reason for the uncertainty of the decision does not lie in the rules, but in the equation's other element: the facts.

After all, what is a fact? The answer is usually: what happened between the parties. But that is a naïve supposition, Frank says. It is not about what *actually* happened between the parties, but what can be *proven* about it. A fact is at most what can be factually established by a judge who is empowered to do so. And judges make all sorts of mistakes in establishing facts, as do juries. But that does not matter, "legally speaking" at least. "For the court-purposes, what the court thinks about the facts is all that matters."[93] Real facts, true facts, "they do not walk in court." The judge can really only guess at the facts ("facts are guesses"), because he receives them from others. "The F is merely a guess about the actual facts."[94]

Some of this has to do with the unreliability of the human mind and human perception as an instrument of registration. A witness is not a photographic plate or a phonographic disk. Things are remembered and forgotten selectively, depending on the person's receptiveness to certain materials. Even when a witness is perfectly honest and forthcoming, their testimony is still highly unreliable. Our construal of a situation is determined by our prejudices and what we expect and hope to see. Frank references a colleague who once told him that 50 percent of all witness testimony is incorrect. People are almost always biased observers. Even when they have no personal stake in the case at all, they are still unreliable as witnesses, in the sense that they quickly come to take the side of the party that asked them to testify. "Human observation is obviously fallible, subjective."[95]

Not only do the *witnesses* distort the facts, but so do the *judges* who receive these "facts" from the witnesses. "The facts as they actually happened are therefore twice refracted—first by the witnesses, and second by those who must 'find' the facts."[96]

92 Ibid., p. 15.
93 Ibid., p. 15.
94 Ibid., p. 16.
95 Ibid., p. 17.
96 Ibid., p. 22.

Law as decision. Realism as decisionism

So far, we have analyzed five characteristics of realism. (i) The realists rebel against the tradition of Langdell. (ii) They put their faith in devising empirical generalizations of judicial behavior. (iii) They are mainly focused on the judge as the competent developer of the law. (iv) Realists are rule-skeptics. (v) Some of the realists also embrace fact-skepticism.

But if the law does not consist of rules—one of the most cherished beliefs in legal theory, from Blackstone to Hart—the question naturally presents itself: what *does* it consist of? Frank concluded based on rule-skepticism that the law consists of *decisions* instead of rules. As such, "decisionism" can be presented as a sixth characteristic of realism.

This is a radical conclusion that, although it emerged naturally from its underlying propositions, only some of the realists ascribed to. We have seen before that Holmes and Gray would not have supported such positions. It is the radical elements from the second generation of realists who wanted to subscribe to it as the inevitable result of their views. Frank comes to this position when he reflects on the classical question of what law is. He begins by saying that an exhaustive definition of the law is impossible. What we can do, however, is ask what law means to the average person (*average man*), not unlike Holmes's "bad man." To an average layman, Frank writes, the law is nothing more than a decision by the judge: "Until a court has passed on those facts no law on that subject is yet in existence." Before the decision, the only available law is the opinion of jurists with regard to the law and the facts, and this is really nothing more than a guess as to what the judge will decide.

That is why law always has to do with judicial rulings, and can be:

(1)   Actual law, meaning a particular decision from the past that relates to that situation
(2)   Probable law, meaning a guess about a future decision.

According to Frank, this view had already been put forward by his great predecessor Oliver Wendell Holmes. Holmes's famous words "The prophecies of what the courts will do in fact, and nothing more pretentious, are what I mean by law," Frank believes comes down to the acknowledgment that

> law is made up not of rules for decision laid down by the courts but of the decisions themselves. All such decisions are law. The fact that courts render these decisions makes them law. There is no mysterious entity apart from these decisions. (...) The "law of a great nation" means the decision of a handful of old gentlemen, and whatever they refuse to decide is not law.

Here, we can make a distinction between "actual law," meaning a particular past judicial decision, and "probable law," a prediction about a future judicial decision.

Frank enlists the great precursor Holmes as a founding father of his own concept of law here, but even from the passages Frank quotes, this is not an open and shut case. Holmes says that law is what judges do. Even so, he could still argue that what judges do is present the *rules* on which they then base their decisions. In other words, Holmes can still have upheld Gray's moderate position and might have distanced himself from Frank's radical view. Holmes himself is unclear—as he so often is—on this point, and so Frank is somewhat presumptuous in gathering prestigious precedents for his radicalism.

We also see decisionism in Taylor. However, Taylor combines the decisionism we find in Frank with an Austinian emphasis on enforceability as a characteristic of law. According to Taylor, only *those* judicial decisions that can be enforced are law. A commentator of Taylor's position rightly speaks of a hybrid form of command-realism because Taylor in effect brings Austin back in through the rear door after Gray had locked him out.[97]

According to Taylor, realism's great defect was that it was never thought all the way through to its "ultimate conclusion." Taylor intends to do so himself. He wants to present us with a "thoroughgoing legal realism," in which he includes such disparate thinkers as Austin and Fuller in his concept of law.[98]

Taylor distinguishes different types of law: (i) divine law; (ii) natural law; (iii) positive law; (iv) customary law; and (v) what he calls "command law." This last type is his focus. He considers it to mean:

> the particular expressed commands addressed to particular persons by any men having the power to enforce them.[99]

As examples he presents: a judge's decision on appeal with regard to a citizen's liability; the enforceable orders of a police officer; and the decision of a department head made within the scope of his authority. From these, we learn that Taylor apparently follows Frank and other realists who view law as *decisions* instead of rules, but also that he advocates a broadening of the realist concept of law (this in agreement with Fuller, whom he names explicitly) by ascribing law-developing activities to all kinds of non-legal organs, and even non-political organs. "Legal realists defined laws as simply the

---

97 J.B. Crozier, "Legal Realism and a Science of Law," pp. 151–167, p. 159.
98 Richard Taylor, "Law and Morality," in: *New York University Law Review*, 43(4) (1968), pp. 611–650, p. 613.
99 Ibid., p. 612.

decisions of the courts," so Taylor writes, "but apparently no one has been willing to confront the implications of the obvious fact that others besides judges have it within their power to issue *binding* decisions."[100]

That is why his concept of law consists of three elements:

(1)   Law as *decision*
(2)   Law as *enforceable* decision
(3)   Law as enforceable decision made by *actors other than judges.*

Law as a concrete decision. According to Taylor, it is impossible to deny that law often involves the individual orders given to some people by other people. These are rarely of a general nature, nor do they need to be in order to be called law: "A law need not be a rule at all."[101] Oftentimes, law is the concrete and individual command one person gives another. For instance, a judge who orders one party to pay restitution to another party. This order from the judge cannot be viewed as a rule, but it certainly is law. By giving this command, the judge establishes a legal obligation for the losing party. The obligation is created *by* the decision; it did not exist *before* the decision.

Inanimate written words, as they are to be found in legal statutes, do not yet bind or force anyone. They have just as little force over us as the Book of Mormon. Only *people* can obligate other people. As such, legislation can only be called law in the derivative sense, that is, as an indication of what some people, often judges, could force other people to do.

Enforceability. Taylor believes that law consists of commands that people actually have to obey. Not in the sense of a normative have to, but factually. In English, the difference is expressed with "must" and "ought," in German with "müssen" and "sollen." The edicts of a government in exile have no legal force, nor do the decisions of the judges of that regime, if this is even imaginable.

> A judicial decision has the force of law simply because it is *enforceable,* that is, because a court has at its disposal the means to compel those named in its decision to act or forbear in accordance with what is commanded.[102]

When this coercive power does not exist, the judicial decision has no legal force, even if all the preconditions for legitimacy and validity have been met. The factual power to force others is not only *necessary* in order to be able to speak of law, but it is *sufficient.* As such, Bishop Hoadly, who Gray

100   Ibid., p. 613.
101   Ibid., p. 620.
102   Ibid., p. 631.

references, presents us with a half-truth. It is not the power to *interpret* laws that produces the element of legal force, but the power to *enforce* them.

Say a highest court declares a certain law forcing school children to read the Bible to be unconstitutional. And say the school management nevertheless requires the children and teaching staff to continue the factual practice of reading the Bible, something that is supported by the local community, in which this practice is customary. According to Taylor, we have to conclude that judicial interpretation is not law to this community. The judge's decision is only an opinion there.

Incidentally, there's no need for imagined examples. The Supreme Court decided that Vigil Hawkins, a black man, could not be denied admission to a school in Florida (Florida ex rel. *Hawkins v. Board of Control*, 347 US 971 (1954)). For nine years, however, various maneuvers by the Florida Supreme Court barred his admission. "Which judicial decision had in fact the force of law for the appellant?" Taylor asks rhetorically.

Actors other than judges. There is no need to stipulate that law can only exist in constitutionally mandated institutions. "Laws are enforceable commands, from whatever source they may issue."[103] Administrative bodies can also make decisions that are binding on others. Taylor notes that Llewellyn had already observed this when he wrote "more often than not, administrative action is, *to the layman affected,* the last expression of the law in the case." As such, there is no such thing as *the* source of valid law. There are countless sources, and the attempt to reduce everything to the legislator is absurd. The person who wants to know if he is allowed to keep chickens in his yard does not need to find out what the sovereign or "Queen in Parliament" thinks of this. He is better off seeing what the county says, or perhaps the local sheriff.

Research into the true determinants of judicial decisions

A seventh characteristic of realism is a logical product of the previous one. When everything focuses on the judge's decision; when, moreover, rules do not guide that judge in his decision; when the judge perceives the facts through a colored lens; then, naturally, the need arises to study judicial behavior in a different way than legal scholars have always been used to. The jurist tries to understand judicial behavior as a form of rule-led behavior, a behavior that can be explained by reference to the *legal* rules. The realists believe this to be impossible, and they advocate a different approach to studying judicial behavior. The seventh characteristic of realism is that they have tried to detect the determinants of judicial behavior by means of a social-scientific approach.

103 Ibid., p. 613.

One of the most important motives of this social-scientific study of law was, of course, that they wanted to provide certainty by researching what hidden factors were influencing the judge. Frank distinguished conscious from subconscious preconceptions as decisive factors in judicial decisions. We can suspect judges of harboring prejudices based on race, religion, politics, and socio-economic background. But it is also possible to look for hidden and often subconscious preconceptions in judges, such as the judge's attitude toward women, unmarried women, women with red hair, brunettes, men with deep voices, or the opposite, and so on.[104] All these factors were studied by the realists. Even the judge's mood was an object of speculation. Could it not have been influenced by his breakfast? Hence "breakfast-jurisprudence," as their critics called the realists' theories.

The determinants of judicial decision-making were, of course, a subject about which it was easy to speculate, but the realists also did serious scientific research in this area. Famous here is the work of Fred Rodell (1907–1980). Entirely in line with the realist position, Rodell believed attention ought to be paid to what a judge actually decides, separate from the reasons he offers for his decision. In this spirit, he studied the decision patterns of two prominent members of the Supreme Court: Justice Hugo Black (1886–1971) and Justice Frankfurter (1882–1965), who held strongly disparate views about how judges should operate.[105] Oftentimes, however, they came to similar conclusions, and it is impossible to explain their decision patterns with reference to their views about judicial methods. In one instance, Black would hold to the literal text of the Constitution, and in the next, he would read meanings into it that only a highly motivated reader would see. In short: the principles judges say they base their decisions on often obscure their real reasons rather than explaining them. Rodell writes that Black's "votes on the Court (...) have been and remain predictable with far greater accuracy from his many-faceted evangelical yet practical humanitarianism, than from any complex of abstract jurisprudential principles."[106] The same is true of Frankfurter.

Since the realists had an interest in all sorts of non-legal factors that influenced the judicial decision, it is not surprising that many chose to do research in the field of sociology of law. New research techniques and methods were used in this field, as well as new developments in statistics and computer science. A new discipline was also developed: "jurimetrics," the study of the development of the law using statistical methods. According to

104 Frank, *Law and the Modern Mind*, p. ix.
105 See on Black: Hugo LaFayette Black, *A Constitutional Faith*, New York: Alfred Knopf 1969.
106 Fred Rodell, "For Every Justice, Judicial Deference Is a Sometime Thing," in: *Georgetown Law Journal Law* (1962), p. 700.

Lee Loevinger (1913–2004), this new science would mean a step forward if it could be applied to legal science.[107] Loevinger is somewhat reminiscent of that other militantly scientistic movement, logical positivism; he writes that

> the problems of jurisprudence are basically meaningless, since they can only be debated but never decided nor even investigated; whereas the questions of jurimetrics are meaningful since they are capable of being investigated, and ultimately answered, even though we may not know the answers now.

Again, it is O.W. Holmes who had already said: "the man of the future is the man of statistics and the master of economics."[108]

Instrumentalism

What we have discussed so far already makes clear that the law was not viewed as an end in itself, but as a means to achieve a certain social goal. On this point, realists found common cause with legal sociologists, both within the United States and outside it, who held similar views. Of the Americans, Roscoe Pound (1870–1964) had a considerable influence on the realists.

According to Pound, it was important to analyze the different public policy goals the legislator ought to realize in the law. The law should serve "social engineering," Pound thought. As such, Pound was, like many realists, a utilitarian. He was pleased to observe, for instance, that the history of the law represents an ever-increasing recognition and fulfillment of human needs and desires by means of social control; ever more comprehensive and efficient protection of social interests; ever more effective reduction of waste; and better prevention of conflicts over essential goods. In essence, it was about a "progressive optimization of social engineering." Llewellyn once characterized the vision of many instrumentalists as follows: "They view rules, they view law, as means to ends; as only means to ends; as having meaning only insofar as they are means to ends."[109]

Robert S. Summers (1933–2019) points out various problems that arise in such an instrumentalist approach to the law. He brings up four objections that go to the heart of the realist undertaking. (1) A legal rule always serves a purpose, according to the instrumentalists. But, so Summers says, highly complex and differing goal structures often underpin most types of

---

107 Lee Loevinger, "Jurimetrics—The Next Step Forward," in: *Minn Law Review*, 33 (1949), p. 455, also in: Lord Lloyd of Hampstead, *Lloyd's Introduction to Jurisprudence*, fifth edition, London: Stevens & Sons 1985, pp. 783–787.
108 Holmes, *Collected Legal Papers*, p. 210.
109 Llewellyn, "Some Realism," p. 1223.

law. The naïve instrumentalist does not acknowledge this, and he easily falls prey to the "one-rule-one-goal" fallacy.[110] This means that they see a single, unambiguously recognizable means-end hypothesis in every legal prescription. However, Summer argues that it is characteristic of many rules that they have more than one goal. (2) A second objection to the realists' instrumentalism has to do with the conclusion that we cannot view law only as an instrument meant to achieve a certain end. According to Summer, we know from interpretation doctrine that the law does not consist only of means, but of means-to-ends constellations. In the teleological interpretation, we assume that we cannot establish what a rule is without knowing what the rule is for. In other words: goals are an integral part of the very definition of the rule. (3) Summers' third argument starts from the assumption that the law is a human artifact and therefore serves some purpose or another. When a rule is of such a flawed design that it cannot serve any purpose in any way, we can say that it is not a legal rule. (4) A fourth argument is that, in the law, means and ends are often hard to distinguish from one another.

Thus, the eighth characteristic of realism can be said to be the fact that the realists cultivated an instrumentalist vision of the law. The law was meant to serve certain social ends.

Perhaps instrumentalism also serves as a suitable introduction to a discussion of what the realists wanted to achieve. Realism has often been presented as a critical movement, a way of thinking about the law that was best characterized by what it opposed. In a certain sense, this is fair, and in some representatives of realism, it is hard to get a sense of the constructive part of their theories. This constructive part perhaps comes out most clearly in their views on the reform of legal education and their reform proposals for the American constitutional system. We will therefore conclude our survey of realism with two characteristics that relate to the implementation of these reforms. First, the realists advocated a different vision of legal science and legal education. Second, they criticized a number of important legal institutions, such as the Supreme Court.

Legal education

Realism also had serious consequences for the contents of the curriculum at the law schools. Realists often complained of a one-sided emphasis on rote-learning the rules and a consistent "neglect of training for constructive participation and leadership in solving the community's problems."[111] W.O. Douglas (1898–1980), later a judge on the Supreme Court (1939), a friend

---

110 Summers, *Het Pragmatisch instrumentalisme*, p. 70.
111 Fryer in William T. Fryer et al., *Legal Method*, St. Paul, MN: West Publishing Co. 1948, p. 1, pp. 2–9.

of Frank's, and closely associated with the realists, said in a 1936 lecture that the law program was no longer in harmony with what had been learned about the workings of the legal field.[112] We now know, Douglas noted, that "hunches,"[113] social views, and other factors that are difficult or impossible to quantify play an important part in the formation of judicial decisions. As such, we should take this into consideration in *legal education*. He refers to Frank, who had written that a judicial decision can never be understood just by looking at laws and precedents. Frank wrote:

> The lawyer will go wrong who believes that (in advising a client, drafting an instrument, trying a case, or arguing before a court) he can rely on the so-called reasons found in or spelled out of opinions to guide him in guessing what courts will hereafter decide.

Douglas approvingly quotes this passage. He who focuses only on written sources is like a botanist who believes he can study a plant by only looking at what is visible above the ground or an anatomist who only examines the outside of the body. The law is about predictions, Douglas writes, again following Frank. And he adds: "A study of the legal literature exemplified by judicial opinions supplies part, but only part, of the material necessary to make such a prediction."[114]

Although he is critical of existing legal education, Douglas is optimistic about the possibilities to change the curriculum. In fact, various steps have already been taken in that direction. Psychologists, economists, political scientists, and representatives from other disciplines are studying the law, and these people have also been given a place in the curriculum. The result of all of this is that the horizons of the law have been widened considerably and that new paths are being explored.

It is sometimes said that this has caused less attention to be paid to hard analysis. But Douglas emphatically denies this. What can be said, however, is that analysis is being done on different types of facts. It is no longer so much about studying "century-old legal precepts" but about studying the "cinema of life."[115] A law professor's job consists of a large part of *research*. And not research in the sense of compiling a corpus juris, but research aimed at staying informed of "the fast-moving stream of human activity."

---

112 William O. Douglas, "Education for the Law," in: William T. Fryer et al., *Legal Method*, St. Paul, MN: West Publishing Co. 1948, pp. 2–9.
113 See: Joseph Hutcheson, "The Judgment Intuitive," in: David M. Adams, ed., *Philosophical Problems in the Law*, second edition, Belmont: Wadworth Publishing Company 1996, pp. 73–81.
114 Douglas, "Education for the Law," p. 4.
115 Ibid., p. 6.

It ought to be said, however, that we find pleas for a broadening of legal education and its field of vision not only in the realists but also in authors who were associated with them, such as Benjamin Cardozo. In his lecture *Our Lady the Common Law* (1939), Cardozo quotes the Dean of Harvard Law School, Lawrence Lowell, who had made a case for a new concept for the law program.[116] The idea that is gaining ground now, according to Cardozo, is that the different disciplines have come to see that they can learn from each other. The physicist understands that he needs the chemist. The zoologist recognizes that he can learn something from the botanist. The economist can learn from the statesman. The notion of a strict separation between the different fields of human knowledge is rejected in a general sense, Cardozo noted. "Something of this same concept of the continuity of knowledge is making its way into the law." He then refers to the fact that, as a judge, he has been confronted with cases in which he had to understand some science, some biology, and some other areas of human knowledge.

A third author who, although strictly speaking not a realist, still had ideas that were related to those of the realists with regard to legal education was Roscoe Pound. Pound also advocated a drastic reform of legal education in the direction of a more interdisciplinary program during this time.[117] He agrees with Holmes, who said that a jurist should know the law. But here the question does arise: what do we mean by "the law"? We could take it to mean *the legal system*. It could also mean *the body of laws*. The law can also be understood as *the process by which the judge makes a decision*. And, finally, we can take *all four* of these as constituting "the law."

How does Pound believe we ought to interpret Holmes's statement? In the latter sense: a jurist should not only know the body of laws but also understand the legal system and the process by which a judge makes his decision. With regard to legal education, a distinction can be made between a *general part* and the specialist *professional expertise* that aspiring jurists should be taught. About the former, Pound says it should include an introduction to the theory of values, the goals of social control, the legal system as a special element of that social control, and an introduction to legal interpretation. About the value of a general introduction to law, Pound says: "General training is no less important than immediate professional training."[118] And also: "The things most urged have been general culture; a grasp of the social sciences, especially in recent years a grasp of the economic order; and an understanding of business organization and methods." Pound emphasizes

---

116 Benjamin Nathan Cardozo, *Selected Writings*, Margaret E. Hall and Matthew Bender, eds., Albany, NY: Broadway 1980 (1947), pp. 87–99.
117 Roscoe Pound, "What Constitutes a Good Legal Education," in: *Law Quarterly Review*, 47 (1931), also in: Fryer, *Legal Method*, pp. 11–16.
118 Pound, "What Constitutes a Good Legal Education?," p. 14.

that it is more about learning certain skills than learning substantive knowledge. What it is really about for Pound is the "power of reason, power to think consecutively, power to weigh and appraise material, with habits of getting to the bottom of things, or going to sources, and of clear thought and expression."[119]

Like all of Pound's reflections, his thoughts on the aims of legal education are so nuanced that no one could possibly take objection to them. He favors one thing, but is reluctant to give up the other. Although nuance is a virtue, it can lead an author to advocate the implementation of two things that are hard to achieve simultaneously. That is problematic. A general education is important, Pound says, as is a great deal of specialist professional expertise. How do these ideals relate to one another? Can they even be reconciled?

The same way, as Kipling said, a sailor has to know his knots, sleeping or waking, so a jurist also has to know a number of things, Pound believes. Besides general knowledge, he then also appears to make a plea for specialist legal expertise. What he favors is the correction of a one-sided emphasis on one of these two things in one period of reflection about the curriculum and a one-sided emphasis on the other in the next period. There used to be a tendency to pay a great deal of attention to factual knowledge. These days, the trend is to underestimate the extent to which a jurist has to have command of a certain set of facts.

Where the realists differed: Frank against predictivism; law as "art," not as science

So much for legal education. It is obvious that such views about legal education are closely related to the realist vision of legal science. As has already been shown here, we can distinguish two visions: a scientistic direction that has great expectations for the development of legal science into a strict discipline and a more humanities-focused approach. It hardly needs to be pointed out that Frank, with his emphasis on uncertainty, cannot be enamored of ideas about legal science as a rigid discipline. He is much more inclined—referencing Aristotle—toward legal science as an art ("ars"). In that context, he opposes Lasswell and McDougal, who had claimed that it ought to be possible to provide a scientific basis for predictions of judicial behavior. According to Lasswell and McDougal, it should be possible to predict what the judge was going to decide in most cases. In order to predict the outcome of a trial, insight into the personality traits of the judges, parties, advisors, witnesses, and members of the jury would be required. After all, what all these actors do is "human" in the sense that it is determined to

119 Ibid., p. 16.

a certain extent by the interaction of their personalities. In his book *Power and Personality* (1948), Lasswell claimed that he could expose a number of factors that were determinative of judicial behavior.[120] But no one who reads that book, so Frank says, will agree that what Lasswell is offering actually enables anyone to predict how a judge will decide in a concrete case. After all, no one, including Lasswell, can predict what will happen on the day of the judge's decision, or on the day before it. A sleepless night, a severe headache, a marital spat—these are all factors that will influence him to a greater or lesser extent.[121] If Lasswell and McDougal are actually capable of "scientifically" predicting how judges will react, they should also be able to tell us *the level of certainty* with which they are able to make these predictions. They should really be challenged the same way Frank challenged Felix Cohen, which is that they should be asked to publish a number of their predictions *before* the judicial decisions in question have actually been made. Then we will wait and see how accurate the predictions are. If they are 80 percent correct, Frank says, he will be deeply impressed with their work, but he strongly doubts that they will achieve such a score.

Frank leveled a similar critique at Loevinger's jurimetrics. Whether it involves Lasswell and McDougal, Cohen, Loevinger, or others, it is always about the overly optimistic nineteenth-century ideal that the social sciences can be grounded in an exact foundation and method in the same way the natural sciences were: "to call the making of social guesses a 'science' has the disvalue of glossing over inescapable difficulties."[122] Of course, it is possible to alter the definition of science so as to enable the classification of legal scholarship as a science. It could be said that science is nothing more than "intelligent observation guided by the best wisdom already in our possession" or "the method of dealing intelligently with all problems." But these are just semantic solutions in order to sell legal scholarship as a science. Not only that, but we also run the risk of flirting with the idea that "legal engineering" could one day become a success. Any form of "social engineering" simply disregards the fact that we are dealing with human beings, and that people are not machines.[123] Let us simply set aside this religion of science of which William James warned us. Scientism has only ever given us the false hope that we could organize legal science on the same basis as the natural sciences, Frank thinks.

Does this mean that we ought to give up on all of legal scholarship's aspirations? No, Frank says. There is no reason to feed to the dogs that which is not good enough for the gods (Tourtoulon). Wise medics have always

120 Harold D. Lasswell, *Power and Personality*, New York: Viking 1948.
121 Frank, *Courts on Trial*, p. 203.
122 Ibid., p. 216.
123 Ibid., p. 217.

known that the practice of medicine uses scientific discoveries but cannot itself be a science. It is an art. The same could be said of law.

In a certain sense, Frank is right when he criticizes the realists' optimistic view that judicial behavior can be predicted. This is, indeed, unlikely. Why would it be possible? The realists have always placed an emphasis on the rejection of "mechanical jurisprudence," but at the same time, they replace it with a different kind of mechanical model for the prediction of judicial behavior, one that is no less optimistic.

Criticism of specifically American institutions: the Supreme Court

Finally, the tenth characteristic of realism: its critique of fundamental American institutions. As is true of so many things, a theory of law can also be recognized by its fruits. In philosophy, and also in legal philosophy, certain foundational principles are frequently repeated. But it is also interesting to see how a certain conception of the law is handled in its practical application. Especially a theory that advertises itself as practical in nature should, in its application, be expected to make a difference to the problem in question. Luckily, the realists wrote many books in which they used the particular treatment of a certain subject to illustrate how a realist view of the subject is distinguishable from its treatment from a different perspective.

One of the most interesting applications of the realist viewpoint is its application to American constitutional history, in particular when it comes to the role of the Supreme Court. It was Fred Rodell who wrote an interesting book about this, *Nine Men* (1955), a book that was representative of the realist movement.[124] We will discuss criticism of the Supreme Court and the functioning of the American constitutional system as the tenth and last characteristic of realism.

About his own history of the Supreme Court, Rodell writes: "It would not spare personalities, yet it would not be content to give its readers the cheap thrill of vicariously peeping through keyholes at undressed Justices."[125] One may wonder, however, which would be preferable, being seen undressed through a keyhole or in the harsh light in which Rodell casts his subjects. Whatever the case, his book is certainly interesting and worth reading.[126] He also notes that he tried not to use too much legal slang, and in this, he

---

124 Fred Rodell, *Nine Men, A Political History of the Supreme Court from 1790 to 1955*, New York: Random House 1955. See also on Rodell: Carel Stolker, *Rethinking the Law School: Education, Research, Outreach and Governance*, Cambridge: Cambridge University Press 2015, pp. 231–232.
125 Rodell, *Nine Men*, p. ix.
126 On Rodell, see also the critical commentary of: Richard A. Posner, *Overcoming Law*, Cambridge, MA, London: Harvard University Press 1995, p. 2.

wholly succeeded.[127] Still, the book is hard to classify. It is a typically realist book, but without the author explicitly naming the presuppositions underlying the method and approach. Realism nevertheless lives on every page.

Nine Men is a history of the Supreme Court in which two elements take center stage. First: the contrast between the two great justices in American history: John Marshall and Oliver Wendell Holmes. The latter is, not surprisingly, the hero of the book. Marshall is depicted as, in a certain sense, an admirable figure, but for the wrong side.

The second element of the book is thematic. It is a flamboyantly written critique of the American constitutional system: a critique of the power of judicial review, the undemocratic character of the American system, and the commingling of law and politics, the latter not as something that should be countered, but as something that—apparently—is an unavoidable part of the system. The position of the Supreme Court is especially targeted here. At the highest levels of the civilian government of the United States, there are (i) Congress, (ii) the president and his cabinet, and (iii) the Supreme Court. Of these three, only one wears a uniform, operates entirely in secret, and is not subject to any democratic control. That is the Supreme Court.

The power of judicial review. Rodell begins with an attack on judicial review. Jefferson had also expressed serious objections to a court that was too powerful. After describing the operation and jurisdiction of the Court, he remarked: "The Constitution on this hypothesis, is a mere thing of wax in the hands of the judiciary which they may twist and shape it into any form they please."[128] Rodell agrees with Jefferson's critique. He quotes Justice Stone, who once said: "The only check upon our own exercise of power is our own sense of self-restraint."[129] Rodell attaches far-reaching consequences to this. It means, he believes, that the old saying that the US government is a government of laws, not of people, is an "undemocratic canard." Rodell explains this as follows:

> Laws do not write or enforce or interpret themselves. Even constitutions are no more than words except as men give them flesh and muscle and meaning in action; then the flesh and muscle are molded and the meaning in action is directed by men.[130]

The idea that the words of the law point in a certain direction is fairly naïve. After all, how to explain that Supreme Court decisions are made by *voting proportions* (5–4, 6–3, 7–2, 8–1)? How to explain that dissenting opinions,

---

127 Rodell, *Nine Men*, p. x.
128 Ibid., p. 5.
129 Ibid., p. 5.
130 Ibid., p. 6.

sometimes by only a single justice, can sound wiser than the majority's judgment? How to explain that the same case can be judged entirely differently than it was some years before?

Prescient was the comment by Charles Evans Hughes before he became Chief Justice of the Supreme Court: "We are under a Constitution, but the Constitution is what the judges say it is."[131]

Sometimes, Rodell does seem to encounter some eminent judges and politicians of integrity and vision. But, he quickly adds, these are the exceptions. For every Marshall, for every Holmes, there is a long list of mediocre characters (just as for every Lincoln and Jefferson there is an army of incompetent statesmen).[132]

One of the most problematic things about the Supreme Court is its lifelong appointments. Since it is the president who nominates the members of the Court, bad appointment policy can leave the country stuck with mediocre justices for a long time. "It has been said that the good a President does is often interred with his bones but his choice of Supreme Court Justices lives after him."[133] It is also said that the Supreme Court follows the elections, only it is the elections of ten years ago.[134]

The American system is not democratic. A second point of criticism that often features in Rodell's critique of the Court is the undemocratic nature of the system, as it is expressed, among other things, in the power of judicial review, but also in other parts of the system. In no way is the American system a true democracy, Rodell says. He offers various reasons for this. First, it has to do with representative democracy. He also finds fault with the idea of entrenched legislation. In a true democracy, the people or the people's representatives ought to be able to easily change *all* laws, including the Constitution. Finally, there is the problem of judicial review. One of the oldest problems for all political philosophers who embrace both constitutionalism and democracy is the question of *who* decides if an act violates the constitution.

---

131 Hughes' statement is a typically realist thing to say, although this perspective can also be found in jurists who have little to do with realism. In the Supreme Court under Chief Justice Rehnquist, such diverse figures as Chief Justice Rehnquist himself and the last "leftist," William Brennan, had a similarly disconcerting view of the law. They did not see the Court as an arena of profound discussions. Every year, Brennan asked his law clerks what they believed the most important rule of the Court to be. When they hesitated or failed to come up with an answer, Brennan held up his fist and opened his hand, spreading his five fingers: "It takes five votes to do anything in the Supreme Court." See: David Savage, *Turning Right, The Making of the Rehnquist Supreme Court*, New York: John Wiley & Sons, Inc. 1992 and Rodell, *Nine Men*, p. 8.

132 Rodell, *Nine Men*, p. 8.

133 Ibid., p. 9.

134 Ibid.

> Whatever men are entrusted with that ultimate decision, especially if they are not elected to that position of trust, their power cannot but be an autocratic power - for it lets them reverse the choice of a contemporary majority and so defeat the democratic will.[135]

As such, the American system is not a true democracy, because it is possible for the will of a minority to thwart the will of the majority.

Law is politics. Rodell also repeatedly argues that law is actually politics. His history of the Court shows that justices had their sights on a lot more than just the Constitution. They all too often stepped up as defenders of big business or some other interest group. A look at the entire history of the Supreme Court demonstrates that it has more often protected the interests of a financial elite than the country's much-lauded civil liberties. "Indeed, the only minority in whose behalf the Justices have regularly and effectively used their power, to block the majority will as expressed in federal laws, is the minority of the well-to-do."[136]

Most US citizens view the Supreme Court with as much reverence as the British view their royal family, Rodell writes. And there are other similarities too. Just as in the case of the royal family, we are talking about a myth.

The *first myth* is that the Court is a kind of coherent, uniform power, a collective mind that operates as a unit within the structure of the government. This myth is supported by another, one could say, supportive presupposition, which is that justices on the Court do not *make* law, but only *establish* what the law is. These myths are carefully maintained. Take this choice of words, for instance: they speak of "the opinion of the Court."

A *second myth* is that those who are appointed as justices suddenly become politically neutral. The assumption apparently is that the moment the robe is donned, a switch is flipped in the mind, effecting a complete change in attitude.

The power the Court wields is, in Rodell's opinion, an irresponsible power in three ways. First, because the members of the Court are accountable to no one but themselves. Second, because they can never affect a positive shift in direction; they are only ever able to reject forms of policy. And third, because they can wield their power without having to explain why.[137]

> In no other nation on earth does a group of judges hold the sweeping political power—the privilege in practice, not just in theory, of saying

---

135 Ibid., p. 21.
136 Ibid., p. 26.
137 Ibid., p. 32.

the last governmental word—that is held by the nine U.S. Supreme Court Justices.[138]

How did the Court accrue this power? At first, it was discussed briefly when the Constitution was drafted. Then, it was further propagated by the Federalists in the first years after the birth of the republic, and Marshall deftly proclaimed it to be standard practice. Finally, various incidents in American constitutional history caused it to grow in strength, and it attained ever more solid stature.[139]

However, we should not make the mistake here of thinking that the Court's power is only exercised when justices invalidate a law. That power is also wielded when they are only "interpreting" laws Congress has passed.

Rodell relates the power of judicial review to the interests of conservative Americans a number of times. Those who favored it were "property-minded" conservative delegates to the Convention, like Alexander Hamilton, James Wilson, Oliver Elsworth, and others. They feared that unchecked power for Congress would mean that all sorts of legislation detrimental to their interests would be passed.

An evaluation of the realists

So far, we have allowed exposé and criticism to run together. However, in order not to interrupt the line of the argument, we have left out points that required a longer discussion. We will end with these now. We will try to shine a critical light on the realists' work on the basis of six points of criticism that are leveled against them.

(a) Were the realists precise enough?

Reading the realists is a pleasure.[140] They stand out because of their tantalizing positions, but also because of their clear and lively style. Holmes enriched legal science with countless adagios that are still regularly quoted in the handbooks, and even those who cannot follow the realist position to its ultimate conclusions admire Holmes's style. Hart once pointedly remarked: "while Holmes was sometimes clearly wrong, he was always wrong clearly."[141]

---

138 Ibid., p. 33.
139 Ibid., p. 34.
140 On this, see also the engaging essay by Raymond Wacks, "Legal Realism," in: Raymond Wacks, *Jurisprudence*, second edition, London: Blackstone Press Limited 1990 (1987), pp. 109–130.
141 Hart, "Positivism and the Separation of Law and Morals," here cited in: Hart, *Essays in Jurisprudence and Philosophy*, pp. 49–87, p. 49.

And yet, Holmes does not present us with a truly fleshed-out theory of law. He was often content to make sweeping statements and turn eloquent phrases; he did not take the trouble to present a fully thought-out vision of the law.

Holmes's style is often praised, but it has been less often observed that his many colorful phrasings contain pieces of wisdom that are rarely applicable on their face. First, there is the problem of their vagueness. It is eloquently phrased: "I do not think that the United States would come to an end." But what view was Holmes trying to refute here? Who is saying that the United States will end without judicial review? Who would dare to make such a pathetic claim? Some writers favor judicial review; others oppose it. But surely no one would argue that the country would go the way of the dodo if something were to change on this point? So, it has to be true that Holmes does not mean what he is literally saying. He probably means that some are *such* enthusiastic defenders of judicial review that they give the impression that they cannot even imagine any other system than the current one.

Another problem with Holmes's aphorisms is the problem with aphorisms in general, including those of famous aphorist Pascal: turn them around, and they usually sound just as good. Pascal said: the heart has its reasons, of which reason knows nothing. Very nice. But turn it around: reason has its passions, of which the heart knows nothing. Is that not just as nice? The same is true of Holmes's sayings. He provides food for thought when he says that the United States would not collapse if there were no judicial review. Upon closer inspection, it is also defensible that the concept of codified higher law that has a normative effect on lower laws, both those of the federation and those of the states, necessarily presupposes a judicial body that can make binding decisions in case of conflicting provisions. That was Marshall's view. Objections can be raised to this, of course, but these objections are not defeated by an aptly worded witticism, a bon mot, or an amusing characterization. That requires arguments, something for which Holmes rarely takes the time.

Oftentimes, Holmes also leaves the impression that he does not do justice to the positions he so smoothly dismisses. It is indeed "revolting to have no better reason for a rule than that it was laid down in the time of Henry IV."[142] But if the view he is criticizing here is the traditionalism of the common-law tradition, then there is much more to be said for it than that a rule happened to have been set down in the time of Henry IV. What the common-law tradition and its inherent conservatism emphasize is that things that have reached a certain age, that have become *tradition*, have emerged intact from a socio-historical struggle for survival.[143] Burke phrased it in the

---

142 Holmes, *Collected Legal Papers*, p. 187.
143 See on this: Gerald J. Postema, *Bentham and the Common Law Tradition*, Oxford: Clarendon Press 1989 (1986); Anthony T. Kronman, "Precedent and Tradition," in: *The Yale*

famous words: "the individual is foolish; the species is wise," to which he added: "when time is given to it." By this, he means that we can view the historical process of development as a process of refinement, of perfecting. Something that has existed for a long time has also managed to survive for a long time and will therefore be a better guiding principle than newly invented ideas with all their attendant teething troubles and imperfections. As such, it is indeed irresponsible to say that a rule from the time of Henry IV deserves our respect just because of its age, but that is not what the common-law tradition is about.

Does Holmes really not know these things, or is he pretending ignorance as a debating tactic? Probably the latter. Not entirely unwarranted are the critiques leveled at Holmes's aphorisms and sayings by one of the leaders of Scandinavian realism, A.V. Lundstedt (1882–1955). About *The Common Law* and Holmes's *Collected Legal Papers* he writes: "here one finds a great many statements, properly speaking intimations rather than reasonings, indicating that the author wishes to free himself from legal ideology."[144]

Incidentally, a certain measure of imprecision is not just characteristic of Holmes's work but also of that of other realists. This is how Llewellyn begins his famous essay *Some Realism about Realism* (1931):

> Ferment is abroad in the law. The sphere of interest widens; men become interested again in the life that swirls around things legal. Before rules, were facts; in the beginning was not a Word, but a Doing. Behind decisions stand judges; judges are men; as men they have human backgrounds. Beyond rules, again, lie effects; beyond decisions stand people whom rules and decisions directly or indirectly touch.[145]

Is this not a spectacular blend of platitudes and vagueries, wholly useless to readers of a scientific essay? Constantly, one is hoping for more and clearer information. Llewellyn notes that there used to be no interest in "the life that swirls around things legal." But whom is he talking about, and why did they lack this interest? Also noticeable is the fact that Llewellyn enjoys turning an elegant phrase, in which, more often than not, he seems more interested in presentation than in precisely expressing what he means. *Some Realism* was written in response to Roscoe Pound's article *Call for a Realist Jurisprudence*. Llewellyn agrees with Pound on a number of points, but he also remarks that Pound "departed in this paper from a practice

Law Journal, 99 (1990), pp. 1029–1068; Martin Krygier, "Law as Tradition," in: *Law and Philosophy*, 5 (1986), pp. 237–262.

144 A. Vilhelm Lundstedt, *Legal Thinking Revisited, My Views on Law*, Stockholm: Almqvist & Wiksell 1956, p. 389.

145 Llewellyn, *Jurisprudence*, p. 42.

he has often followed, of indicating, in each instance when he presented a view, precisely whose view it was, and precisely where that person has set it forth."[146] But what Pound is accused of here can also be laid at the feet of the realists.

(b) How original were the realists?

A second point that is often discussed in the literature is the question of how original the realists were. Precursors can, of course, always be identified. Rumble names Holmes, James, and Dewey.[147] Another possible name here could be Pound, who wrote in 1910: "Let us look the facts of human conduct in the face. Let us look to economics and sociology and philosophy, and cease to assume that jurisprudence is self-sufficient. (...) Let us not become legal monks."[148] In *The Need of a Sociological Jurisprudence*, he phrases it as follows:

> the modern teacher of law should be a student of sociology, economics, and politics as well. He should know not only what the courts decide and the principles by which they decide but quite as much the circumstances and conditions, social and economic, to which these principles are to be applied (...) Legal monks who pass their lives in an atmosphere of pure law, from which every worldly and human element is excluded, cannot shape practical principles to be applied to a restless world of flesh and blood.[149]

In other respects, too, Pound can be viewed as a precursor to the realists, such as with regard to his views about legal interpretation. What Pound was concerned with was "equitable application of law"; he explicitly distinguished this from the mechanical deduction of positions from certain premises. The supporters of modern legal scholarship, so Pound believed, view a legal rule as a guideline that leads to the correct result, but they also stipulate that the judge must have some freedom to do justice to individual cases.[150]

Incidentally, Llewellyn did not deny the realists' debt to Pound. In 1960, he wrote about Pound's pioneering work that it is the basis "of our

---

146 Ibid., p. 45.

147 Rumble, *American Legal Realism*, p. 4.

148 Roscoe Pound, "Law in Books and Law in Action," in: *American Law Review*, XLIV (1910), p. 35, cited in: Rumble, *American Legal Realism*, p. 10.

149 Pound, "The Need of a Sociological Jurisprudence," p. 611, cited in: Rumble, *American Legal Realism*, p. 13.

150 Roscoe Pound, "The Scope and Purpose of Sociological Jurisprudence," I, in: *Harvard Law Review*, XXIV(8) (June 1911), p. 515, pp. 591–619.

forward-looking thought of the '20's and '30's [sic] and has provided half of the commonplace equipment on and with which our work since has builded [sic]."[151]

The realists wanted to succeed where Pound, to their minds, had failed. In what ways did they progress further than Pound? Rumble sees it like this: (1) first, the empirical work they did must be acknowledged. (2) The realists also had the effect of stimulating further research.[152]

(c) Were the realists consistent?

Frank's work in particular seems somewhat uneven because, in his critique of the legal profession, he adopts such radical positions that he is forced to distance himself in his more constructive passages from what he wrote in the more critical parts.

For instance, in his critique of the myth of legal certainty and the impersonal performance of judges, he emphasizes the judge's personal input so strongly that, in his constructive passages about what judges ought to do, he is confronted with his own pessimism with regard to what is possible.

This can be illustrated by what Frank writes about judicial interpretation. When a judge tries to determine the goal of the legislator, the judge has to distance himself as much as possible from his own ideas about policy. Frank offers a good reason for this: because the goal of the legislator is to put into words the result of a process that brought together a multitude of conflicting interests. When Frank himself was involved in a case, he was invited to leave the legislator's language for what it was and view the legislator's goal as irrelevant to the current state of affairs, all "to achieve what we might regard as a more just result." He answered as follows:

> Such a remaking of the legislation, would require consideration of questions of legislative policy bearing on fiscal and economic matters and on administrative convenience; to discharge that task efficiently we would be obliged to hold a sort of Congressional Committee hearing, at which all interested persons would be heard, so as to be sure that our amendments would not entail unforeseen and undesirable results. We have no power to embark on such an enterprise.[153]

In effect, Frank is voicing a traditional view about legal interpretation that distances itself from too much judicial input. Blackstone and other representatives of the traditional model of legal interpretation would entirely

---

151 Llewellyn, *Jurisprudence*, p. 496.
152 Rumble, *American Legal Realism*, p. 21.
153 Frank, *Courts on Trial*, p. 302.

agree with such a passage. It is certainly surprising, however, that it is *Frank*, of all people, supporting these ideals, when his previous chapters have just extensively explained how it is impossible for the judge to distance himself from policy considerations and attempts to dispense justice objectively.

This odd paradox is found often in Frank's work. How Frank summarizes his ideas about judicial interpretation is equally surprising in light of his critical passages: "Awareness and public acknowledgement by judges of their legislative power may well induce restraint in exercising it."[154] This, too, points to a highly nuanced view of the law-finding process: "A judge who publicly admits that at times he cannot help legislating, is likely to be far more restrained when doing so."

All of this points to a certain emphasis on judicial self-restraint, a conviction that we also find in Holmes. But how does such a passage relate to other things Frank said in which he seems to want to do away with all the certainty, predictability, traditions, and conventions?

A well-meaning interpreter of Frank's will probably say that he first had to challenge overly rosy positions on judicial impartiality in order to then replace them with a kind of purified plea for judicial modesty. But the cynic, or "realist," could say that most of Llewellyn's ideas are too vague to expose their inconsistencies, and Frank's are too clear to hide their inconsistencies from view.

Perhaps some things can also be explained by the personal development of the author, who started out with a very radical view, as expounded in *Law and the Modern Mind*, but nuanced this in his later development, such as in *Courts on Trial*.

In this later book, we also find a fairly nuanced and sympathetic discussion of natural law; something that is unexpected on the basis of Frank's earlier work. In the later work, he presents a fully formed vision of natural law, in which he notes that natural law could be invoked in countless cases. When Henry VIII wanted to divorce his wife, he appealed to natural law, but the Pope refused to cooperate on the same grounds. Natural law has often been invoked to justify slavery, but also to argue the injustice of slavery. Natural law has been used to justify polygamy, but also to reject it. Bodin deduced from natural law a legitimation of absolute monarchy, but later writers appealed to natural law to reject any claim of absolutism. That is why it has been said that: "Natural Law is simply that law of which the person using the phrase approves."[155] And it is also why it is incorrect to claim that when we abandon natural law, we are preaching a form of cynicism.[156] It is much more honest to openly state which values you uphold

---

154 Ibid., p. 306.
155 Ibid., p. 349.
156 Ibid., p. 350.

and expose them to criticism from others than to grant them an aura of legitimacy by presenting them as "natural law."[157]

So far, this is fairly critical of natural law thinking. But Frank does not mean to entirely discredit the natural law tradition. He writes:

> At its best, Natural Law has symbolized the unquenchable, human desire for norms or standards of justice by which to evaluate existing, legal rules, contrasting the "is" with the "ought to be." We need a symbol for the demand that statutes should be repealed, and judge-made rules abandoned or modified, when they obstruct valued moral aims, for the demand that human institutions be altered when they work injustice.[158]

And, indeed, no one can object to this. Incidentally, Frank does also say: "I suggest Justice as a better symbol than Natural Law."

(d) Were the realist ideas about legal education "realistic"?

At first glance, not many objections can be leveled against Frank's ideas about legal education. He advocates the introduction of the social sciences to the legal curriculum, a greater focus on the practice of the law, and more attention paid to the facts as a part of the law-finding process and therefore as a relevant object of study for legal scholars. Who would oppose this? His views about legal education are somewhat similar to Pound's, but that sets us on the path of a reservation that one could formulate about both Frank and Pound when it comes to legal education. One might wonder whether their ambitions are not overly lofty, whether their expectations of what is possible are actually "realistic." They want law *teachers* to be people who have mastered the principles of all the social sciences *and* who have significant practical experience *and* who are scientifically talented enough to integrate these different areas of science and experience *and* who are able, moreover, to educate students about these things in an inspiring manner. That sounds marvelous, of course, but is it realistic? Who has all these different qualities?

Similar objections can be leveled at what they expect from *students*. It is, of course, great if a student learns the law, as well as all these social sciences, as well as being a frequent visitor to court cases in order to see the law in action. But where are students supposed to find the time? Much of what Frank writes sounds excellent, but is it "realistic"?

157 Ibid., p. 353.
158 Ibid., p. 365.

The impression that he is asking for *too much* is heightened when we read that, besides the things already named, a law student should also become highly versed in "the need for embodying democratic ideals and values in the legal rules."[159] The ideal law student is an accomplished technician and an interdisciplinary problem solver, not to mention someone who further develops the law in the light of the ideals of a constitutional democracy.

(e) Were the realists "fair" in their criticism?

Anyone paraphrasing what Rodell writes in his book *Nine Men* is constantly tempted to quote him—so beautiful are his characterizations, so well-chosen his words. As the Rector of Leiden University Carel Stolker makes clear in his *Rethinking the Law School* (2014), Rodell was also very critical of the style of his colleagues. In "Goodbye to Law Reviews" (1936) Rodell wrote: "There are two things wrong with almost all legal writing. One is its style. The other is its content."[160] As one may expect, Rodell's *Nine Men* is one of the most interesting histories of the Supreme Court.

However, the fact remains that most of his generalizations are highly contestable and almost never accompanied by justifications. Is it true that the person who *interprets* always also *detects*? Is it the case that the words of the Constitution are in no way a restriction on judges' discretionary powers? Is it the case that judicial review is necessarily an undemocratic factor in the American constitutional system or can review and democracy somehow be reconciled?[161] Is it the case that Marshall always defended the rich? Is it the case that the idea of a government of laws, not of people is dashed if judges have the power of judicial review? The claims are all made with great confidence, but all of them are subject to all sorts of views and theories that Rodell pays no attention to whatsoever. Indeed, discussion with others is something Rodell generally avoids in his book. He dispenses *strong opinions* with gusto, but never engages in debate with concrete thinkers, identified by name, who defend the positions he sets out to disprove.

A second point of criticism that could be made against Rodell is that his book approaches the history of the Supreme Court from a purely negative or critical angle. Rodell only focuses on the system's faults; not once does he even try to discuss the system's virtues. In that respect, his book is a good counterpoint to Lord Bryce's *The American Commonwealth*, in which the arguments supporting the American system are eloquently—like

159 Ibid., p. 239.
160 In Fred Rodell, "Goodbye to Law Reviews," in: *Virginia Law Review*, 23(1) (1936), p. 38, here quoted in: Carel Stolker, *Rethinking the Law School: Education, Research, Outreach and Governance*, Cambridge: Cambridge University Press 2015, p. 231.
161 This was attempted by: Eugene V. Rostow, "The Democratic Character of Judicial Review," in: *Harvard Law Review*, 66 (1952), pp. 193–224.

Rodell, though at a slower pace—discussed.[162] Bryce carefully and fastidiously argues that review is a necessary element of the concept of higher law, that the power of interpretation needs to be accompanied by a plea for judicial self-restraint, and that democracy and review can be reconciled.

Bryce's work could really be viewed as a reconstruction of the American system according to Marshall's ideas, while Rodell offers a reconstruction based on the ideas of Holmes. Rodell assumes the error of the Marshallian perspective, however, rather than actually proving it.

A third point of criticism is that it is often unclear from which perspective Rodell characterizes something as a negative. In fact, he seems *impossible* to please. Take his view of the diligence or reticence with which the Supreme Court sometimes accepts cases. If the Court is *anything*, Rodell says, it is a *brake*. It can never be an "affirmative force"; it is always a negative force. "It cannot create, it cannot initiate, it cannot put into action any government policy of any kind."[163] The only thing judges are able to do is say "yes" or "no" to a particular law or form of policy. And he then adds: "Failure to use the power to govern is one way of governing."[164]

Rodell is right about this, but why is it such a problem? Based on his own ideas about the undemocratic nature of judicial review, it should be seen as a good thing that the Supreme Court works only as a brake and not as an institution that can introduce legislation of its own. In fact, the "brake-function" is what the Court ought to limit itself to. It is the legislator who ought to offer new alternatives when the judge has identified unconstitutionality in the existing system.

Fourth, it can be said that, although Rodell's book is still an interesting read, his commentary is outdated in the sense that the position of the American system is no longer unique. Of course, this does not mean that his criticism of the American system is flawed, but it does mean that he cannot criticize the American system *for being so unusual*, as he regularly does. In no other country does the judge have such far-reaching powers, Rodell believes. And indeed, when he wrote his book, that was true. But since then, the American system, with a constitution containing higher law and the related power of judicial review, has been adopted by many other countries. Germany adopted it, as did other states in Europe. Even in England, the doctrine of the "sovereignty of Parliament" is teetering, and there are calls for a "Bill of Rights for Britain."[165] The constitutional model that is so pop-

162 James Bryce, *The American Commonwealth*, two volumes, New York: Macmillan 1926 (1893). Those in search of a modern parallel could look at: F.A. Hayek, *The Constitution of Liberty*, London, Henley: Routledge and Kegan Paul 1976 (1960).
163 Rodell, *Nine Men*, p. 11.
164 Ibid., p. 19.
165 See: Leslie Scarman, *English Law: The New Dimension*, London: Stevens & Sons 1974; Ronald Dworkin, *A Bill of Rights for Britain*, London: Chatto & Windus 1990. On

ular nowadays—so dominant that it is possible to, paraphrasing Fukuyama, speak of the end of constitutional history—is the model in which:

- a distinction is made between regular, everyday law and higher law set down in a constitution;
- the higher law is safeguarded by the courts.

This model became so dominant after the Second World War that it may be possible to speak of a General Constitutional Pattern of the Modern Age (GCP).[166]

(f) Can the law be studied as a de facto pattern of behavior?

Finally, a word about the realists' factual approach. Some go so far as saying this is the death blow to the entire realist project. Hart, Kelsen, and others who view the law as a normative entity are of this opinion. The normative character of the law, the law as a system of normative rules or principles, is mostly ignored by the realists. It has been said that the realist has an "addiction to brute fact."[167]

The fiercest critic of realism was Hermann Kantorowicz, a prominent representative of the *Freie Rechtslehre*, which is related to the realist approach to the law. In 1934, Kantorowicz published a critique of realist philosophy that would set the stage for much of the later criticism.[168] The most serious shortcoming of predictivism, Kantorowicz said, lies in the fact that the realists confuse the concept with one of its elements. Say we agree with Holmes and his followers, Kantorowicz writes, that law is what the courts do. Does that not come down to the same thing as saying "religion" is what the churches preach, "science" is what the universities teach, "medicine" is what the doctor prescribes, a "shoe" is what the cobbler makes? This is simply putting the cart before the horse. After all, "church" cannot be defined without "religion," "university" not without "science," "doctor"

---

these attempts, see also: C.M. Zoethout, *Constitutionalisme, Een vergelijkend onderzoek naar het beperken van overheidsmacht door het recht* [Constitutionalism; A Comparative Study in Restraining Governmental Power], Arnhem: Gouda Quint 1995, pp. 152–169.

166 See on this: Paul Cliteur and Afshin Ellian "Constitutional Democracy as a Legitimate Form of Government," in: Paul Cliteur and Afshin Ellian, *A New Introduction to Jurisprudence*, London, New York: Routledge 2019, pp. 36–75.

167 Lord Lloyd of Hampstead, *Lloyd's Introduction to Jurisprudence*, p. 694.

168 H. Kantorowicz, "Some Rationalism about Realism," in: *Yale Law Journal*, 43 (1934), pp. 1240–1253, also cited in: Hermann Kantorowicz, *Rechtswissenschaft und Soziologie, Ausgewählte Schriften zur Wissenschaftslehre*, Karlsruhe: Verlag C.F. Müller 1962, pp. 101–117.

not without "medicine," and "cobbler" not without "shoe." As such, law is not what the courts do; courts are the institutions that execute law.[169]

This notion has been reformulated countless times in critiques of realism. Always, the critique comes down to the assertion that the rule-perspective simply cannot be done away with. The realists wanted to study the law as the behavior patterns of judges. But, as it has often been said to the realists, judicial behavior as a purely objective datum simply does not exist without making reference to the law in the books. Without reference to a legal system, the behavior of judges cannot even be identified as the behavior of a judge acting in his official capacity. Kelsen also made this point. Law would not be "law" if it consisted only of descriptive generalizations of behavior patterns.[170]

In a certain sense, that critique is warranted. It is not clear, however, to what extent realism is wounded by it. The realist can say, after all, that he does not deny the normative character of the rules, but that he is calling attention to the fact that this does not, or only very minimally, enable us to explain judicial decisions. Critics will then reply that this means that the realist is taking a non-scientific approach to the law. Legal science is essentially dissolving into empirical forensic psychology. Again, though, we can ask to what extent the realist is impacted by this blow. He could say that empirical forensic psychology can tell us more interesting things about the law than traditional legal science can. And perhaps this was true during a certain phase in the development of legal thought. These days, many of the insights realists emphasized have become commonplace, but they did need to be brought to the fore in order to attain that status. In that sense, realism is also a movement that is a victim of its own success, or, less dramatically put, it was a revolutionary movement that saw most of its program realized and thus lost its reason for existing.

On the basis of these considerations, we can appreciate realism as representative of an approach to the law for which there was a need during a certain period, as a correction to the overly idealistic and naïve conceptions of the law. But that is as far as realism's impact goes. It is not an integral philosophy of the law and the legal field. As a comprehensive doctrine, realism fails. Incidentally, this is not an insight about which, looking back, we ought to conclude that criticism of realism is an accompanying phenomenon of its history. Lon Fuller,[171] in particular, was one of the fiercest critics of

---

169 Kantorowicz, "Some Rationalism," p. 1250.
170 Hans Kelsen, *General Theory of Law and State*, Cambridge: Translation Wedberg 1945, p. 162ff.
171 Fuller, *The Law in Quest of Itself*; L.L. Fuller, "American Legal Realism," in: *University of Pennsylvania Law Review*, 82 (1934), pp. 429–462; Lon L. Fuller, "American Legal Philosophy at Mid-century," in: *Journal of Legal Education*, 6(4), 1954, pp. 457–485. A defense of the realists can be found in: M. McDougal, "Fuller v. the American Realists: An Intervention," in: *Yale Law Journal*, 50 (1941), pp. 827–840.

realist thought from the very beginning, but he certainly was not the only one. Lord Lloyd of Hampstead phrases a common critique[172] of the realist philosophy as follows:

> in law, as in other intellectual spheres, there are signs of a reaction, connected with the feeling that empiricism and positivism are not enough, and that some new *mystique* must be found to underpin the *ethos* of man and human society.[173]

The word *mystique* is, in all its vagueness, perhaps not the most obvious of concepts through which to express a certain dissatisfaction with the realist approach. It ought to be clarified, in any case. Perhaps the following clarification is acceptable. Realism wants to make an empirical, business-like, sometimes cynical study of the law as the "behavior patterns" of those involved in legal practice. But does this approach to the law not suffer from a similar failing as the "black letter man's" strategy for studying the law?[174] According to Holmes, the "black letter man" makes the mistake of seeing and studying the law as no more than the black letters on the paper of the legal provision, the will, the contract, or any other document in which the law is manifested. Such an approach to the law is too one-dimensional, too limited; it lacks the context within which the printed letters acquire perspective and meaning, so the realist says.

But is the realist not guilty of a similar one-sidedness? To him, the law is nothing more than the empirical patterns of those involved in its practice. But do these empirical patterns mean anything at all free from the rules, principles, and ideals to which they are, in some way or another, related?[175]

---

172 He attributes this to, among others: Fuller, Hall, Northrop, and Goodhart. See: Lord Lloyd of Hampstead, *Lloyd's Introduction to Jurisprudence*, p. 695.

173 Ibid., p. 695.

174 This is thought out well by: N.E. Simmonds, *The Decline of Juridical Reason, Doctrine and Theory in the Legal Order*, Manchester: Manchester University Press 1984; N.E. Simmonds, "Law as a Rational Science," in: *Archiv für Rechts- und Sozialphilosophie*, 66 (1980), pp. 535–556.

175 For an accentuation of the need for a moral approach to judicial interpretation, see: Ronald Dworkin, "The Moral Reading of the Constitution," in: *The New York Review of Books*, 21 March 1996, pp. 46–51.

Chapter 3

Rationalism, empiricism, and logical positivism

A methodological journey through a permanent reversal of doubt and certainty

> "Knowledge" is a vague concept for two reasons. First, because the meaning of a word is always more or less vague except in logic and pure mathematics; and second, because all that we count as knowledge is in a greater or less degree uncertain, and there is no way of deciding how much uncertainty makes a belief unworthy to be called "knowledge," any more than how much loss of hair makes a man bald.[1]

> The pregiven world is the horizon which includes all our goals, all our ends, whether fleeting or lasting ... All our theoretical and practical themes, we can also say, lie always within the normal coherence of the life-horizon "world." World is the universal field into which all our acts, whether of experiencing, of knowing, or of outward action, are directed.[2]

The first two chapters of *A New Introduction to Legal Method* are dedicated to the status of legal scholarship as a science or scientific discipline. In the previous two chapters, we have dealt with the status of legal scholarship in general (Chapter 1) and a famous skeptical movement in legal thought, i.e., American realism (Chapter 2), which demolishes all pretension of the scientific character of legal scholarship. In the next two chapters, we will go deeper into the scientific method in general. We will do this by reflecting on the work of one of the most well-known philosophers of science in the twentieth century, viz. the Austrian thinker Karl Popper (1902–1994). The present Chapter 3 is a preparation for the next one, which discusses essentialism. More or less, criticism of essentialism was also one of the basic features of the American realists but Popper's critique of essentialism is more thoroughgoing and therefore more challenging and interesting for us. Popper's attack on essentialism is all the more important because legal

---

1 Bertrand Russell, *Human Knowledge. Its Scope and Limits* (1948), London, New York: Routledge 2009, p. 91.
2 Edmund Husserl, *The Crisis of European Sciences and Transcendental Phenomenology*, Evanston: Northwestern University Press 1970, p. 144.

DOI: 10.4324/9781003282570-4

thought has often been reproached for its inveterate essentialism. So essentialism will be our focus in the next two chapters.

In the final two chapters of this book, we will come back to legal science and scholarship again. This will be done in particular in relationship with the judicial decision.

We cannot understand Karl Popper's attack on essentialism, though, without paying some attention to rationalism, empiricism, and positivism. In doing so, we do not intend to extensively reconstruct the critical debates in which Popper found himself.[3] That in itself can fill an entire book. What we will present here is a condensed reflection of the foundations of Popper's thinking and a description of the discourse to which Popper's methodology stands in opposition.

During the nineteenth century and the first half of the twentieth century, intense debates raged in the academic world about scientific knowledge and how knowledge can be acquired. In effect, the entire late modern period is characterized by studies into, and discussions about, fruitful methods of thought and research. Ancient philosophical methods were once again up for debate: observations[4] and normative statements about reality. In this context, logical reasoning (and especially its validity) is a key issue. Countless books and articles have been written about this impressive history of philosophy and the philosophy of science. It is not our intention to retell or problematize the entire history of methodological thought here. Our aim is merely to describe the context of Karl Popper's methodological thought without getting lost in the details. In the beginning, there were two academic tribes: rationalists and empiricists. They each had a favorite method for the acquisition of knowledge: deduction and induction.

Rationalism and empiricism

It was the philosophy of René Descartes (1596–1650) that paved the way for the mathematization of knowledge. Although Descartes begins with doubt, he ends with the establishment of limits to our knowledge—limits, therefore also, to the certainty with which we can make claims.

The first rule of the Cartesian methodology holds that in all examinations and studies, the mind must be focused on formulating a reliable and true judgment.[5]

---

3 See, for example: Imre Lakatos and Alan Musgrave, eds., *Criticism and the Growth of Knowledge*, Cambridge: Cambridge University Press 1970; Imre Lakatos, *The Methodology of Scientific Research Programmes* (Philosophical Papers volume 1), Cambridge: Cambridge University Press 1999; Thomas Kuhn, *The Structure of Scientific Revolutions*, Chicago: The University of Chicago Press 2012.
4 *Wahrnehmen* in German, meaning to accept something as true.
5 René Descartes, "Rules for the Direction of the Mind," in: *The Philosophical Writings of Descartes* (volume I), Cambridge: Cambridge University Press 2005, p. 9.

The second rule posits the achievement of certainty as the touchstone for science and philosophy: "We should attend only to those objects of which our minds seem capable of having certain and indubitable cognition."[6]

So, there are three core concepts: *cogitare*, thinking (as knowing); *cogitatus*, things that are known; and *cogitatio* (plural *cogitationes*), thinking. Because the senses can deceive us, Descartes looked for an instance in which certainty can be found, a foundation on which it can be based.

This Cartesian radicalism marks the beginning of the late modern period in thought. According to Edmund Husserl (1859–1938), the break Descartes makes with the past can be illustrated as follows: "the ancient world was not acquainted with this sort of thing, since the Cartesian *epoché* and its ego were unknown." So what is this fundamental change Descartes introduced? Again, according to Husserl, it was "a completely new manner of philosophizing which seeks its ultimate foundations in the subjective."[7] In this, there is only room for *cogitare*, thinking as knowing, *cogitatus*, things that are known, and *cogitatio*, thinking. The I (ego) as a subject is the ultimate instance of the *cogitare*:

> Since now I do not have a body, these are mere fabrications. Sense-perception? This surely does not occur without a body, and besides, when asleep I have appeared to perceive through the senses many things which I afterwards realized I did not perceive through the senses at all. Thinking? At last I have discovered it—thought; this alone is inseparable from me. I am, I exist—that is certain. But for how long? For as long as I am thinking. For it could be that were I totally to cease from thinking, I should totally cease to exist.[8]

The title of Descartes' second meditation clearly reveals his starting position, in which he posits that "the nature of the human mind" is more easily known than the human body. Of course, at that time, more was known about logic and mathematics than about the human body. At the same time, he establishes a hierarchy that places the mind above the body, because he does not attribute the power of self-movement, such as the power of sensation and even thought, to the body ("quite foreign to the nature of a body").[9] In case there exists an all-powerful deceiver who is producing deceptive observations, we ought to look for an indisputable foundation for the I that perceives and judges things:

6 Ibid., p. 10.
7 Husserl, *The Crisis of European Sciences and Transcendental Phenomenology*, p. 81.
8 René Descartes, "Meditations on First Philosophy," in: *The Philosophical Writings of Descartes* (volume II), Cambridge: Cambridge University Press 2005, p. 18.
9 Ibid., p. 17.

The fact that it is I who am doubting and understanding and willing is so evident that I see no way of making it any clearer. But it is also the case that the "I" who imagines is the same "I." … Yet I certainly seem to see, to hear, and to be warmed. This cannot be false; what is called "having a sensory perception" is strictly just this, and in this restricted sense of the term it is simply thinking.[10]

The absoluteness of the subject, the I that is able to think, is inseparable from the I that perceives itself and the world. The I becomes the act of thinking, and vice versa. Man's existence is defined in a non-religious, strictly rational sense: the thinking thing! Being nothing, death, occurs when thinking ceases to exist. Here, we see the contours of a methodological approach whose influence continues well into our time. We even have a name for it: *artificial intelligence*. Artificial thinking presupposes that the thing cannot think on its own, but only through the addition of an algorithm, a complicated logical construct. The body of a computer consists of electronic parts, but to Descartes, what remains of a person beyond or even prior to the I, the thinking thing, seems to be a terrifying nothing! Beyond thinking, insofar as thinking was able to pass itself on, everything is transient. In the Middle Ages, we find this radical, almost atheistic transience in the Persian poet, mathematician, and philosopher Omar Khayyam (1048–1131):

> And, as the Cock crew, those who stood before
> The Tavern shouted—"Open, then, the Door!
> You know how little while we have to stay,
> And, once departed, may return no more."
>
> Ah, make the most of what we yet may spend,
> Before we too into the Dust descend;
> Dust into Dust, and under Dust to lie,
> Sans Wine, sans Song, sans Singer, and—sans End![11]

Thinking, which we might also call *mind* in this time, is uncoupled from perceptions: the mathematization[12] of thought. Descartes' theory of knowledge rationalizes everything, especially research methodologies that lack empirical foundations. Here, as well as in another great rationalist, Gottfried

---

10 Ibid., p. 19.
11 Accessed 8 June 2020, https://poets.org/poem/rubaiyat-omar-khayyam-excerpt.
12 *Discours de la méthode. pour bien conduire sa raison, et chercher la vérité dans les sciences. plus La Dioptrique. Les Meteores et La Geometrie qui sont des essais de cette méthode* [Discourse on the Method of Rightly Conducting One's Reason and of Seeking Truth in the Sciences and in addition the Optics, the Meteorology and the Geometry, which Are Essays in this Method], Paris: Fayard 1986.

Leibniz (1646–1716),[13] we see the birth of modern rationalism, which is really deductive and mathematical in nature. It is no coincidence, therefore, that both philosophers made fundamental contributions to mathematics and geometry. Bertrand Russell[14] rightly notes that, after Descartes and Leibniz, two opposing movements sprang up in the theory of knowledge: the continental idealism of the rationalists and British empiricism.[15] The rationalists had an immediate and revolutionary impact on all the sciences. Physics changed: with Galileo Galilei, Edmund Husserl believed, the mathematization of physics had begun. Galileo idealized (formal) mathematics.[16]

The universality of science has its roots in the "reshaping of mathematics," so Husserl believed.[17] Is reason the only source of knowledge? And if that is the case, what is the status of the observable, empirical world? Empiricism puts the observable world first. That is where knowledge begins. Francis Bacon (1561–1626) begins his *Novum Organum* (The New Organon) with an empirical approach:

> Man, being nature's servant and interpreter, is limited in what he can do and understand by what he has observed of the course of nature—directly observing it or inferring things [from what he has observed]. Beyond that he doesn't know anything and can't do anything.[18]

Man does not interpret nature by means of an idealized mathematical method but through observations. In his second proposition, Bacon defends the importance of instruments in science. After all, according to Bacon,

---

13 In "Monadology," Leibniz makes a clear distinction between facts and norms, or deductive and inductive knowledge: "There are also twee kinds of truth: those of reasoning and those of fact. Truths of reasoning are necessary, and their opposite is impossible; those of fact are contingent, and their opposite is possible. When a truth is necessary, the reason for it can be found by analysis, by resolving it into simpler ideas and truths until we arrive at the basic ones." G.W. Leibniz, "Monadology (1714)," in: *G.W. Leibniz. Philosophical Texts*, London: Oxford University Press 1998, p. 272.

14 In his study on Leibniz, as early as 1900, Russell noted the concept of identity in Leibniz's logic: "The notion that all *a priori* truths are analytic is essentially connected with the doctrine of subject and predicate. An analytic judgment is one in which the predicate is contained in the subject. The subject is supposed defined by a number of predicates, one or more of which are singled out for predication in an analytic judgment. Thus Leibniz as we have just seen, gives as an instance the proposition: 'the equilateral rectangle is a rectangle' (N. E. p. 405; G.v. 343). In the extreme case, the subject is merely reasserted of itself, as in the propositions: 'A is A,' 'I shall be what I shall be.'" Bertrand Russell, *The Philosophy of Leibniz*, Nottingham: Spokesman 2008, p. 17.

15 Bertrand Russell, *History of Western Philosophy*, London: Routledge 2005, p. 516.

16 Husserl, *The Crisis of European Sciences and Transcendental Phenomenology*, pp. 23–43.

17 Ibid., p. 21.

18 Francis Bacon, *The New Organon: Or True Directions Concerning the Interpretation of Nature*, p. 4. See: www.earlymoderntexts.com/assets/pdfs/bacon1620.pdf.

neither the bare hand nor the unaided mind are capable of much. Tools are necessary for intellect (reason) and for observation. This is called the *instrumentalization* of science.

British empiricism owes a great deal to John Locke (1632–1704). Locke revolutionizes the discussion about reason by introducing a new term, namely *understanding*.[19] Understanding is a comprehensive term: it encompasses reason, but also comprehension in the conventional sense. It resembles eyes that enable sight, as well as the necessary condition for sensory observations.[20] Locke also seeks to provide a basis for "certainty of our knowledge." As such, there are "no innate principles in the mind." After all, the mental state of children demonstrates that there are no innate ideas and concepts. Knowledge is the result of experience. To Locke, mathematics is a way to teach the mind to adopt the habit of reasoning in a concentrated and coherent way. The sources of knowledge? The most important one of these is sensation: observations and experiences. That is where ideas or concepts come from.[21]

Perception and thinking converge in understanding:

> The power of thinking is called the understanding, and the power of volition is called the will, and those two powers or abilities in the mind are denominated faculties. Of some of the modes of these simple ideas of reflection, such as are remembrance, discerning, reasoning, judging, knowledge, faith, etc.[22]

Locke uses terms like *faculty*, which would later be used extensively by Kant. According to Locke, perception is "the first faculty of the mind." This is also the most basic idea we have of reflection. Here, this refers to thinking. Perception itself is observation, sensory observation.[23] Reflection is wholly

---

19 "Since it is the understanding that sets man above the rest of sensible beings, and gives him all the advantage, and dominion, which he has over them; it is certainly a subject, even for its nobleness, worth our labour to inquire into." John Locke, *An Essay Concerning Human Understanding*, London, New York: Penguin Books Classics 1997, p. 53.

20 "It is an established opinion amongst some men. That there are in the understanding certain innate principles, some primary notions, κοιναὶ ἔννοιαι (*koinai ennoi*, common notions), characters, as it were stamped upon the mind of man, which the soul receives in its very first being; and brings into the world with it. It would be sufficient to convince unprejudiced readers of the falseness of this supposition, if I should only show (as I hope I shall in the following parts of this discourse) how men, barely by the use of their natural faculties, may attain to all the knowledge they have, without the help of any innate impressions, and may arrive at certainty, without any such original notion or principles." Ibid., p. 59.

21 "The better to conceive the ideas, we receive from sensation, it may not be amiss for us to consider them, in reference to the different ways, whereby they make their approaches to our minds, and make themselves perceivable by us." Ibid., p. 123.

22 Ibid., p. 129.

23 "What perception is, everyone will know better by reflection on what he does himself, when he sees, feels, etc. or thinks, than by any discourse of mine. Whoever reflects on what

connected to observation and experience; he who does not perceive anything has nothing on which to reflect. He also makes a distinction between simple ideas and complex ideas. Simple ideas are the foundation of our thinking; they constitute a kind of depiction of our impressions. Complex ideas, on the other hand, are "acts of the mind." Here, simple ideas (which are the product of sensory observations) are combined, which is how abstractions are created:

> I call complex, such as are beauty, gratitude, a man, an army, the universe, which though complicated of various simple ideas, or complex ideas made up of simple ones, yet are, when the mind please, considered each by itself, as one entire thing, and signified by one name.[24]

Locke combines the problem of strictly idealized rationality or the working of reason with empirical reality. With Locke, the history of epistemology evolves. This epistemological approach is later questioned as well, however. But what can we build on the foundation of observations and their result, data? Contrary to Locke, Popper believes the answer is nothing. He says this because pure, uninterpreted observations do not exist:

> they do not exist: there are no uninterpreted "data"; there is nothing simply "given" to us uninterpreted; nothing to be taken as basis. All out knowledge is interpretation in the light of our expectations, our theories, and is therefore hypothetical in some way or other.[25]

The empiricism and razor-sharp skepticism of David Hume (1711–1776) were extraordinarily beneficial to the development of science and philosophy. Hume's philosophy is a further development of the British empiricism John Locke started. Locke's complex ideas could be explained by the laws of the association of ideas: resemblance and diversity, spatial-temporal proximity, and causality. The empiricists were concerned with the integration of ideas in the empirical world, or, in other words, in the connection between ideas and their real-world origins: "All the perceptions of the human mind resolve themselves into two distinct kinds, which I shall call impressions and ideas."[26] The perceptions we perceive with the most intensity and force, Hume calls *impressions*. And ideas? Those he calls "the faint images of these in thinking and reasoning." He uses a remarkable example to illustrate this:

---

passes in his own mind, cannot miss it: and if he does not reflect, all the words in the world, cannot make him have any notion of it." Ibid., p. 142.

24 Ibid., pp. 159–160.

25 Karl Popper, *Realism and the Aim of Science*, London, New York: Routledge 2005, p. 102.

26 David Hume, *A Treatise of Human Nature*, Oxford: Oxford University Press 2003, p. 7.

the perceptions his book leaves with the reader. This is not about feeling or seeing, but the experience we have in our minds after reading Hume's book. A simple idea, on the other hand, corresponds to a simple impression. Red is red: the idea of red corresponds with the impression of the color red.[27]

Hume's general proposition views ideas, or concepts, as a representational relationship of empirical experiences or observations: a representational relationship between object and concept: "From this constant conjunction of resembling perceptions I immediately conclude, that there is a great connexion betwixt our correspondent impressions and ideas, and that the existence of the one has a considerable influence upon that of the other."[28] This is the beginning of a picture theory of reality and thought. But ideas as a result of an initial impression (such as pain or joy) evoke certain impressions:[29] pain as an experience is transformed into an idea, and then the idea of pain makes us experience the impression of pain: "So that the impressions of reflection are only antecedent to their correspondent ideas; but posterior to those of sensation, and derived from them."[30] Here, Hume tries to show the primacy of experience through a causal link between experience and reflection. Hume furthers empiricist thought by addressing the probability of knowledge.

Certain knowledge is the result of a logically necessary deduction. Here, he is speaking of the sciences that possess a "perfect of exactness"[31] (we would call these the *exact sciences*). Arithmetic and algebra fall into this category. As such, they are perfect examples of normative reasoning. But probable knowledge is a kind of subjective observation: "Thus all probable reasoning is nothing but a species of sensation."[32] The principle behind this conviction is that all cases we have not observed must necessarily resemble cases we *have* observed. Hume talks about probability in a way that is very familiar to us. He distinguishes two types of assessments on the basis of probabilities: a calculation of the odds and a calculation based on causes.[33] With British empiricism, science is introduced to a new method of thought, namely "probability." The question of what ought to be the starting point of an enquiry caused discord between science and philosophy: concrete

---

27 "One general proposition that all our simple ideas in their first appearance are derived from simple impressions, which are correspondent to them, and which they exactly represent." Ibid., p. 9.

28 Ibid., p. 9.

29 "It is evident, that there is a principle of connection between the different thoughts or ideas of the mind, and that, in their appearance to the memory or imagination, they introduce each other with a certain degree of method and regularity." David Hume, *An Enquiry Concerning Human Understanding*, Oxford: Oxford University Press 1999, p. 101.

30 Hume, *A Treatise of Human Nature*, p. 11.

31 Ibid., p. 51.

32 Ibid., p. 72.

33 Ibid., p. 86; Hume, *An Enquiry Concerning Human Understanding*, p. 131.

observations or universally formulated propositions or rules. Once, however, science and philosophy were connected, and so the epistemological
question was posed in both disciplines. Hume had already established what
the starting point of philosophy, or more accurately, of an enquiry ought
to be: "A man must be very sagacious, who could discover by reasoning,
that crystal is the effect of heat, and ice of cold, without being previously
acquainted with the operations of these qualities."[34] Skeptical thought continues, without or without empiricism. According to Popper, Hume is the
first thinker who convincingly addressed the problem of induction, or infinite regression (*regressus in infinitum*).[35] This is about the inference from the
impression to the idea. It is easy, Hume writes, to observe "that in tracing
this relation, the inference we draw from cause to effect."[36] But how many
concrete observations have to occur before a necessary causal connection or
a logical explanation can be established? This is the problem of induction:
a universal limit for observations and data in order to come to a definitive
theory or explanation is not available:

> From the mere repetition of any past impression, even to infinity, there
> never will arise any new original idea, such as that of a necessary con-
> nexion; and the number of impressions has in this case no more effect
> than if we confined ourselves to one only.[37]

Although in Hume, only the representation of impressions remained, George
Berkeley's skeptical thought did away with the world altogether, and with
reality. Berkeley (1685–1753) sought to correct the inconsistency of empirical thought, and especially that of John Locke.[38] Berkeley's foundational
claim is that everything we observe (in whatever way, simple or complex
[composite], inner or outer observations) only reflects certain states of our
mind, or in other words, our consciousness.[39] It is impressive to see how
Berkeley explains and juxtaposes the complex questions from the history of

---

34 Hume, *An Enquiry Concerning Human Understanding*, p. 113.
35 Karl Popper, *The Two Fundamental Problems of the Theory of Knowledge*, London, New
York: Routledge 2009, p. 35.
36 Hume, *An Enquiry Concerning Human Understanding*, p. 61.
37 Ibid., p. 62.
38 An example of this is what he said about "words becoming general": "By observing how
ideas become general, we may the better judge how words are made so." George Berkeley,
Principles of Human Knowledge and Three Dialogues, Oxford: Oxford University Press
2009, p. 13.
39 "After what hath been said, it is I suppose plain, that our souls are not to be known in the
same manner as senseless inactive objects, or by way of idea. Spirits and ideas are thing
so wholly different, that when we say, they exist, they are known, or the like, these words
must not be thought to signify anything, common to both nature. There is nothing alike or
common in them." Ibid., p. 88.

the theory of knowledge. This idealism, the modern idealism, is furnished with empirical arguments in order to take aim at the rational and empirical methods.[40] Russell believes that Berkeley's arguments are largely sound and that they prove that our sense-data cannot be proven to exist independent of us.[41] Our knowledge of ideas and reality is based on participation in the divine; it is God himself who is showing us all these representations.[42] This is where science and philosophy in the rationalist and empiricist sense ends. This was considered unsatisfactory. It would have meant that not only the fate of metaphysics (the queen of all sciences) but also that of philosophy and science as a whole were at stake.

The confrontation between the theories of knowledge of Leibniz and Descartes (the rationalist method) on the one hand and Locke and Hume (the empirical method) on the other, brought science and philosophy to a dangerous crossroads. Immanuel Kant (1724–1804), the German philosopher from Königsberg, is the first great systematic thinker of the late modern period because he developed a systematic and consistent theory of knowledge about all philosophical (scientific) domains. Kant's three Critiques (his main works) are still relevant today.[43] And Kant's political philosophy has been a source of inspiration[44] to many, just a few of whom are the three neo-Kantian philosophers Ernst Cassirer (1874–1945), Hans Kelsen (1881–1973), and Jürgen Habermas (b. 1929). In the following section, we in no way attempt to lay out Kant's entire epistemology. We intend instead to discuss the major themes in the relationship between rationalism and empiricism.

The Kantian synthesis and logical positivism

The *Critique of Pure Reason* (*Kritik der reinen Vernunft*) begins with a rhetorical observation about the state of thought:

> Human reason has the peculiar fate in one species of its cognitions that it is burdened with questions which it cannot dismiss, since they are

---

40 Ayers rightly asks how we should qualify Berkeley: as an empiricist or a rationalist: "Berkeley's first aim was to demonstrate that, after all, a proper understanding of our dependence on sense and imagination for the objects of knowledge will carry us away from materialism, rather than towards it. That purpose appears directly opposed to a famous purpose of Descartes' *Meditations*, to lead the mind away from the senses." Michael Ayers, "Was Berkeley an Empiricist or a Rationalist?" in: Kenneth P. Winkler, ed., *Berkeley. The Cambridge Companion to Berkeley*, Cambridge: Cambridge University Press 2005, p. 57.
41 Bertrand Russell, *The Problems of Philosophy*, Oxford: Oxford University Press 1912, p. 38.
42 Berkeley, *Principles of Human Knowledge and Three Dialogues*, p. 90.
43 Immanuel Kant, *Critique of Practical Reason*, New York: Prometheus Books 1996; Immanuel Kant, *Critique of Judgement*, New York, London: Hafner Press 1951.
44 Immanuel Kant, *The Philosophy of Law*, Clark, NJ: The Lawbooks Exchange Ltd. 2010; Immanuel Kant, *Political Writings*, Cambridge: Cambridge University Press 1991; Immanuel Kant, *Anthropology History, and Education*, Cambridge: Cambridge University Press 2012.

given to it as problems by the nature of reason itself, but which it also cannot answer, since they transcend every capacity of human reason. Reason falls into this perplexity through no fault of its own. It begins from principles whose use is unavoidable in the course of experience and at the same time sufficiently warranted by it. With these principles it rises (as its nature also requires) ever higher, to more remote conditions.[45]

Here, Kant repeats an expression from Plato about the embarrassment regarding the expression *being*.[46] Two millennia later, Kant says about human reason that it "falls into this perplexity through no fault of its own."[47] Human reason is barely able to answer the question it poses to itself. Metaphysics was shrouded in darkness and contradictions. This brought forth dogmatists, to whom empiricists like Locke responded in turn.

Kant is looking for an answer with regard to the limits of our knowledge: what can I know? He wants to mark the boundaries of those things that lie outside the reach of our knowledge. With what can these boundaries be marked: only by our sensory experiences? Kant's first and most important observation is that all our knowledge begins with experience. Yet, those who believe that Kant is merely defending empirical knowledge here will be disappointed. No knowledge precedes experience in time: it always begins with experience. But not all knowledge comes from experience: "though all our knowledge begins with experience, it by no means follows that all arises out of experience."[48] We should not lose sight of the fact that our sensory observations are also mixed with subjective experiences. As such, there are two types of knowledge: *a priori* and *a posteriori* (straight from experience). The *a priori* knowledge that is entirely free from all that is empirical Kant calls "pure."[49]

The method of doing research or knowing is actually of paramount importance for the achievement of a valid and true research result. That is why Kant distinguishes between synthetic and analytical judgments:

> In all judgments in which the relation of a subject to the predicate is thought (if I consider only affirmative judgments, since the application

---

45 Immanuel Kant, *Critique of Pure Reason*, Cambridge: Cambridge University Press 1998, p. 99 (Aviii).

46 Later in the twentieth century, this would become the beginning of the main work of Martin Heidegger: *Being and Time*, Albany, NY: State University of New York Press 2010, p. xxix.

47 "In diese Verlegenheit gerät sie ohne ihre Schuld." Immanuel Kant, *Kritik der reinen Vernunft* [Critique of Pure Reason], Frankfurt am Main: Suhrkamp 1974, p. 11; Kant, *Critique of Pure Reason*, p. 99 (Aviii).

48 Kant, *Kritik der reinen Vernunft*, p. 45 (B.1); Kant, *Critique of Pure Reason*, p. 136 (B.2).

49 Kant, *Kritik der reinen Vernunft*, p. 46 (B.3); Kant, *Critique of Pure Reason*, p. 137 (B.3).

to negative ones is easy), this relation is possible in two different ways. Either the predicate B belongs to the subject A as something that is (covertly) contained in this concept A; or B lies entirely outside the concept A, though to be sure it stands in connection with it. In the first case I call the judgment analytic, in the second synthetic.[50]

A synthetic judgment is not made on the basis of logically necessary relationships: this pen is blue. Analytical judgments, on the other hand, are based on formal-logical relationships of necessity: someone who is single is unmarried. They are internally constituted by concepts. Analytical judgments have a formal, normative character. It is also important to note that *a priori* knowledge exists independent of experience. *A posteriori* knowledge, on the other hand, is gained through experience. In these terms, the rationalist (formal-logical) and empirical (sensory experience) methods are already revealing themselves.

Analytical judgments are *a priori* and based on the law of non-contradiction. All experience judgments—judgments that are based on experience—are synthetic and lead to the growth of knowledge. In the analytical proposition, the predicate is a part of the subject: "a tall man is a man," or "an equilateral triangle is a triangle." But synthetic propositions are comprised of experience: Caesar was a great general. However, unlike other philosophers, Kant does not assume that all synthetic propositions are the result of experience. This is actually where Kant's epistemology begins: How could a general rule be deduced from a concrete experience? Because if all knowledge were synthetic, then pure mathematics and physics (*physica pura, rationalis*, or, in other words, fundamental physics) would not be possible. Einstein would never be able to formulate his theory of relativity. So it is about the general validity of propositions; laws cannot just be deduced from experience. An experience represents an individual, private event, one that does not necessarily reveal a necessary and universal rule. When we say the ball is round, then the predicate expresses something that was already contained in the subject: the term *ball* includes roundness. Experience judgments as such are synthetic, Kant believes.

So, do *a priori* synthetic propositions exist? In other words: How is synthetic knowledge possible *a priori*? Mathematical judgments are synthetic judgments,[51] Kant believes. To illustrate, he uses the example of 5 + 7 = 12, which is an *a priori* judgment, because it is true necessarily and everywhere; it is not comprised of an individual experience.[52] At the same time, this is not an analytical claim, because 12 is not already contained in five and

50 Kant, *Critique of Pure Reason*, p. 130 (B.11).
51 Ibid., p. 143 (B.14).
52 Ibid., p. 144 (B.16).

seven. And Kant's assertion becomes even clearer as the numbers get larger. That is how Kant reaches the conclusion that *a priori* synthetic judgments are possible. In addition, there are two other terms that are important for answering the question if *a priori* synthetic judgments are possible: time and space.[53] Time and space are not objects, not empirical terms that arose from an "exceptional experience." Time and space are a necessary *a priori* representation that is the foundation of all outer appearances:

> Space is a necessary representation, a priori, which is the ground of all outer intuitions. One can never represent that there is no space, al though one can very well think that there are no objects to be encountered in it. It is therefore to be regarded as the condition of the possibility of appearances, not as a determination dependent on them, and is an a priori representation that necessarily grounds outer appearances.[54]

Space determines the form of all appearances (phenomena) and precedes all experiences. When it comes to inner sensoriality, time is nothing more than the shape of the inner sensoriality of observing ourselves and our inner state.[55] Time and space are two sources of cognition on which Kant believes synthetic knowledge can be based.

In this fashion, Kant builds up a comprehensive system of knowledge and scientific methods within which universally valid and necessary propositions are characterized as *a priori* synthetic. Rationalism (a system of universal, necessary, valid propositions that are deductive) is connected to empirical reality (synthetic experiences). And he draws another hard line: about the "thing in itself" (*Ding an sich*), or the *noumenon*, we can know nothing.[56] Kant's century casts a very long shadow. All philosophies of the

---

53 Ibid., p. 157 (B.38).

54 Ibid., p. 158 (B.39).

55 "Time is nothing other than the form of inner sense, i.e., of the in tuition of our self and our inner state. ... For time cannot be a determination of outer appearances; it belongs neither to a shape or a position, etc., but on the contrary determines the relation of representations in our inner state. And just because this inner intuition yields no shape we also attempt to remedy this lack through analogies, and represent the temporal sequence through a line progressing to infinity, in which the manifold constitutes a series that is of only one dimension, and infer from the properties of this line to all the properties of time, with the sole difference that the parts of the former are simultaneous but those of the latter always exist successively. From this it is also apparent that the representation of time is itself an intuition, since all its relations can be expressed in an outer intuition. Time is the *a priori* formal condition of all appearances in general." Ibid., p. 163 (B.50).

56 "I call a concept problematic that contains no contradiction but that is also, as a boundary for given concepts, connected with other cognitions, the objective reality of which can in no way be cognized. The concept of a noumenon, i.e., of a thing that is not to be thought of as an object of the senses but rather as a thing in itself (solely through a pure understanding), is not at all contradictory; for one cannot assert of sensibility that it is the only possible

nineteenth century and the first half of the twentieth century are reactions to Kant's philosophy of knowledge, ethics, esthetics, religion, politics, and law. Starting at the end of the nineteenth century, Kant's epistemology and Newton's physics end up on the operating table of science. Here, we will first take a closer look at the positivist movements.

The positivism of August Comte (1789–1857) was a romantic and naïve idealization of the (positive) factual world and observations; it limited the job of science to what is visible and reveals itself to the researcher.[57] In this view, science will have to devote itself to describing facts and relationships established by observation. However, simply arranging facts is not science. That is why language, logic, and mathematics returned to the academic debates at the end of the nineteenth century. The German mathematician and logician Gottlob Frege focused on fundamental logical concepts.[58] He devised fundamental connections between mathematics and logic, and he examined the rules of evidence in both fields. Before that, he made a distinction between everyday language and the formalist language of logic that is more suited to science.[59] In his *Begriffschrift* (1879), he expounds on his idea of a formal language modeled on arithmetic, while at the same time he sets out to prove that arithmetic[60] can be reduced to logic. He rejected symbolical logic, which forms the basis of our formal logic. "A is A" or "Venus is Venus" does not contain information, but "the Morning Star is the Evening Star" does. After all, they refer to the same planet (Venus), but they still have different meanings. In "On Sinn and Bedeutung," Frege wrote that

> the Bedeutung of a proper name is the object itself which we designate by using it; the idea which we have in that case is wholly subjective; in between lies the sense, which is indeed no longer subjective like the idea, but is yet not the object itself.[61]

kind of intuition. ... The concept of a noumenon is therefore merely a boundary concept, in order to limit the pretension of sensibility, and therefore only of negative use." Ibid., p. 350 (B.310 and B.311).

57 Auguste Comte, *Introduction to Positive Philosophy*, Cambridge: Hackett Publishing Company 1998.

58 Joan Weiner, "Understanding Frege's Project," in: *The Cambridge Companion to Frege*, Cambridge: Cambridge University Press 2010, pp. 32–62.

59 "I believe I can make the relationship of my *Begriffsschrift* to ordinary language clearest if I compare it to that of the microscope to the eyes. ... Likewise, this *Begriffsschrift* is an aid devised for particular scientific purposes and should therefore not be condemned because it is no good for others." Gottlob Frege, "Begriffschrift. A Formula Language of Pure Thought Modelled on that of Arithmetic," in: *The Frege Reader*, Oxford: Blackwell Publishing 1997, p. 49.

60 Later, in 1903, Bertrand Russell tried to prove in a large study that mathematics and logic are identical. See: Bertrand Russell, *Principles of Mathematics*, London: Routledge 2010, p. xxxi.

61 Frege, *The Frege Reader*, p. 155.

Positivism, insofar as it sought to be a science and formulate universally valid propositions and rules, had to acquire a logical component. That is how logical positivism entered academic debates. The philosophy of science as a new discipline was born in Vienna in the 1920s. The group that developed this philosophy was also called the *Wiener Kreis* (Vienna Circle).[62] These were its most important members: the physicist Moritz Schlick (1882–1936),[63] the logician Rudolf Carnap (1891–1970), the mathematician Philipp Frank (1884–1966), and the historian Viktor Kraft (1880–1975). The logical positivism that took shape was a movement of logicians and other philosophers of science. Its main purpose was to rid science and philosophy of metaphysics. Positivism represented this idea: that science and philosophy should deal in empirical facts, so there should be no room for speculative deductions. Still, they considered positivism to be an insufficient basis on which to build a strict philosophical methodology for science. The universally necessary propositions cannot simply be deduced from facts.

In 1929, the positivists produced a scientific manifesto titled "Wissenschaftliche Weltauffassung. Der Wiener Kreis."[64] The Viennese positivists drew the attention of scientists and philosophers in various European capitals. In their manifesto, they argued against the upsurge of theological and metaphysical thought in Europe as a result of the economic crisis.

Before the academic debates brought an end to the Wiener Kreis, the *Anschluss* of Austria with Nazi Germany brought a de facto end to the development of this group: many of them had to flee Germany or Austria. The logical positivists did not oppose empirical methods, but they did want to furnish them with a universal logical foundation. The modern formal logic of Frege was the right instrument for this. In his *Der Logische Aufbau der Welt* (*The Logical Structure of the World*), Carnap seeks to refine and clarify the logical method:

> The present investigations aim to establish a "constructional system," that is, an epistemic-logical system of objects or concepts. The word "object" is here always used in its widest sense, namely, for anything about which a statement can be made. ... It is the main thesis of construction theory that all concepts can in this way be derived from a few

---

62 Friedrich Stadler, "The Vienna Circle. Context, Profile, and Development," in: *The Cambridge Companion to Logical Empiricism*, Cambridge: Cambridge University Press 2007, pp. 13–40; Ali Süleyman, Üstünel, *An Introduction to Analysis on Wiener Space*, Berlin: Springer Verlag 1995; Dieter Hoffmann, "The Society for Empirical/Scientific Philosophy," in: *The Cambridge Companion to Logical Empiricism*, Cambridge: Cambridge University Press 2007, pp. 41–57.

63 In 1936, Moritz Schlick was murdered by a student who had Nazi sympathies.

64 Accessed 9 December 2021, http://neurath.umcs.lublin.pl/manifest.pdf.

fundamental concepts, and it is in this respect that it differs from most other ontologies (*Gegenstandstheorie*).[65]

So, what David Hume and other empiricists were lacking, Carnap[66] believes he can construct: logical foundations.

According to the logical positivists, there are also meaningless empirical propositions: "all bachelors are unmarried," or "all circles are round." The formal truth of these claims has no meaning in reality, which is why it can be proven in a logical construct without reference to reality. They are analytical propositions. Here, we have an example of a proposition that does have meaning: "the stone is in Switzerland." That is why Carnap says: "These sentences are unquestionably meaningful; it makes no difference whether they are true or false."[67] A scientific proposition is true when it has been empirically proven. In order to be able to say that all ravens are black, one has to look for empirical proof. If enough proof has been gathered, the proposition is correct.[68] This is grounded in the verifiability principle. How much evidence is enough for verification? Here, we enter the domain of inductive probability, and that does not offer enough of a handhold for the formation of a scientific theory. After all, only verifiable propositions can form the building blocks for a theory. The verifiability principle holds that when there is no logical proof available, evidence must be sought in empirical reality. As such, the propositions (such as "all As have the characteristics of Bs") must be empirically tested. In Carnap, the construction of structures acquires a reductionist bent:

> According to the explanation given above, if an object a is reducible to objects b, c, then all statements about a can be transformed into statements about b and c. To reduce a to b, c or to construct a out of b, c means to produce a general rule that indicates for each individual case how a statement about a must be transformed in order to yield a statement about b, c. This rule of translation we call a construction rule or constructional definition.[69]

Differently put: the sense of a proposition consists of the method of its verification, which has an intersubjective nature: it must be verified by more

65 Rudolf Carnap, *The Logical Structure of the World and Pseudoproblems in Philosophy*, Chicago: Open Court Classics 2005, p. 5.
66 See, on the neo-Kantian origins of Carnap's philosophy: Alan Richardson, *Carnap's Construction of the World. The Aufbau and the Emergence of Logical Empiricism*, Cambridge: Cambridge University Press 1998, pp. 116–158.
67 Carnap, *The Logical Structure of the World and Pseudoproblems in Philosophy*, p. 54.
68 Ibid., p. 179.
69 Ibid., p. 6.

than one person. That is why logical positivists embrace experimentation. However, this confirmation principle excludes a fair number of natural laws and physics theories from science for lack of sufficient empirical confirmation. The logical positivists believed they had solved the problem of induction by means of the verifiability principle.[70]

Critical rationalism: *The Open Universe*

In 1986, his autobiography ends with these final words, which are really an appeal to all people: "Open your eyes and see how beautiful the world is, and how lucky we are who are alive."[71] These were the words of Karl Raimund Popper (1902–1994), a genius philosopher of science from Austria.[72] In 1934, Popper caused a truly seismic shift within the circle of logical positivists, but later also in the wider world of science. In that year, his book *Logik der Forschung* appeared in Vienna.[73] Initially, it did not receive much attention due to the political unrest in Europe, followed by a world war, but in 1959, his main work was translated into English: "The logic of scientific discovery."[74] Afterward, he will defend his theory in various books and essays. As early as 1934, he wrote that a philosopher, as opposed to a scientist, will not encounter any organized structure, "but rather something resembling a heap of ruins … he cannot appeal to the fact that there is a generally accepted problem-situation."[75] Popper rejects two methods for theory formation: inductive confirmation (Carnap) and hard evidence through observation. The latter is impossible because theories and

---

70 Although later, in 1974, Carnap posits that a logical foundation can be found for induction in relation to probability: "The main points that I wish to stress here are these: both types of probability—statistical and logical—may occur together in the same chain of reasoning. Statistical probability is part of the object language of science. To statements about statistical probability we can apply logical probability, which is part of the metalanguage of science. It is my conviction that this point of view gives a much clearer picture of statistical inference than is commonly found in books on statistics and that it provides an essential groundwork for the construction of an adequate inductive logic of science." Rudolf Carnap, *An Introduction to the Philosophy of Science*, Mineola, NY: Dover Publications 1995, p. 39.

71 Karl Popper, *Unended Quest. An Intellectual Autobiography*, London: Routledge 2002, p. 233.

72 Although he did not always act in harmony with his lofty principles. This was especially noticeable when he refused to sign a petition on behalf of Salman Rushdie when the British author was struck by a death verdict of the Iranian dictator Khomeini. See: Paul Cliteur and Dirk Verhofstadt, "Popper, Karl Raimund," in: Paul Cliteur and Dirk Verhofstadt, eds., *Het atheïstisch woordenboek*, Antwerpen/Utrecht: Houtekiet 2015.

73 Karl Popper, *Logik der Forschung. Zur Erkenntnistheorie Der Modernen Naturwissenschaft*, Wien: Springer Verlag 1935.

74 Karl Popper, *The Logic of Scientific Discovery*, London: Routledge 1999.

75 Ibid., p. 13.

viewpoints precede all observations. That our senses can mislead us does not require illustration; it is evident. In the area of sense-data, too, Russell taught us as early as 1914 that there is a difference between hard data (basic facts) and all other facts.[76] He considered doubt and further study to be an utmost necessity if one did not wish to end up living in fairy tales. Gestalt psychology also comes to mind here. In 1927, Russell rightly noted about objectivity and perception that "it is not to be supposed in any case that perceiving an object involves knowing what it is like. That is quite another matter." Russell is concerned with the idea that perception in itself "reveals the character of an object," which is a delusion.[77] Popper, too, wanted scientists to start to avoid delusion. In the end, philosophy is about cosmological problems or questions that allow us to understand ourselves and the world, Popper believes. To this, we could add fundamental scientific research (such as in physics, mathematics, biology, or chemistry).[78]

Popper succinctly and clearly describes the methodological revolution he sought to bring about in his introduction:

> The method I have in mind is that of stating one's problem clearly and of examining its various proposed solutions *critically*. I have italicized the words "*rational discussion*" and "*critically*" in order to stress that I equate the rational attitude and the critical attitude.[79]

Instead of *logical positivism*, the new theory of knowledge is called *critical rationalism*. It is rationalist because it is based on formal-logical analysis,[80] and it is critical because it wants to subject all existing theories, laws, and hypotheses to a permanent critical analysis. Nothing is sacred to critical rationalism: "No doubt God talks mainly to Himself because He has no one worth talking to. But a philosopher should know that he is no more godlike than any other man."[81] So, philosophers must also have the courage to enter into critical debate about their theories.[82] Knowledge is a search for truth, but not for certainty. Popper always stayed true to this maxim. What is truth? In the light of Kant's epistemology, Popper defines it like this:

---

76 Bertrand Russell, *Our Knowledge of the External World*, London: Routledge 1914, pp. 75–79.
77 Bertrand Russell, *An Outline of Philosophy*, London: Routledge 2009, p. 76.
78 Popper, *The Logic of Scientific Discovery*, p. 15.
79 Ibid., p. 16.
80 Popper says about this: "The logical content of a statement of theory may be identified with what Tarski has called its 'consequence class'; that is, the class of all the (nontautological) consequences which can be derived from the statement of theory." See: Popper, *Unended Quest. An Intellectual Autobiography*, p. 24.
81 Popper, *The Logic of Scientific Discovery*, p. 17.
82 About the "critical attitude," see: Karl Popper, "Towards a Rational Theory of Tradition," in: *Conjectures and Refutations*, London: Routledge 2002, p. 164.

"A theory or a statement is true, if what it says corresponds to reality."[83] This notion of truth is not unlike what Alfred Tarski once claimed about formalized languages: "A true sentence is one which says that the state of affairs is so and so, and the state of affairs indeed is so and so."[84] In order to really serve the truth or the search for truth, we have to have the courage to be extremely critical: "Science, scientific knowledge, is therefore always hypothetical: it is conjectural knowledge. And the method of science is the critical method: the method of the search for and the elimination of errors in the service of truth."[85] The first problem Popper had to solve was the problem of induction.

Induction is a research method, an empirical method, in which claims are made on the basis of observations or empirical experiences with the aim of capturing them in a universal, generalizing proposition. We see that all coffee beans are brown; from these various observations, we try to distill a general rule or proposition: from concrete individual to abstract general. Induction has to do with how we can acquire knowledge directly: the sense-data are data that lead to an inference. In 1912, Bertrand Russel rightly characterizes the method of bringing together different observations in order to distill a rule from them in terms of expectation and probability.[86] Induction produces a verification for our expectations, which we characterize as probability. The induction principle cannot be proven with an appeal to experience: a pattern or statement is deduced from observed facts ("all As"), but what has not been observed ("all unobserved As") is also a part of the probabilities. Experience only corroborates the observed facts.[87] So what has not been observed through experience is still possible unless that possibility is excluded. But the inductive method can never exclude that which cannot be observed. The possible cannot be confirmed or denied.[88]

83 Karl Popper, "Knowledge and the Shaping of Reality. The Search for a Better World," in: *In Search of a Better World. Lectures and Essays from Thirty Years*, London: Routledge 2000, p. 5.

84 Alfred Tarski, *Semantics, Metamathematics*, Oxford: Clarendon Press 1956, p. 155.

85 Popper, "Knowledge and the Shaping of Reality. The Search for a Better World," p. 4.

86 "Do *any* number of cases of a law being fulfilled in the past afford evidence that it will be fulfilled in the future? If not, it becomes plain that we have no ground whatever for expecting the sun to rise to-morrow, or for expecting the bread we shall eat at our next meal not to poison us, or for any of the other scarcely conscious expectations that control our daily lives. It is to be observed that all such expectations are only *probable*; thus we have not to seek for a proof that they *must* be fulfilled, but only for some reason in favour of the view that they are *likely* to be fulfilled." Russell, *The Problems of Philosophy*, p. 96.

87 Ibid., p. 106.

88 In 1959, Russell added a footnote to his analysis with regard to induction from 1912. In this note, he says: "The conclusion is that scientific inference demands certain extra-logical postulates of which induction is not one." Bertrand Russell, *The Basic Writings of Bertrand Russell*, London: Routledge 2009, p. 127.

According to Popper, induction consists of a singular (or individual) statement as a result of one or more observations. And when this singular statement is converted into a universal statement like a hypothesis, theory, or
law, the logical, analytical operation begins. Popper detects a major problem in this conversion, the problem of induction:

> Now it is far from obvious, from a logical point of view, that we are
> justified in inferring universal statements from singular ones, no matter
> how numerous; for any conclusion drawn in this way may always turn
> out to be false; no matter how many instances of white swans we may
> have observed, this does not justify the conclusion that all swans are
> white.[89]

The principle of induction is synthetic, and the negation of it is not self-con-
tradictory. Inductive information[90] cannot provide solid ground for a universal statement. A calculation of probabilities does not solve the problem
of verification. In his critique of induction, Popper is inspired by[91] Hume's
skepticism with regard to the senses.[92] In effect, Hume posits that we cannot
build a logically valid line of reasoning on the basis of cases we cannot experience or observe. On the basis of an imaginary comparison between what
we do experience and what we suspect (probability) but cannot experience,
we cannot make logically valid and thus universal pronouncements about
all these cases.[93] Popper came to the conclusion that "no number of true test
statements would justify the claim that an explanatory universal theory is
true."[94] Again: this is not about the truth or falsity of universal laws, theories, or statements that were arrived at on the basis of induction.

As such, singular statements cannot lead to a theory in a deductive line
of reasoning. Nor does verification prove the truth or validity of a deduced
theory. However, there is another way to examine the validity of theories
or other universal statements, Popper's method: if a theory has not been
falsified, it means it is provisionally true. The emphasis is on provisionality;
after all, it is not the job of science to look for confirmation of a theory, but

89 Popper, *The Logic of Scientific Discovery*, p. 27.
90 In addition, inductive reasoning would also end in an infinite regress.
91 Karl Popper, *Objective Knowledge. An Evolutionary Approach*, Oxford: Oxford Univer-
    sity Press 1979, p. 3.
92 "Thus to resume what I have said concerning the senses; they give us no notion of contin-
    ued existence, because they cannot operate beyond the extent, in which they really operate.
    They as little produce the opinion of a distinct existence, because they neither can offer it
    to the mind as represented, nor as original." Hume, *A Treatise of Human Nature*, p. 128.
93 Ibid., pp. 138–144.
94 Popper, *Objective Knowledge. An Evolutionary Approach*, p. 7; But at the same time,
    Popper believes that "the assumption of the truth of test statement sometimes allows us to
    justify the claim that an explanatory universal theory is false." Ibid.

to see if it can be falsified. The criterion for demarcation between science and pseudoscience is not the verifiability but falsifiability of a theory, law, or statement.[95] It is an asymmetrical system between two extremes. What determines science's objectivity? Popper does not build his theory of objectivity on the logical validity of a deductive statement. The objectivity lies in the intersubjective testing of a theory.

In *Die beiden Grundprobleme der Erkenntnistheorie*, which preceded *Logik der Forschung*, Popper schematically lays out the different positions, including his own. There are three possibilities: (1) classical rationalism, which is strictly deductive and rationalist (Descartes and Spinoza); (2) classical empiricism, which is inductive and empirical (the logical positivists); and (3) inductive rationalism, which is a combination of 1 and 2. Popper placed Wittgenstein in the third category. His own position is this:

> Finally, the view advanced here combines a strictly deductivist standpoint with a strictly empiricist one. Like rationalism, this view assumes that the most general statements (axioms) of natural science are (tentatively) adopted without logical or empirical justification. However, unlike rationalism, they are not a priori assumed to be true (in view of their self-evidence), but are adopted only as problematic, as unjustified anticipations or tentative assumptions (conjectures). They are corroborated or refuted, in strictly empiricist fashion, only by experience: by deducing statements (predictions) that can be empirically tested in a direct manner.[96]

The ultimate falsification takes place in empirical research. We do have to distinguish between justification and decision. The verdict, the judgment about whether a theory or statement is true or untrue, Popper compares to a trial by jury. There too, the jury has to test the theories and the resultant indictment, which can be deduced from the law, in relation to the facts.[97]

The positivists oppose the idealists' and especially the rationalists' assertion that they ignore objective facts. Logical positivism tried in vain to unite these two worlds. Popper's critical rationalism does not strive for certainty, but rational, empirical scientific rigor. In that case, there are two phases

---

95 Popper, *The Logic of Scientific Discovery*, p. 40.
96 Karl Popper, *The Two Fundamental Problems of the Theory of Knowledge*, London: Routledge 2012, pp. 16–17.
97 "By its decision, the jury accepts, by agreement a statement about a factual occurrence—a basis statement, as it were. The significance of this decision lies in the fact that from it, together with the universal statements of the system (of criminal law) certain consequences can be deduced. In other words, the decision forms the basis for the application of the system; the verdict plays the part of a 'true statement of fact.'" Popper, *The Logic of Scientific Discovery*, pp. 109–110.

in research: the context of discovery and the context of justification. The discovery phase does not require strict rational grounds. After all, how discoveries are made changes with the times. Incidentally, a hypothesis about gravity can also be formulated after seeing a falling apple. But the second phase requires logical justification. The legitimation of knowledge, and thus of deductive statements, requires its own specific procedure. A logical positivist settles for counting all the ravens that are black in order to be able to say that all ravens are black. Here, concrete observation is held up as the basis for a theory. But the moment the first non-black raven is found, the theory crumbles. However, here the theory is based on concrete observations, namely this or that raven (deduction). How could it be proven that all ravens were observed?

So, verification is not sufficient ground upon which to base a deductive statement. That is why Popper posits that it is not observation but theory that is the foundation of knowledge. Empirical research then has to determine whether the theory is falsifiable. In this, the method of trial (theory formation) and error (falsification),[98] guessing and disproving, is used.[99] This does not happen automatically. A viewpoint is required in order to test something in empirical reality. Theories, hypotheses, knowledge of related matters, and scientific principles serve as this viewpoint for research. Science does not search for probable theories, Popper taught us, but explanations for strong and unlikely theories. It is a learning process, in which the refutation of a theory is, in and of itself, a victory for science. And that which is not falsifiable cannot be scientifically investigated; it falls outside the domain of science.[100] Now that we have an insight into Popper's theoretical framework, in the upcoming section, we will discuss another aspect of Popper's philosophy of science, namely his attack on essentialism.

98 Imre Lakatos believes that Popperian falsifiability does not provide a solution to the demarcation between science and pseudoscience. See: Lakatos, *The Methodology of Scientific Research Programmes*.

99 So, (wherever possible) empirical consequences are deduced from a theory: *modus tollens*, if p then q; not q, so not p.

100 Popper's philosophy is a theory of trial and error, of conjectures and refutations: "It made it possible to understand why our attempts to force interpretations upon the world were logically prior to the observation of similarities." Karl Popper, "Science: Conjectures and Refutations," in: *Conjectures and Refutations*, London: Routledge 2002, p. 60.

Chapter 4

Popper's critique of essentialism and the scientific outlook

And its thinking is a thinking on thinking[1]

Aql, wa āqil wa magul, thought thinking thought[2]

Under the banner of their radical and politically correct "anti-essentialism" march ancient religious taboos, the luxury of the pampered husband, ill health, ignorance, and death.[3]

In the first chapter of *A New Introduction to Legal Method*, we reflected on the scientific method in general. The second chapter was devoted to one of the most famous skeptical attacks on legal science in the United States, namely that of the American realists. The third chapter is about the work of the most famous philosopher of science of the twentieth century: Karl Popper. In this fourth chapter, we will mainly address Popper's critique of essentialism.

An introduction

There is a terrifying enemy stalking the halls of academia. *Another* enemy! And since the second half of the previous century, this enemy of thinkers and politicians has had a name: *essentialism*. It goes hand in hand with its twin brother, *historicism*. And those who are accused of this have to answer

---

1 Aristotle, *Metaphysics* (translated and edited by Jonathan Barnes, volume 2), Princeton: Princeton University Press 1991, p. 1698 (1074b, 30).
2 This Aristotelian rationalist thought was also subscribed to by Al-Farabi. See on this: Majid Fakhry, *Al-Frarabi. Founder of Islamic Neoplatonism*, Oxford: One World 2002, p. 81; Abu Nasr Al-Farabi, *Mabadi' ārā ahl al-madinat al-fādilah* [On the Perfect State], Cairo: Hindawi 2016, p. 16; Aristotle, "Metaphysics," in: Jonathan Barnes, ed., *The Complete Works of Aristotle. The Revised Oxford Translation* (volume 2), Princeton: Princeton University Press 1984, p. 1698.
3 Martha Nussbaum.

DOI: 10.4324/9781003282570-5

for themselves. In this chapter, we discuss whether criticism of essentialism holds water. We believe it does not, at least not in the way it was formulated by Karl Popper.

But can we even do without essentialism? Especially for legal science, this question is pressing. Jurists work with definitions. What is theft? What is manslaughter? When is it possible to speak of deception? Can legal science do without this never-ending search for "essences"? A legal-ethical concept like *murder* has the essence of a clearly delineated definition: the intentional, unlawful, and premeditated killing of a person. It would be absurd to accuse a jurist of "essentialist thought" when he is trying to determine the essential characteristics of the crimes set down in the Criminal Code. In that sense, jurists, judges, prosecutors, and legal scholars at universities are always "essentialists" in the contested sense of the word: they need to reflect on the delineation of definitions. Of course, a jurist knows that there is no definition of *theft* or *murder* written in the sky by God's own hand, or that such definitions are waiting to be discovered in some Platonic realm of ideas.

Nevertheless, the charge against jurists is widely shared. Bertrand Russell (1872–1970), who shares Popper's philosophy, goes so far as to write about jurists that they have in common with communists and religious believers that they believe they can deduce their truths from "inspired books." These books contain definitions or essences of certain concepts from which absolute truths can de deductively derived: "Deduction from inspired books is the method of arriving at truth employed by jurists, Christians, Mohammedans, and Communists."[4] Russell views this method of deducing truths from definitions as the opposite of the true scientific method. He associates the latter with the name of Galileo (1564–1642). It is not until the seventeenth century, until Galileo's work, that we started making scientific progress. Russell puts exceptional stock in the significance of Galileo: "Science as an important force begins with Galileo."[5] Galileo's method was empirical. He observed what he saw around him. He did not deduce conclusions from established definitions or essences. That is why Russell says: "Those who believe in deduction as the method of arriving at knowledge are compelled to find their premises somewhere, usually in sacred books."[6] What are we to think of this attack on essentialism? Are Russell and Popper right? Is it true that the deductive method, applied to certain definitions or essences, is the opposite of the scientific method?

It is remarkable that Russell and Popper's critique has some resemblance to the critique of deductive thought and the associated "formalism" by the

4 Bertrand Russell, *The Scientific Outlook*, London: George Allen & Unwin Ltd 1954 (1931), p. 33.
5 Ibid., p. 9.
6 Ibid., p. 33.

American thinkers. Like the realists, Popper and Russell also favor a more empirical approach.

Perhaps we ought to start with a philosopher who has had a significant impact on the anti-essentialist thought of the French postmodernists, and therefore on our time: Michel Foucault (1926–1984). In a series of books, Foucault constructed "essences." He did not use this word, but he did distinguish essential characteristics of sexuality and the Western way of life. Because this ran so strongly counter to the reigning prejudice that "generalizing" and "essentialist thought" is wrong, he felt compelled to answer for himself before the tribunal of anti-essentialism and anti-historicism.[7]

For legal science, this debate about essentialism and anti-essentialism is of great importance. If jurists could not spend significant attention to definitions or strive to treat them as precisely and carefully as possible, legal science would be crippled. "There is no such thing as universal rights" and "a constitution has no fixed anchor points": these are things that can be heard among legal scientists who have been influenced by postmodernism, just as some Arabists will say "there is no such thing as Islam." And those who want to argue that universal rights (or Islam) certainly do exist are often met with a fancy academic slur: essentialism. Oddly enough, this slur is only used in response to analyses *critical* of Islam; apparently, positive reflections on Islam are not essentialist in nature.[8] The same discourse surrounds universal rights.

That is why we want to focus on Popper's critique of essentialism in this chapter. After all, anti-essentialists use his critique as a foundation for their theories and analyses. This analysis inevitably harks back to medieval and ancient philosophy. The battle against essentialism also affects philosophers of Islam, because all their ideas would fall under the heading of essentialism.

---

7 Michel Foucault, *The History of Sexuality. Volume I: An Introduction*, New York: Pantheon Books, 1978, pp. 150–151.

8 Islam and political Islam have fundamental characteristics, essentials that distinguish Islam from other worldviews, religions, or ideologies. When it comes to Muslims, we want to refer to the fundamental distinction introduced by Afshin Ellian, which is the distinction between (i) Muslims, (ii) Islam, and (iii) political Islam. Muslims are not the same as Islam. According to the official dogmas, Islam is perfection and a Muslim is a human being, with all the flaws that this entails. Political Islam, finally, is a legal, political, and sometimes also military manifestation of Islam. The term *Islamism* is synonymous with political Islam. This resembles the stern message of the German-Syrian scholar of Islam Bassam Tibi in his book about Islamism: "The first message of this book is that there is a distinction between the faith of Islam and the religionized politics of Islamism, which employs religious symbols for political ends. Many will deny this distinction, including most prominent Islamists themselves. There is no doubt that many Islamists hold the sincere conviction that their Islamism is the true Islam. In fact, however Islamism emanates from a political interpretation of Islam: it is based not on the religious faith of Islam but on an ideological use of religion within the political realm." Bassam Tibi, *Islamism and Islam*, New Haven, London: Yale University Press 2012, p. vii.

After we have described Popper's critique of essentialism, we will discuss criticisms of Popper's conception of essentialism by Martha Nussbaum, David Oderberg, and Brian Ellis. It will become clear that we share Popper's critique of essentialism where it concerns the duplication of reality (Plato). However, we will defend a realistic form of essentialism in line with the phenomenological approach. It is the realistic, nuanced forms of essentialism especially that constitute fertile soil for science, philosophy in general, and legal science in particular. Nevertheless, we consider Popper's critical rationalism, the Popperian theory of science with regard to epistemology, correct and true. We also share his core criticism of totalitarianism and his defense of the open society. Yet, we disagree with his critique of essentialism, as will become clear in this chapter. We wish to present a modification, a fine-tuning of the critique of essentialism. Islamic scholars like Abdulkarim Soroush also wrote about the essences of Islam.[9] Soroush's essentialism derives from Aristotelian metaphysics, that is to say, essences and accidents (attributes that may or may not belong to a phenomenon).[10] We are not concerned here with people's individual faith.[11] We do not get into that.

Finally, we will end this chapter with some conclusions and propositions. We will argue that the balance between "explaining" and "understanding" ought to be the ultimate epistemological goal in the humanities. Perhaps we are not so far removed from Popper in this, because in "Realism and the Aim of Sciencee," he used this remarkable phrase: "Our modified essentialism."[12] Why? In Popper's own words:

> I do not doubt that we may seek to probe deeper and deeper into the structure of our world or, as we might say, into properties of the world that are more and more essential, or of greater and greater depth.[13]

Popper's critique of essentialism

The *casus belli* for continental philosophy was posited as early as Plato. As such, ontology and its development have occupied a prominent place in

9 Abdulkarim Soroush, *The Expansion of Prophetic Experience. Essays on Historicity, Contingency and Plurality in Religion*, Leiden, Boston: Brill 2009; Abdolkarim Soroush, *Bast-e tadjrebeh Nabavi* [The Expansion of Prophetic Experience, fourth edition], Teheran: Moa'seseh Farhangi-e Sarat 2003, p. 16.
10 See: Aristotle, *Metaphysics*, among others, numbers: 1015–1017; Aristotle, "Metaphysics," 1984, pp. 1603–1608.
11 See about individual convictions in comparative perspective: Ruud Koopmans, *Das verfallene Haus des Islam: Die religiösen Ursachen von Unfreiheit, Stagnation und Gewalt*, Munich: C.H. Beck 2020.
12 Karl Popper, *Realism and the Aim of Science*, London, New York: Routledge 1999, p. 137.
13 Ibid., p. 137.

thought and research since ancient history. Plato classifies the ontological question by raising the following penetrating issue, which Martin Heidegger will later repeat: "For manifestly you have long been aware of what you mean when you use the expression 'being' ['seiend']. We, however, who used to think we understood it, have now become perplexed ['sind Wir in Verlegenheit gekommen']."[14] Now, two millennia later, Heidegger does not only pose the same question, but he also wonders if we have come up with an answer. But a few lines on, Plato himself presents the central question of ontology:

> Well then, must we not, so far as we can, try to learn from those who say that the universe is one, what they mean when they say "being"? ... Do you say that one only is? We do, they will say ... Well then, do you give the name of being to anything? ... Is it what you call "one," using two names for the same thing, or how is this?[15]

If someone posits the identity of "name" and "thing" in combination with the verb *to be*, that person will be forced to either recognize that the name does not refer to anything, or, if he insists that the name is something, that the name is only the name of a name, and of nothing else. Since only unity consists of one, it is also, in itself, unity of the name, Plato says. The concept *being* as a general term is indefinable, which is why Heidegger poses the question about the sense of being.[16] The definition of general terms and their level of reality is already food for philosophical debate. It is not for nothing that Heidegger characterizes his own phrasing as inelegant and unmanageable: "We may remark that it is one thing to report narratively about *beings* and another to grasp *beings* in their *being*. For the latter task not only are most of the words lacking but above all the 'grammar.'"[17] In scientific analysis, grammar functions, organizes, and judges through the verb *to be*: to be true or to be untrue! But Popper wants to escape the prison of *being* without breaking with the verb and its grammar.

Popper uses the term *methodological essentialism* to characterize the position of Plato and many of his students and followers "that it is the task of pure knowledge or 'science' to discover and to describe the true nature of things, i.e. their hidden reality or essence."[18] The term *essentialism* is a

---

14 Martin Heidegger, *Being and Time*, Albany, NY: State University of New York Press 2010, p. xxix.
15 Plato, "The Sophist," in: *Plato Theaetetus. Sophist* (translated by Harold North Fowler.), Cambridge, MA: The Loeb Classical Library, Harvard University Press 2006, p. 365 (244b).
16 Heidegger, *Being and Time*, p. 37.
17 Ibid., p. 36.
18 Karl Popper, *The Open Society and Its Enemies (1. Plato)*, Princeton: Princeton University Press 1971, p. 31.

construction (actually a reconstruction) of Popper's, with which he intellectually confronts ancient and medieval philosophy and its influence in the late modern period: from Plato to Ibn Sina (Avicenna) and Heidegger.

We have to note here that the Latin word *essentia* is as ambiguous as the Greek word *ousia*: both can mean *being* as well as *that which is* (essence).[19] The duplication of reality in sensory and true reality (forms, ideas, *eidos*, or *idea* are objectively perfect structures) brings with it an epistemological question or problem. In the *Phaedo*, Plato says that if something is beautiful, it takes part in beauty (or the Beautiful itself).[20] The world looks like the depiction of something else, of the archetype. Being, knowledge of being, that is the truth.[21] Several categories are posited: truth-opinion, truth-probability, being-appearance, being-becoming, thinking-being, and being-to be. Real knowledge is possible on the basis of intellectual intuition, not on the basis of observations. With this perspective, it is possible to approach the truth (or in Popper's words "the essence") of an idea. The science of ideas—outside of time and space—can only be acquired, it is said, in a strictly rationalist, abstract fashion. That is why mathematics, geometry, and logic have an important place in this philosophical thought, as well as in later ones. The intelligible (that which is only knowable to reason) whole then consists of purely intelligible forms and mathematical objects that correspond with pure and mathematical thought. Being the eternal same will become the eternal recurrence of the same in Nietzsche. As such, dialectics is the method that penetrates all the way into this absolute goal by eliminating hypotheses.[22]

We think that with Plato, the first serious step was taken in the direction of the rationalization of reality in its totality. Plato therefore turns against poetry and poets, and not because they did not perform their task well. Nor did Plato harbor hatred of literature itself. He was opposed to mythology (*mythos*) through literature. It is Ernst Cassirer (1874–1945) who opened our eyes to the historical weight of rationalization in Plato. In his 1949 book *The Myth of the State* (*Vom Mythus des Staates*), he demonstrates that

19 L.M. de Rijk rightly writes that this problem was already visible in Augustine: "Augustine, whose use of language had an enormous influence on medieval thought and speech, who uses the term *summa essentia* (highest Being, highest Essence) to refer to God." See: L. M. de Rijk, *Middeleeuwse wijsbegeerte. Traditie en vernieuwing* [Medieval Philosophy. Tradition and Renewal], Assen: Van Gorcum 1981, p. 191.

20 Plato, "Phaedo," in: *Plato Euthyphro. Apology. Crito. Phaedo. Phaedrus* (translated by Harold North Fowler), Cambridge, MA: The Loeb Classical Library, Harvard University Press 2006, pp. 343–345 (100).

21 Plato, "Timaeus," in: *Plato Complete Works* (translated by Donald J. Zeyl), Indianapolis, Cambridge: Hackett Publishing Company 1997, p. 1235 (29).

22 Plato, "Republic," in: *Plato Complete Works* (translated by G.M.A. Grube, rev. C.D.C. Reeve), Indianapolis, Cambridge: Hackett Publishing Company 1997, pp. 114–1149 (533–534).

myth is an aspect of language: language contains general terms that are ambiguous.[23] Cassirer attributes Plato's distaste for poetry to his battle with *mythos*.[24] The *phronēsis* (practical wisdom) then becomes the condition for moderation and balance (*sōphrosynē*),[25] and because politics is also a part of Plato's ontological worldview, the replacement of *mythos*[26] by *logos* could also lead to moderation (an important virtue). The poets mislead people with their "bizarre" tales of gods, so Plato believes. The true God is one. In Plato's philosophy, the birth of monotheism or *tawhid* (but here in Plato, outside of religion) can be observed. Apparently, Popper was not interested in such an analysis; he initially took aim at the essence. In a fairly simple fashion, Popper marked the field of battle: essentialism throughout the entire history of philosophy. Plato is the producer of this essentialism, which is why Plato is the greatest enemy to Popper. Plato introduced something in the history of Western thought that we can rid ourselves of only through the most strenuous effort.

In Popper's view, Plato's methodological essentialism mostly applied to the essence of sensory objects, which can be found elsewhere in the Forms. Although not all essentialists[27] applied Plato's method in full, they believed that "it is the task of pure knowledge or 'science' to discover and to describe the true nature of things, i.e. their hidden reality or essence."[28] So it is about the essence, its definition, and its name. With this methodological essentialism, which seeks to discover essences by means of definitions and descriptions, Popper juxtaposes methodological nominalism. In this method, one does not search for the true nature of a thing. Popper's nominalism describes "how a thing behaves in different circumstances" in order to discover patterns.[29] Here, the description and the explanation of things and events are central, as, finally, is the search for universal laws and patterns.

Popper's nominalism will never ask questions like: what is energy? What is movement? What is an atom? Instead, his nominalism will pose

---

23 Ernst Cassirer, *The Myth of the State*, New Haven, London: Yale University Press 1974, p. 18.
24 Ibid., p. 66ff.
25 Ibid., pp. 75–76.
26 Ernst Cassirer, *The Philosophy of Symbolic Forms. Volume 2: Mythical Thought*, New Haven, London: Yale University Press 1955, pp. 29–30.
27 Popper says he does not take a position on the metaphysical problem of universals, so he only applies the term *nominalism* to methodology. Despite the Aristotelian critique of Plato, in which the essences and the things come together, Popper mostly views this as a significant transformation: Plato's pessimism (the essences are not here) versus Aristotle's optimism, in which the essence of a thing is identical with its ultimate purpose. The *causa finalis*, the final cause, lies inside the phenomenon itself, not outside of it. See: Popper, *The Open Society and Its Enemies*, 1971 (volume 2), p. 5.
28 Ibid. (volume 1), p. 31.
29 Ibid. (volume 1), p. 32.

questions starting with the word *how*: How does a planet move? He makes the transition from *what-questions* to *how-questions*. But is a successful, well-delineated philosophical or scientific research method possible without what-questions?

Next, we will show that Popper himself is not always loyal to his absolute dogma about how-questions. Of course, Popper's aim is exact knowledge. That domain is dominated by the exact, empirical sciences, which is why he comes to the conclusion that methodological nominalism has nowadays been almost universally accepted in the natural sciences.[30] Here, the question arises of what nominalism actually is. Popper claims not to take a position on the metaphysical problem of universals,[31] which is why he only applies the term *nominalism* to methodology. In *The Poverty of Historicism* (1957), Popper again explains why essentialism goes hand in hand with historicism. Here, he refers to the discussion about universals. The philosophical problem of universals was a topic of intellectual debate in the Middle Ages.[32] This concerned the nature of universal terms. So, again, the views of Plato and Aristotle about universal terms like red, white, beauty, human being, and justice were at the center of attention. Rightly, Bertrand Russell points out in his *The Problems of Philosophy* (1912) that Plato's Theory of Forms was an attempt to clarify and solve the problem of universals:

> When we examine common words, we find that, broadly speaking, proper names stand for particulars, while other substantives, adjectives, prepositions, and verbs stand for universals. Pronouns stand for particulars, but are ambiguous: it is only by the context or the circumstances that we know what particulars they stand for. The word "now" stands for a particular, namely the present moment; but like pronouns, it stands for an ambiguous particular, because the present is always changing.[33]

Russell uses the following example to illustrate: "Charles I's head was cut off." Charles I is a proper noun (the name of an individual), but the common noun *head* and the verb *to cut off* are universals.

To Plato, ideas[34] existed in a separate world. Aristotle rejected the Realm of Ideas (or "Forms"): "Therefore the Forms will be substance; and the

30 Ibid. (volume 1), p. 32.
31 Ibid. (volume 2), p. 290.
32 Gyula Klima, "The Medieval Problem of Universals," in: Edward N. Zalta, ed., *The Stanford Encyclopedia of Philosophy*, https://plato.stanford.edu/entries/universals-medieval/#Bib, Gyula Klima, "Nomainalist Semantics," in: *The Cambridge History of Medieval Philosophy* (volume I), Cambridge: Cambridge University Press 2014, pp. 159–172.
33 Bertrand Russell, *The Problems of Philosophy*, Oxford: Oxford University Press 1912, pp. 145–146.
34 In his Metaphysics (Alpha), Aristotle summarizes Plato like this: "Things of this other sort, then, he called Ideas, and sensible thing, he said, were apart from these, and were all called

same terms indicate substance in this and in the ideal world."[35] On the other hand, Aristotle did think that form and matter are connected to one another, like actuality and potential: in predisposition (potentiality) and in action (completion). Aristotelian ontology is teleological through and through: "for all these are for the sake of the end, though they differ from one another in that some are instruments and others are actions."[36] On the one hand, *being* and *that which is* mean something we say is "a possibility" and, on the other, something we say is "an actuality."[37] An archeological study into universals and nominalism inevitably takes us back to the Middle Ages, the time of Neoplatonism, the inductive resistance in the margins of the natural sciences with an appeal to Aristotelian physics. This latter group has an interest in promoting nominalism.

In Aristotle, the universal concepts[38] become, in some sense, *immanent*. That is, they are situated in this world.[39] This also makes the empirical approach to reality possible. Nevertheless, the question was how universal concepts are possible: the relationship between a universal concept such as *man* and the concrete, individual man. The intellectual discussion that emerged about this was focused on two movements: realism[40] and nominalism. The realists, like Johannes Scotus (810–877),[41] did not attribute reality to individual things but to universal concepts.[42] This nomenclature is

---

after these; for the multitude of things, which have the same name as the Form exist by participation in it." See: Aristotle, "Metaphysics," 1984, p. 1561 (987b).

35 Ibid., p. 1566 (991a).

36 Ibid., p. 1600 (1013b).

37 "Again 'being' and 'that which is,' in these cases we have mentioned, sometimes mean being potentially, and sometimes being actually." See: Aristotle, "Metaphysics," 1984, p. 1606 (1017b).

38 In rejecting Plato's Theory of Forms, Aristotle uses various arguments, but the most important one is this: "Again it must be held to be impossible that the substance and that of which it is the substance should exist apart; how, therefore, can the Ideas, being the substances of things, exist apart?" See: Aristotle, "Metaphysics," 1984, p. 1567 (991a).

39 Boethius (480–525) formulated the research question as follows: genera and species either exist in reality or just in our minds. Do they exist in reality? Or do the universals, the universal concepts that only exist as thoughts in our minds, represent things in reality? This is the core question about which realists and nominalists will later clash. See: John Marenbon, *Medieval Philosophy. An Historical Land Philosophical Introduction*, London: Routledge 2007, pp. 34–37.

40 Conti views the following thinkers as moderate realists: Thomas Aquinas, Henry of Ghent, Simon of Faversham, John Duns Scotus, Thomas of Sutton, Giles of Rome, and Walter Burley. See: Alessandro D. Conti, "Realism," in: Robert Pasnau and Christina van Dyke, eds., *Cambridge History of Medieval Philosophy* (volume 2), Cambridge: Cambridge University Press 2014, p. 648.

41 He is the prototype of a Platonic thinker. See: Bertrand Russell, *History of Western Philosophy*, London: Routledge 1996, p. 378.

42 Timothy B. Noone, "Universals and Individuation," in: Thomas Williams, ed., *The Cambridge Companion to Duns Scotus*, Cambridge: Cambridge University Press 2003, pp. 100–128.

somewhat confusing. The medieval research question was once aptly formulated by De Rijk:

> The flip side of the ontological question is the matter of universals: what gives Plato and Aristotle and us the right to furnish a universal term such as *man* with predicates of A and B, when these are not referring to the same concrete individual (man)? Even if the universal term refers to the platonic Idea or the Aristotelian *eidos* (in the sense of individual denotation), what is such a connotation that makes the term suited to being attributed to more than one individual? Is the connotatum (significatum) used in an unambiguous sense in the distinguishing predicates?[43]

This issue should not be simplistically interpreted as a battle between the followers of Plato and Aristotle. After all, both great philosophers could be used to justify arguments on all sides, especially considering the distortion of both philosophers' ideas in the Middle Ages due to the incorporation of Christianity in the intellectual debates of scholasticism. In the East, too, philosophers of Islam were engaged in the debate about *wūjud* (existence, being, presence) and *maahiyya* (essence). A good example of this is a passage at the beginning of *Al-Shifa* (*The Book of Healing*) by Avicenna.[44] In the *Ente et Essentia* (on Being and Essence), Thomas Aquinas appeals to *Al-Shifa* in determining his position about realism and nominalism.[45] In this context, Popper defends nominalists and argues in favor of the proposition that universal concepts as a semantic property of names (*nomina*)—the plurality of things under a common name—exist.

Not just Popper, but Wittgenstein also took a position in this medieval dispute. In his *Philosophical Investigations* from 1945, Wittgenstein addresses general words that appear in a multitude of concrete things. In thesis 30 he says: "The ostensive definition explains the use—the meaning—of the word

---

43 De Rijk, *Middeleeuwse wijsbegeerte*, p. 227.

44 "As for substance, it is clear that its existence, inasmuch as it is only substance, is not connected with matter. Otherwise, there would be no substance that is not sensible. As for number, it would apply to (both) sensible and non-sensible things. Thus, inasmuch as it is number, it is not attached to sensible things." See: Avicenna, *The Metaphysics of The Healing* (a parallel English-Arabic text), Provo, UT: Brigham Young University Press 2005, p. 8; Avicenna, *Isharat Va Tanbihat* (volume I, *The Book of Directives and Remarks*), Teheran: Soroush Press 2009, p. 247

45 "Hence it happens that some things are specifically the same and numerically different. But the essence of the simple is not received is matter, so there cannot be any multiplication of it. Nor in such substances do we find many individuals of the same species. There are as many species as there are individuals, as Avicenna expressly says." See: Thomas Aquinas, "On Being and Essence," in: Thomas Aquinas, *Selected Writings*, London: Penguin Books 1998, pp. 41–42.

when the overall role of the word in language is clear."[46] The ostensive definitions are necessary when the words in question could be interpreted differently or inaccurately if the definition were not there. The use of a word in different circumstances for different things does not imply that the word has an essence. For instance, the word *game* is used in different combinations: the Olympic Games and card games. There are commonalities between these things, but the word *game* does not have an essence, otherwise, all combinations containing the word would have the same meaning. According to Wittgenstein, the rules of the game constitute an "instrument of the game itself."[47] The word *play* is an activity that contains some resemblances or likenesses, and when we look at different forms of playing, we see the resemblances and likenesses appearing and disappearing.[48] What Wittgenstein did stress in his language-game analysis is the commonality of words. This brings us back to the heart of the problem of when we ought to furnish the commonality with the universality of a status.[49] No one could have suspected that the "battle over universals" would become a point of contention in the philosophy of science that would acquire such a clear political dimension. Popper further reflects on this problem in the earlier mentioned work *The Poverty of Historicism* (1957). In order to prevent confusion, he changes *realism* into *essentialism*, because the medieval realists are really the idealists. This will become the new framework for the battle of universals: essentialism versus nominalism. According to Popper, this fight began with Plato and Aristotle, as was briefly and succinctly described earlier.

Popper acknowledges that every science uses universal terms, such as *energy, evolution, justice, state, carbon*, or *speed*.[50] There are also exceptional or individual names, such as the *First World War, Alexander the Great*, and so on. Popper does not argue with this. And how could he? We do not only use concepts to refer to individual things, but also to indicate abstract qualities. However, according to Popper, essentialists attribute an intrinsic characteristic to a universal term like *white*, namely whiteness. They do not, or not sufficiently, realize that whiteness does not exist in

---

46 Ludwig Wittgenstein, *Philosophical Investigations*, London: Basil Blackwell 1986, p. 30.

47 Ibid., p. 26ff.

48 Ludwig Wittgenstein, *Philosophical Investigations*, Chicester: Wiley-Blackwell 2009, pp. 18–19.

49 Rudolf Carnap will describe the universal terms as abstract entities. Carnap sought to solve the problem of universals pragmatically: "The acceptance or rejection of abstract linguistic forms, just as the acceptance or rejection of any other linguistic forms in any branch of science, will finally be decided by their efficiency as instruments, the ratio of the results achieved to the amount and complexity of the efforts required." See: Rudolf Carnap, "Empiricism, Semantics and Ontology," in: *Revue Internationale de Philosophie*, 4 (1950), p. 40.

50 Karl Popper, *The Poverty of Historicism*, London: Routledge 1961, p. 27.

the same way that white things in the world do. They do confer a kind of higher status on the essence of whiteness. Popper places himself in a long tradition of Locke, Hume, Mill, and other empiricists who are not partial to this. Popper also posits that the essentialists use the universal concept (the characteristic of whiteness) as an object.[51]

He does not only turn against Plato but mostly opposes Aristotelian essentialism, which is also why he opposes Avicenna (Ibn Sina, 980–1037) and Al-Farabi (872–950). Popper's explanation of Aristotelian philosophy with regard to universal concepts in the context of Aristotle's metaphysics is somewhat one-sided because Aristotle in particular created unity of *potential being* and *actual being* with his theory. In Plato, it would have been different: "whiteness" has its own existence in a separate world of ideas. After all, "whiteness" can only manifest as a form or idea. Now we come to the heart of the Popperian critique: because the essentialists believe in the existence of essences, they believe that this is also important for science. As such, science must penetrate these essences. So far, it is mainly Plato who is the object of Popper's criticism. After this, Popper also directs his criticism toward the followers of Aristotle, therein noting that, as mentioned before, they pose what-questions (what is matter?). Methodological nominalists, such as Popper himself, on the other hand, ask how-questions like: "how does this piece of matter behave?"[52] In the natural sciences, essentialism is not common, Popper notes.

In the social sciences, however, essentialism rules the roost. The social sciences first seek to penetrate the essence of social units like classes and groups, the state, and the law in order to then explain them, asking, for instance: what is the state?[53]

At the time of the Cold War, Popper mostly debated Marxists. There is no getting around the fact that Popper's critique was mostly aimed at Marxism and Neo-Marxism. Still, he universalizes his criticism and applies it to all social sciences. The question that arises here is this: was he only concerned with Marxism? This is Popper's answer:

> Essentialism may have been introduced on the ground that it enables us to detect an identity in things that change, but it furnishes in its turn some of the most powerful arguments in support of the doctrine that the social sciences must adopt a historical method, that is to say, in support of the doctrine of historicism.[54]

Popper—rightly—opposes a determinist interpretation of history that, worse still, also claims to be able to make predictions about revolutions,

51 Ibid., p. 28.
52 Ibid., p. 29.
53 Ibid., p. 30.
54 Ibid., p. 34.

class struggles, and so on in the name of the social sciences. The law of historical developments was depicted as a kind of divine providence; it is an eschatological way of thinking. In effect, History itself took the place of God in a number of worldviews. This is certainly the case in the theories of Marx and Engels: history commands the classes to move. Both derived their understanding of history from Hegel. Hegel's dialectical thought combined with materialist thought resulted in the materialist-dialectical movement of history. This historicism, which regards history as a well-written theatrical performance, is actually far removed from real history. Popper's critique of essentialism is aimed at historicism as a source of totalitarian thought and action. We see the same criticism from other philosophers, such as Claude Lefort and Hannah Arendt, who are focused on the contingency in history and the contingent events. In the following paragraphs, we will try to develop a discourse about the derailing of anti-essentialist thought.

The critique of the critique of essentialism

The Popperian critique of essentialism contains many different layers:

(1) the discussion about the battle between realists and nominalists in the Middle Ages
(2) the critique of Plato's Realm of Ideas
(3) disputes in the philosophy of language about the picture theory of language interpretation, and realms of meaning, and finally
(4) the critique of totalitarian ideologies.

Popper's philosophy is a logical continuation of an anti-metaphysical tradition. As early as 1651, Thomas Hobbes leveled a withering attack against scholasticism and especially also Aristotelian thought. In *Leviathan*, Hobbes observes that the ability to reason logically emerged from our use of language.[55] But Aristotle's *Metaphysics* was written with the use of language too. According to Hobbes, "scarce anything can be more absurdly said" in all of natural philosophy than that book.[56] This "foolish" metaphysics was blended together with the Scriptures to prove that essences exist in the world that are independent of bodies: "abstract essences," or in other words, "substantial forms."[57] But suppose, Hobbes writes, "that there were a language without any verb answerable to *est*, or *is*, or *be*."[58] The people

---

55 Thomas Hobbes, *Leviathan*, Cambridge: Cambridge University Press 2000, p. 459.
56 Ibid., p. 461.
57 Ibid., p. 463.
58 Ibid., p. 464.

who spoke this language would "be not a jot less capable of inferring, concluding, and of all kind of reasoning, than were the Greeks and Latins [Romans]." A very intriguing question! Such language once actually existed: Arabic. However, the philosophers of Islam were forced to write in the lingua franca of the time, regardless of where they came from or if their native language was Arabic.

In his substantial book about formal logic, the Iranian philosopher and logician Mohammed Khansari reflects on the problem of *being* in Arabic. Incidentally, his book is written largely in Arabic because he explains classical logic with the use of philosophical texts by philosophers of Islam (especially from the Middle Ages). Here, he also addresses all of Eastern scholasticism. The problem of language reared its head in ontology and in propositional logic: affirmation and negation. The verb *to be*, as it exists and functions in the Indo-Germanic languages, Greek, Latin, or Persian, did not exist in Arabic. Khansari explains how the great philosophers of Islam solved this problem by using loanwords and adverbs (*huwa, hiya*)[59] and converting them into a particular grammatical construction. Here, he quotes from a work by Al-Farabi in which Farabi explains how, in the conversion of Greek philosophy into Arabic, his predecessors came up with a linguistic solution for the verb *to be*.[60] So, the term *being* is necessary in order to explain, understand reality, and judge. Nothing and no one can escape *being*!

Hobbes's attack on ontology, because that is what it is about in the end, was, in essence, an attack on theology; after all, as he said, the theologians' writings were little more than "insignificant trains of strange and barbarous words."[61] The "obscure language" of scholasticism, Aristotle's books about metaphysics, ethics, and politics, are taught to support the Pope and Catholic clergy, Hobbes believes.[62] So, the verb *to be*, or ontology, has various aspects linked to different times: political, cultural, religious, and scientific aspects. And what is true of Hobbes's writings here is also true of Popper's. Popper's attack on the verb *to be* in the context of essentialism is also not unambiguous. There are concepts and categories that, as universal notions sometimes precede sensory perception: *a priori* versus *a posteriori*, analytical versus synthetic concepts and numbers. It was Immanuel Kant

---

59 "the complete absence of the copula in Semitic languages, saying that these languages are 'still unable to express the thought adequately.' ... were the pronouns *huwa* and *hiya*, the interrogative/indefinite *mā* and *anna*." See: Lenn E. Goodman, *Avicenna*, updated edition, Ithaca, London: Cornell University Press 2006, pp. 106–107; Michael Leezenberg, *Islamitische filosofie. Een geschiedenis* [A History of Islamic Philosophy], Amsterdam: Bulaaq 2001, p. 92.

60 Mohammad Khansari, *Mantiq-e Suri* (volume 2), Teheran: Agah Uitgeverij 1980, p. 22.

61 Hobbes, *Leviathan*, pp. 472–473.

62 Ibid., p. 477.

who posited that we cannot know certain objects, but we still have to be able to think:

> Yet the reservation must also be well noted, that even if we cannot cognize these same objects as things in themselves, we at least must be able to think them as things in themselves. For otherwise there would follow the absurd proposition that there is an appearance without anything that appears.[63]

In order to attribute objective validity (reality) to this, Kant believes more is required than just thought.

Popper believes the what-questions, as described earlier, to be utterly superfluous. However, science is not just the technique of answering how-questions through the use of data, observation, or measurement. For instance, *Grand Design* (2010), by Stephen Hawking (1942–2018), starts with these types of questions: "How can we understand the world in which we find ourselves? How does the universe behave? What is the nature of reality? Where did all this come from?"[64] Hawking believes these are *the* philosophical questions, but, so he says, philosophy is dead!

If Hawking is right and philosophy is dead, Popper contributed to this with his bitter war against essentialism. However, Hawking begins with a what-question and other questions that lead to more what-questions:

> To understand the universe at the deepest level, we need to know not only how the universe behaves, but why. Why is there something rather than nothing? Why do we exist? Why this particular set of laws and not some other?[65]

Here, one of the greatest physicists and mathematicians of our time poses the same question as the German philosopher Martin Heidegger had decades earlier: "Why are there beings at all instead of nothing?"[66] That is indeed the question.[67] It speaks volumes that Hawking asks more or less the same question in 2010. Apparently, the philosophical-ontological questions are not yet dead!

63 Immanuel Kant, *Critique of Pure Reason*, Cambridge: Cambridge University Press 1998, p. 115 (B.XXXVI).
64 Stephen Hawking and Leonard Mlodinow, *The Grand Design*, New York: Bantam Books 2010, p. 5.
65 Ibid., pp. 9–10.
66 Martin Heidegger, *Introduction to Metaphysics*, New Haven, London: Yale University Press 2000, p. 1
67 "Why are there beings at all instead of nothing? That is the question. Presumably it is no arbitrary question. 'Why are there beings at all instead of nothing?'—this is obviously the first of all questions." See: ibid., p. 1, and Heidegger, *Being and Time*, p. 39.

The elementary things also still exist. As Ernst Cassirer taught us, we have to acknowledge the ambiguity of words. The word *water* can be used in all sorts of ways, not least metaphorically. Nevertheless, water has an elementary scientific essence: H_2O.[68] It is necessary to pose the scientific question "what is water?" A legal-ethical word like *murder* has a clearly delineated definition: the intentional, unlawful, and premeditated killing of a person. It would be absurd to accuse a jurist of "essentialist thought" when he or she is trying to determine the essential characteristics of the crimes set down in the Criminal Code. In that sense, jurists, judges, prosecutors, and legal scholars at universities are always "essentialists" in the contested sense of the word: they need to reflect on the delineation of definitions. Of course, a jurist knows that there is no definition of *theft* or *murder* written in the sky by God's own hand, or that such definitions are waiting to be discovered in some Platonic realm of ideas. Because whether a death constitutes a murder depends on the elements of the definition, a definition that was devised by people, in democratic states by a democratically controlled legislator, not one that was derived from some revelation. In a democracy, a law is the expression of the will of the people. In a theocracy, a law is the expression of the will of God (or of those who claim to speak on God's behalf).[69] We began this chapter of *A New Introduction to Legal Method* with a quotation from Bertrand Russell: "Deduction from inspired books is the method of arriving at truth employed by jurists, Christians, Mohammedans, and Communists."[70] This was an amusing witticism, but we now recognize that it is also misleading. The "inspired book" to which Russell refers is something very different for jurists than it is for religious believers. In a democracy, a book of laws is created by the people. As such, the deductions the judge makes on the basis of this book constitute the drawing of conclusions from something the people *themselves* have established. This kind of deduction is very different from the deduction a theologian makes based on the supposed will of God. In a democracy, the book of laws is based on *self-determination* or *autonomy*, on the community imposing laws on

---

68 Martin says about this example: "To say that something is water is to say neither that is something that has the chemical constituency H_2O (that is, the essential property of water) nor that it is something that has all (or many) of the accidental properties (wet, colorless, tasteless, etc.). What follows is that no descriptivist account of the meaning of this general term is correct, that is, that the attribution of this general term is not semantically equivalent to the attribution of any description. Well, then, what do we mean by 'water'. … General terms apply to an open-ended set of things, some of which we have never had any contact with." See: Robert Martin, *The Meaning of Language*, Cambridge, MA: The MIT Books 1994, pp. 200–201.

69 See more extensively about this: "The separation of church and state," in: Paul Cliteur and Afshin Ellian, eds., *A New Introduction to Jurisprudence: Legality, Legitimacy, and the Foundations of the Law*, London, New York: Routledge 2019, pp. 75–114.

70 Russell, *The Scientific Outlook*, p. 33.

itself. Theological deduction is based on *heteronomy,* on another authority imposing the law.

It can also be phrased like this: the Platonic essences are constructed in a different sphere of being, on the other side of this world. The legal essences are established by us, ourselves. Various factors, such as time and culture, are important in this. Still, even when a death is not classified as a murder, the essence of the term *murder* remains intact. A term like *social class* also has a delineated, formalist essence: a group of people who are connected in some (economic, political, religious, or ethnic) way. We see this when Marx poses this question to a social class (a group of workers) based on their economic position: how could the workers be emancipated? In answering this how-question, Marx posits his theories about a violent revolution. Here, especially, Popper's criticism of Marx decries the lack of a how-question as the foundation of the revolution.

In recent decades, nuanced theories have been developed about the concept of "essence." In *Scientific Essentialism* (2001), Brian Ellis makes a distinction between two major "worldviews." The first is the mechanical worldview, like that of Descartes, Newton, Locke, Hume, and even Kant. According to this worldview, what happens in the world depends "essentially on what the laws of nature happen to be."[71] So it does not depend on what things are or under what circumstances they exist. The second "worldview" is essentialism, which Ellis defends. He wants to prevent the ascension of a new medieval Aristotelian school. He appeals to quantum physics and demonstrates that the distinction between different chemical elements is real and absolute. So, the laws were born of essential, constitutive aspects of elements interacting with one another.[72] Scientific essentialism enables the making of distinctions in the world of real objects.[73] This ontological approach regularly appeals to the natural sciences. About the social sciences Ellis observes that its practitioners are strictly anti-essentialist. He comes to the following conclusion about this:

> They associate essentialism with just about everything that is bad in social theory and practice—for example, with racism, social Darwinism, sexism, and other positions that play down the roles of culture, circumstances, education or oppression in the formation of character.[74]

71 Brian Ellis, *Scientific Essentialism*, Cambridge: Cambridge University Press 2001, p. 1.

72 "According to scientific essentialism, therefore, all of the law of nature, from the most general (for example, the conservation laws and the global structural principles) or the more specific (for example, laws defining the structures of molecules of various kinds, or specific laws of chemical interaction) derive from the essential properties of the object and events that constitute it, and must hold in any world of the same natural kind as ours." Ibid., p. 4.

73 See the chapter on "powers and dispositions" in ibid., pp. 106–140.

74 Ibid., p. 177.

It is not assumed in scientific essentialism that the attitude or ability of people is determined by biological or other inherited structures. Besides this scientific essentialism, there is also the "real essentialism."

The latter philosophy of science was developed by David Oderberg in the book *Real Essentialism* (2007). Oderberg begins his book with a polemical observation: "That there are at least some things in the world that have essences is a proposition to which more philosophers are prepared to subscribe than there once were."[75] He also notes that, since the 1970s, and especially due to the scientific publications of Saul Kripke and Hilary Putnam, there has been a revival of essentialism. Oderberg opposes the illusion of a search for inner structures subscribed to by Ellis, Kripke, and Putnam.[76] He searches for the form: "The central concept deployed to carry out this explanatory work is that of form. Form is decidedly not hidden or inner structure."[77] Inner structures do exist, but they are not a necessity. Michelangelo's David does not have an inner structure, but it is an entity with a form. "Real essentialism" is not a revival of Plato's true reality because it is concerned with things that are and terms that are knowable and definable and interpretable. In his mathematical, metaphysical study, he seeks to show that his real essentialism, unlike nominalists who believe in individual essences (*haecceities*), postulates essences (*quiddities*) universally.[78] Popper's methodological concern[79] with regard to essentialism has to do with the curtailment of the growth and development of science. Essentialism supposedly slowed this down, because the attention paid to essences prevents the formulation of general theories, which Popper believes is at the heart of scientific growth. Conversely, Oderberg posits that essentialism is a positive stimulus for scientific progress. After all, an essentialist should not look for the most universal classification, but for the most specific classification of characterization:

> The most specific characterization is what marks gold off from everything else in the universe and so explains the features that give it its particular identity in the scheme of reality. It is logically possible for ultimate specificity to be reached without reaching an ultimate level of generality.[80]

---

75 David Oderberg, *Real Essentialism*, New York, London: Routledge 2007, p. 1.
76 Ibid., p. 13. See also: Hilary Putnam, *Mind, Language and Reality, Philosophical Papers* (volume 2), Cambridge: Cambridge University Press 1975; Saul Kripke, "Identity and Necessity," in: M. Munitz, ed., *Identity and Individuation*, New York: New York University Press 1971, pp. 136–164; Nathan Salmon, *Reference and Essence* (second edition), New York: Prometheus Books 2005, pp. 253–264.
77 Oderberg, *Real Essentialism*, p. 16.
78 Ibid., p. 21.
79 Karl Popper, *Objective Knowledge*, Oxford: Clarendon Press 1979, p. 196.
80 Oderberg, *Real Essentialism*, pp. 34–35.

To an essentialist looking for inner structures, H_2O is the essence of water. However, to real essentialism, that is only part of its essence: there are many more possible structures to be found in the discovered essence. In addition, the real essentialist does not search for endless hidden structures, like a movement called *hidden structure essentialism* does.[81] With this, Oderberg demonstrates that the growth of science would not be hampered if scientists were only focused on essences and not on the formulation of scientific theories. The essences and the formulation of scientific theories do not necessarily have to get in each other's way.

Popper's radical rejection of any form of essence and all what-questions is viewed as a problem, particularly in the fields of politics, ethics, and the law. Although Popper opposes moral and political relativism, his anti-essentialist dogma does lead to moral relativism. Martha Nussbaum pointed out the ethical and political consequences of anti-essentialism, and so also of the Popperian approach. In "Human Functioning and Social Justice: In Defense of Aristotelian Essentialism" (1992), she joins the critique of Putnam and others.[82] Putnam was concerned about the ethical implications of a philosophy of science that suffers from "method fetishism."[83] Nussbaum made a name for herself in the world of philosophy with her detailed study of Aristotle.[84] However, she was confronted at the time by intellectuals who viewed criticism of the human rights situation in developing countries as an "essentialist" and therefore reprehensible perspective, as "essentialist talk of human functioning and human capability." In short, there is no such thing as a universal "human" and there are therefore also no "human rights." Such notions are only the essentialist ideas of Westerners. This critique of human rights is very old; it was being voiced by American cultural anthropologists even before the Universal Declaration of Human Rights (1948) was adopted by the United Nations.[85]

Nussbaum writes that "essentialism is becoming a dirty word in the academy and those parts of human life that are influenced by it."[86] Really, she

81 Ibid., p. 36.
82 Martha Nussbaum, "Human Functioning and Social Justice: In Defense of Aristotelian Essentialism," in: *Political Theory*, 20(2) (May 1992), pp. 202–246.
83 Hilary Putnam, "Reason and History," in: *Reason, Truth and History*, Cambridge: Cambridge University Press 1991, p. 188ff.
84 Martha Nussbaum, *Aristotle's De Motu Animalium*, Princeton: Princeton University Press 1978.
85 Statement on Human Rights, in: *American Anthropologist*, 49 (1947), pp. 539–543.
86 Nussbaum, "Human Functioning and Social Justice: In Defense of Aristotelian Essentialism," p. 205. The most famous modern-day representative of this tradition is the cultural anthropologist Clifford Geertz: Geertz, Clifford, "Anti Anti-Relativism," in: *American Anthropologist*, 86 (1984), pp. 263–278. Bassam Tibi reports on a discussion between Clifford Geertz and Ernest Gellner that took place in Amsterdam in 1994. Gellner argued in favor of "reviving the ideals of the Enlightenment against the challenge of

says, essentialism is a dirty word! She experienced this as an impediment to an effective dialogue about the protection of the rights of women and minorities, and to social justice. All her opponents, so anti-essentialists, spoke with "a certain air of superiority." Especially in the debates about ethics, this superiority was used as the foundation for an attack on metaphysical (but scientific) "real" essentialism and "internalist" essentialism.

Previously, we have discussed both essentialist positions. Nussbaum simply joins Putnam and others in their defense of universalism. She positioned herself in contrast to Bork's. The conservative American judge and legal scholar Robert Bork (1927–2012) believes there is no such thing as universal values:

> There is, he says, no principled way to distinguish the pain of a living being who is being tortured from the pain caused to a religious conservative by the knowledge that some couples in the state of Connecticut are using contraception.[87]

This is indeed the ultimate consequence when we consider everything to be contingent. This way of thinking leads to subjectivism, which renders human rights meaningless as soon as they are applied to people outside the own group. In *Reason and History* (1981), to which Nussbaum appeals, Putnam writes that no relativist wants to be a relativist on all subjects.[88] It is an astute remark by Putnam.[89]

Nussbaum accepts the criticism of essentialism when it comes to essentialists' unwillingness to accept the diversity between peoples and cultures. Her essentialist philosophy parries the criticism with an appeal to "basic human functions." *Needless to say*, this is extraordinarily essentialist because she offers a definition, or at least accepts the existing definitions, of the human being and human capabilities. Nussbaum posits that this is more an empathic concept than a metaphysical one: the recognition of the other as a human being despite all our differences.[90] All people die someday. Death is universal and essential for mankind, as is the fact that our bodies have comparable needs when we are alive: food, clothing, sex, mobility, and so on.

---

neo-fundamentalisms." The relativist Geertz, however, criticized this kind of "enlightenment fundamentalism." Geertz called for respect for "the cultural peculiarity of the other," to which Gellner replied "then one has to respect Hitlerism as 'the peculiarity of the Germans.'" Geertz viewed this critique as "unfair." See: Tibi, *Islamism and Islam*, p. 52.

87 Nussbaum, "Human Functioning and Social Justice: In Defense of Aristotelian Essentialism," p. 211.

88 Putnam, "Reason and History," p. 158.

89 See also: Cliteur and Ellian, *A New Introduction to Jurisprudence*, pp. 153–214.

90 Nussbaum, "Human Functioning and Social Justice: In Defense of Aristotelian Essentialism," p. 215.

We also share the ability to experience pain and pleasure, cognitive abilities, practical reason, and more. With this, Nussbaum paints a picture of the essence of mankind with the help of metaphysical ethics:

> The Aristotelian essentialist claims that a life that lacks any one of these, no matter what else it has, will be lacking in humanness. So it would be reasonable to take these things as a focus for concern, in asking how public policy can promote the good human beings. The list is, emphatically, a list of separate components.[91]

The question, however, is whether the empathic element adds anything to a philosophy-of-science debate about essentialism. Nussbaum ties political consequences to her Aristotelian essentialism: the need for essentialism in government policy. Her advocacy of essentialism in politics concludes with compassion as a shared characteristic of humanity.[92] Nussbaum returns, *de facto* and *de jure*, to the beginnings of philosophy: the universal terms, the universality of man, and therefore also the general terms.

In a discussion with an economist, she concluded that

> in the end, the confidence of the radical economist is unshaken: we are both victims of basic essentialist thinking, who fail to recognize the beauty of otherness. … Under the banner of their radical and politically correct 'anti-essentialism' march ancient religious taboos, the luxury of the pampered husband, ill health, ignorance, and death.[93]

A historically embedded and sensitive essentialism is what Nussbaum argues for, at least in 1992.

In 2012, Nussbaum refocused on the issues she had addressed 20 years before in "Human Functioning and Social Justice: In Defense of Aristotelian Essentialism" (1992). She did so in her book *The New Religious Intolerance: Overcoming the Politics of Fear in an Anxious Age*. Here, seemingly without noticing it, Nussbaum employs exactly the same kind of reasoning her opponents used in 1992. She takes the positions she herself had criticized so vehemently in 1992. In 2012, she suddenly becomes a critic of *universalism* and *essentialism*. Now, two decades later, she attacks the critics of the burka. Is the burka denigrating to women?

Nussbaum's answer takes the form of comparisons.

According to Nussbaum, sexual depictions, pornography, nude pictures, or very revealing clothing turn women into "things." She also believes that plastic surgery denigrates women: "Every time I undress in the locker room

---

91 Ibid., p. 222.
92 Ibid., p. 239.
93 Ibid., p. 204.

of my gym, I see women bearing the scars of liposuction, tummy tucks, breast implants."[94] And these are alterations to the female body that women have done to please men. These perceived improvements to their bodies *turn them into*, or allow them to *continue to be*, an object of desire to men.

Is this comparison convincing? Is getting breast implants comparable to being forced to wear a burka in countries where the theocratic government proscribes and violently enforces this?

Of course, an aesthetic ideal fueled by advertising can have a negative effect on women's self-image, but to suggest that Western women are just as oppressed as women in Iran because of this is simply absurd. A few differences are readily apparent when these examples are more closely scrutinized. We will limit ourselves to two points.

First, there is a difference between the reactions of the government and society to women not conforming to the practices that are compared in Iran and the Western countries. Breast augmentation is allowed in Western countries because the women who have one believe it makes them more attractive to men, but men in the Western world cannot *force* women to have the procedure done. In Iran, this is different, *mutatis mutandis*. In Iran, wearing a veil is not something that is recommended to women by advertising: the apparatus of the state forces women to conform to this obligation. Women who refuse end up in prison. There are no women in Dutch prisons who refused to get breast implants. That would, incidentally, create serious capacity problems. If Nussbaum's examples are taken to their extremes, it is possible to say that Western women would be just as oppressed as women in Saudi Arabia or Iran if they were dragged away by the religious police, brought to special clinics, and forced to undergo breast enlargement surgery. Only if the women in Nussbaum's dressing room can tell such a tale do her comparisons make any sense. Beauty treatments, and even surgical procedures that are freely chosen, cannot be compared to a burka, the wearing of which has to be enforced by divinely mandated police action.

A second reason why Nussbaum's comparison seems strained is that the reason why women in Iran wear the burka is fundamentally different from why women in the Western world get breast implants. Women in Iran who wear burkas do this in order to be *less attractive* to other men. They have to hide everything that makes them attractive as women. Women in the Western world who get breast implants do it especially to be *more attractive* to men. In the Western world, the specifically feminine is cultivated—albeit sometimes in too explicit a fashion. In Iran, it is suppressed.

Apparently, Nussbaum has been seduced by the comparison because, in both cases, it is the *interests of men* that inspired both practices. In the case

---

94 Martha Nussbaum, *The New Religious Intolerance: Overcoming the Politics of Fear in an Anxious Age*, Cambridge, MA, London: The Belknap Press of Harvard University Press 2012, p. 115.

of the burka, this is the man's interest to have full, exclusive possession of his wife, a possession that cannot even be infringed upon by the looks of other men, and in the case of the breast implants, it is the interest of the man to enjoy the sight of a woman with unnaturally perfect breasts.

The Dutch writer F. Springer (1932–2011), author of *Teheran: een zwanenzang* [Teheran: A Swan Song], a 1991 novel about the Iranian revolution of 1979, understood the ideology of the Shiite fundamentalists who reintroduced the burka after it had been banned by Reza Khan (1878–1944). Springer writes:

> Reza Khan, the father of this shah, was a grim cavalry man who rode into Tehran in 1924 with a band of ruffians, placed himself on the throne, cut down rebellious tribes in the interior, forbade the women of Persia to wear the veil, and, as a crowning achievement, established the Pahlavi Dynasty. He was possessed of a feverish urgency to transform the backward country into a modern society, but the Second World War interfered, and Reza Shah ended his life in exile in Johannesburg.[95]

Put plainly: Nussbaum's comparison makes no sense. Nussbaum asks us, on the basis of "politeness," to restrain ourselves when it comes to condemning the burka. The true meaning of the symbol eludes her. What she also does not see is that social change sometimes requires decisive measures. If Europeans had behaved politely in the nineteenth and twentieth centuries with regard to the values of misogynistic Christianity, no woman could ever have become a professor in the first place.

As the feminist Alice Schwarzer (*b.* 1942) understands well, a battle is being waged inside and outside of the Islamic world for the position of women.[96] Nussbaum would do well to align herself with *this kind* of feminism. She can find inspiration from the French feminists Chadortt Djavann,[97] Jeanette Bougrab,[98] and Caroline Fourest,[99] or from the Italian

95 F. Springer, *Teheran: een zwanezang* [Teheran: A Swan Song], Amsterdam: Querido 1991, p. 42.

96 Alice Schwarzer, *Die Antwort* [The Answer], Cologne: Kiepenheuer & Witsch 2007; Alice Schwarzer, ed., *Die Grosse Verschleierung: für Integration, gegen Islamismus* [The Great Veil: For Integration, Against Islamism], Cologne: Kiepenheuer & Witsch 2010.

97 Chadortt Djavann, *À mon corps defendant, l'occident*, Paris: Flammarion 2007; Chahdortt Djavann, *La muette*, Paris: Flammarion 2008; Chahdortt Djavann, *Bas les voiles!* Paris: Gallimard 2003; Chahdortt Djavann, *Comment lutter efficacement contre l'idéologie islamique* [How to Effectively Fight Islamic Ideology], Paris: Éditions Grasset 2016.

98 Jeanette Bougrab, *Ma république se meurt* [My Republic Is Dying], Paris: Éditions Grasset 2013; Jeanette Bougrab, *Maudites* [Cursed], Paris: Albin Michel 2015; Jeanette Bougrab, *Lettre d'exil: La barbarie et nous*, Paris: Le Éditions du Cerf 2017; Jeanette Bougrab, *Lettre aux femmes voilées et à ceux qui les soutiennent*, Paris: Les éditions du Cerf 2019.

99 Caroline Fourest, *Quand la gauche a du courage: chroniques résolument progressistes et républicaines*, Paris: Éditions Grasset 2012; Caroline Fourest, *Génie de la laïcité* [The Genius of Secularism], Paris: Éditions Grasset 2016.

Oriana Fallaci.[100] These women are demanding control and authority over and protection of their bodies in and outside of the public space.[101] Does the legal order have a role to play here? It was Nussbaum herself who, in 1992, argued in favor of the universality of rights based on an essence of humanity, an essence of humans that is the same for all people. Human rights, as they were set down in the *Universal Declaration of Human Rights* (1948), apply to all people on the basis of an essence of what it is to be human, even if relativists like Clifford Geertz and others do not approve.

The incoherence of incoherence (*Tahafut al-Tahafut*)

"Without sensibility no object would be given to us, and without understanding none would be thought. Thoughts without content are empty, intuitions without concepts are blind." These are the words of Immanuel Kant.[102] There must be objects that are observed, and that which has been observed has to be put into words in order to be understood. Therefore, there is a balance between the general and the concrete, the universal and the individual. When we defend a realistic form of essentialism, we are also defending the position of philosophers of Islam such as Ibn Rushd of Averroes (1126–1198). *Tahafut al-Tahafut* (The Incoherence of Incoherence)[103] is the title of the famous philosophical polemic he co-authored with Al-Ghazali (1058–1111), who, in his own book *Tahafut al-Falasifa* (The Incoherence of Philosophers),[104] considered philosophy to be unnecessary and in conflict with religion, that is: Islam. Al-Ghazali was a philosopher who wanted to put an end to philosophy in general, and Popper is a philosopher of science who wants to put an end to a particular form of philosophy, namely the ancient and medieval philosophies about ontology—except his own philosophy of

---

100 Oriana Fallaci, "Ayatollah Khomeini," September 1979, in: Oriana Fallaci, ed., *Interviews with History and Conversations with Power*, New York: Rizzoli 2011, pp. 172–262; Oriana Fallaci, "Mohammed Riza Pahlavi," October 1973, in: Oriana Fallaci, *Interviews with History and Conversations with Power*, New York: Rizzoli 2011, pp. 151–172; Oriana Fallaci, *Entretien avec moi-même—L'Apocalypse*, Paris: Éditions du Rocher 2007.

101 Afshin Ellian, "De sterfelijke god en de eeuwige terugkeer naar gelijkheid. Gelijkheid en vrijheid, maar voor wie en tot hoever?" [The Mortal God and the Eternal Return to Equality. Equality and Freedom, but for Whom and How Much?], in: Jasper Doomen and Afshin Ellian, eds., *De strijd van gelijkheid en vrijheid* [The War of Equality and Freedom], Den Haag: BJU 2015, pp. 25–48.

102 Kant, *Critique of Pure Reason*, p. 115 (B. 75), pp. 193–194.

103 Averroes, *Averroes' Tahafut Al-Tahafut* [The Incoherence of Incoherence], Cambridge: Cambridge University Press 1987.

104 "The source of their unbelief is in their hearing high-sounding names such as Socrates, Hippocrates, Plato Aristotle, and their likes and the exaggeration and misguidedness of groups of their followers in describing their minds." Al-Ghazali, *The Incoherence of the Philosophers, A parallel English-Arabic text*, Provo, UT: Brigham Young University Press 2000, p. 2.

science. The title of this section is ambiguous, and, at the same time, it is a tribute to Averroes and his apology for philosophy and science.

Historicism was the core of Popper's critique of the determinist philosophy of Hegel and especially Marx. This determinism in the name of freedom, or reason, or the class struggle brings forth a totalitarian movement. Popper did not say that parts or passages from Hegel or Marx's philosophy are not inspiring. Nor does Popper claim that there are no events that inevitably lead to certain situations. The deterministic view of history is applied in particular to the whole of history, not to individual events in a certain time or era. It is important to make this clear, otherwise, a misconception might arise that theoretical history or a theory of history is useless. Even Popper admits that "there are a few correct elements in historicism."[105] The Enlightenment or other historical periods could be philosophized about or theorized in a justified way. Without this theorization, all that remains are literary stories, persons, and events. What Popper does not want to acknowledge, however, is the fact that the Hegelian philosophy of history also made a positive contribution to the theorization of history. In the end, Popper also comes to the conclusion that there is room for "a more detailed study of the logic of situations."[106] Incidentally, without some form of the theorization of history, a philosophical analysis of totalitarian regimes and movements would not be possible. See on this Hannah Arendt's monumental study *The Origins of Totalitarianism* (1951).[107] Finally, Popper also produces all sorts of theories on progress, such as liberalism and democracy, in which a number of determinants can be found. Nevertheless, this is not historicism. After all, historicism implies that history in its totality is determined by a general providence.

The logic of the situation sounds empirical, but this is a normative proposition in the end: the logic is normative. And that which is normative has a general character. Yes, this brings us back to universal terms. There are no essences, but there are universal terms. And these terms are not all empty. With his theory of incoherence, Popper addresses the philosophies of Plato and Aristotle and Hegel and Marx. Apparently, Popper does find essences in the philosophies of philosophers and the theories of theoreticians that he can extensively analyze and critique. Are these essences because they were theoretically devised? No, they are ideas that Popper views as comprising certain essences. For instance, in describing and explaining the emergence and development of the open society, Popper devises a kind of "essence" for

---

105 Popper, *The Poverty of Historicism*, p. 149.
106 Ibid.
107 The first two parts are based on detailed historical studies on the basis of which she develops her theories. See: Hannah Arendt, *The Origins of Totalitarianism*, New York: Harvest Book 1979.

the open society and the closed society: the tribal magical versus the demo-cratic society. He tries to escape the above-mentioned incoherence by posit-ing that he is not claiming that this method is scientific because a historical interpretation can never be tested as rigorously as a regular hypothesis: "The interpretation is mainly a *point of view*, whose value lies in its fertility, in its power to throw light upon the historical material."[108] However, the term *point of view* really cannot be the foundation for such a comprehensive theory about democracy and the open society. He was probably criticized for this at the time because, in 1961, he published a new afterword to his book. In it, he notes that transcending the dualism of facts and metrics was crucial in the Hegelian philosophy of identity:

> All standards are historical: they are historical facts, stages in de devel-opment of reason, which is the same as the development of the ideal and of the real. There is nothing but fact; and some of the social or historical facts are, at the same time, standards.[109]

If "reason" is replaced here with "democracy and the open society," a phi-losophy of identity also threatens to emerge from historical facts, the only difference being that Popper refuses to accept the consequences of this. Not only that, but Popper was able to reveal the essences of totalitarianism, of the totalitarian regime. He looked for essences in ideas and even in real-world political phenomena like regimes, and he found them.

Popper reconstructs Plato and Aristotle in order to understand the essence of their thought. They are, after all, the enemies of the open society! The essence? Popper can argue that this is about ideas, not about reality. Ideas can have essences. After all, ideas consist of theories and universal terms. But it is Popper himself who teaches us that these ideas can be dangerous. Plato and Aristotle's ideas, as essentialist frameworks, have contributed to totalitarian thought and thereby the birth of totalitarian movements and regimes. So it can be said that Popper believes that ideas can be realized, in other words, that ideas can materialize in the real world. The philosophical ideas were realized, or materialized, or have at least contributed in some fashion to the totalitarian manifestation in the real world. If that were not the case, Popper's book would have been wholly unnecessary. Ironically, the relationship between idea and reality could be explained in a Platonic or Aristotelian way. The Platonic version: the philosophical ideas of essential-ism and historicism have always existed independent from human action. However, those who have transformed the open society into a closed society have participated in these ideas. And the second, Aristotelian version: the

---

108 Popper, *The Open Society and Its Enemies (1. Plato)*, p. 171.
109 Ibid. (volume 2), pp. 394–395.

forms already existed in man or in history, and at some point, their potential was actualized. Or, as Popper himself says about Aristotle: "The form or essence of anything developing is identical with the purpose or end or final state towards which it develops."[110] Plato and Aristotle would probably find this application of their ontology laughable, and they would be right! This absurd situation was created by Popper himself: Plato and Aristotle's dangerous ideas have been realized, actualized, after 2000 years. Popper's methodological problem is not solved here by the use of the term *point of view* to describe the open society and explain totalitarianism. After all, Popper has created one thing, a whole, a manifestation of history that includes Plato and Aristotle's philosophical ideas. Again, this is not about the philosophical critique of Plato and Aristotle; this is about the enemies of the open society and the eventual effect of their ontology (essentialism) in the real world of politics; after all, Popper emphasized that historicism and essentialism go hand in hand. So, these are not worldviews or religions, because they exist expressly to change the real world.

The incoherence becomes even more glaring when we take a closer look at his discussion of democracy or the closed community. In this domain, Popper asks the what-questions (although they are hidden in long sentences). What is democracy? What is an open society? What is a closed society? Also, in a (fictional) polemic with Friedrich Engels, he explains what democracy is, listing all the elements that constitute democracy and its parameters.[111] In his essay "Three Views Concerning Knowledge" (1963), Popper again criticizes essentialism.[112] He posits that essentialism looks for the essential nature of things, for the reality behind the phenomena. And this is interpreted as the "ultimate explanation."[113] This critique was credibly parried by Oderberg: the ultimate explanation of a thing does not need to contain the highest possible generalization: "It is logically possible for ultimate specificity to be reached without reaching an ultimate level of generality."[114]

Popper assumes that essentialism in general, regardless of its form, tries to elevate theories to where they are beyond all doubt. When we are talking about a thing, we are no longer talking about theories. The acknowledged definition of water is true as long as it is not refuted. And if essences are a part of a theory, then its thesis and premises ought to be true. An essentialist explanation or description that places itself outside of time and space and that can never be tested is, indeed, not science at all, and certainly

---

110 Ibid., p. 5.
111 Ibid., pp. 160–162. See in addition the same essential approach with regard to the closed society: Ibid. (volume 1), pp. 171–176.
112 See on this also: Popper, *Realism and the Aim of Science*, pp. 135–138.
113 Karl Popper, *Conjectures and Refutations*, London, New York: Routledge 2002, p. 140.
114 Oderberg, *Real Essentialism*, p. 35.

not philosophy. Popper's requirement of testability also holds for essences. Popper reveals his true intention, thereby bringing a small ray of light to the darkness:

> Thus my criticism of essentialism does not aim at establishing the non-existence of essences; it merely aims at showing the obscurantist character of the role played by the idea of essences in the Galilean philosophy of science. In other words, my criticism tries to show that, whether essences exist or not, the belief in them does not help us in any way and indeed is likely to hamper us; so that there is no reason why the scientist should assume their existence.[115]

This is clarifying. Popper's true critique of essentialism turns out to be that we can never use the essence of a phenomenon *against* empiricism. However, we should attempt to discover essence *on the basis of empiricism*. And the essences we discover when we do that can always be adapted in the light of new empirical developments. Would these get in our way when we find out what the essence or construct of a certain phenomenon is? Would it be unimportant to know what the essence or essential structure of a disease is? Few deny the validity of a fundamental critique of Platonic essentialism. However, it is Popper himself who, in his article "Three Worlds" from 1978, sows confusion about his views. In this article, he challenges the thinkers who have a monistic or dualist worldview. He introduces three worlds: the first consists of "physical bodies"; the second is the psychological, mental world; and the third world consists of the products of human reason, such as language.[116] So Popper's third world, which consists of language, is not materialized, which is why he acknowledges that he might be charged with granting substance to non-existent things. However, what he seeks to show is that the third world has reality: "They may be real in that they may have a causal effect upon us, upon our world 2 experiences, and further upon our world 1 brains, and thus upon material bodies."[117] The mental world (2) is "thought process," and the world of language (3) is "thought contents." There is therefore a logical and even causal relationship between the phenomena of these worlds. Do these worlds constitute the return of Plato through the side door of epistemology? An unpleasant question for someone who transforms Plato's duality into a trinity! Transcendental thought is back as well:

---

115 Popper, *Conjectures and Refutations*, p. 141.
116 Accessed 9 December 2021, https://tannerlectures.utah.edu/_documents/a-to-z/p/popper80.pdf; see also: Karl Popper and John C. Eccles, *The Self and Its Brain. An Argument for Interactionism*, London, New York: Routledge 1977, pp. 36–50.
117 Accessed 9 December 2021, https://tannerlectures.utah.edu/_documents/a-to-z/p/popper80.pdf p. 150.

Man is certainly part of nature, but, in creating World 3, he has transcended himself and nature, as it existed before him. And human freedom is indeed part of nature, but it transcends nature—at least as it existed before the emergence of human language and critical thought, and of human knowledge.[118]

Popper argued that essentialism discovers our "ordinary world" as a facade behind which the true world is hidden.[119] But according to the later Popper,[120] hidden behind our ordinary world is language, which owes its existence to another world: the mental world.[121]

Criticism, including Popper's critique of essentialism, has spurred thought and science. But the issue here is the radical, absolute rejection of essentialism in all forms. This radical rejection not only has scientific but also ethical and political consequences. Because it fosters moral relativism. Martha Nussbaum's polemic, discussed earlier, showed the serious moral and political consequences anti-essentialism could have: the rejection of the universality of human beings;[122] the protection of women,[123] minorities, and homosexuals in other parts of the world; and the dialogue about social justice in and outside of the West, among other things. Popper later realized, because of the furor around his critique of essentialism, that his radicalness could stimulate moral and political relativism. In an afterword from 1961 to *The Open Society and Its Enemies* entitled "Facts, Standards, and Truth: a Further Criticism of Relativism,"[124] he posits that the most important philosophical ill of our time is intellectual and moral relativism.[125] In

---

118 Karl Popper, *The Open Universe. An Argument for Indeterminism*, London, New York: Routledge 2007, p.130.

119 Popper, *Conjectures and Refutations*, p. 154.

120 See on this: Popper and Eccles, *The Self and Its Brain*, pp. 86–88.

121 In his intellectual autobiography (1992), he revisits the three worlds: "I think that I was always a Cartesian dualist (although I never thought that we should talk about substances); and if not a dualist, I was certainly more inclined to pluralism than to monism." These and other words he uses on this subject further add to the confusion. See: Karl Popper, *Unended Quest. An Intellectual Autobiography*, London, New York: Routledge 2002, p. 218.

122 See: P.B. Cliteur, "Cultuurrelativisme als uitdaging voor de universaliteit" [Cultural Relativism as a Challenge to Universalism], in: P.B. Cliteur, ed., *De filosofie van mensenrechten*, second edition, Nijmegen: Ars Aequi Libri 1999, pp. 43–65.

123 See on this: Machteld Zee, *Choosing Sharia: Multiculturalism, Islamic Fundamentalism & British Sharia Councils*, The Hague: Eleven, 2015; Machteld Zee, *Heilige identiteiten: Op weg naar een shariastaat?* [Sacred Identities: Moving Towards a Sharia State?], Amsterdam: Querido 2016.

124 Popper, *The Open Society and Its Enemies* (volume 2), Princeton: Princeton University Press 1971, pp. 369–396; Karl Popper, *In Search of a Better World. Lectures and Essays from Thirty Years*, London: Routledge 2000, p. 5.

125 Popper, *The Open Society and Its Enemies* (volume 2), p. 369.

his contribution, he tries, wherever possible, to blame others, such as the existentialists, for relativism.[126] In his lecture in 1982 titled "Knowledge and the Shaping of Reality: the Search for a Better World," he does not mince words in his critique of relativism. At this time, all these relativists are like criminals to Popper:

> The philosophical relativism that hides behind the 'old and famous question' What is truth?' may open the way to evil things, such as a propaganda of lies inciting men to hatred. ... Relativism is one of the many crimes committed by intellectuals. It is a betrayal of reason and of humanity.

It is all a beautiful philosophical expose in which he nevertheless refuses to accept his own contribution to relativism (his absolute rejection of essentialism). Without some form of essentialism, we would have nothing but inductive methods and empiricism. The problem with inductive methods and their probability function was analyzed brilliantly by Popper himself in *The Logic of Scientific Discovery* (1934).[127] It has already been proven that a scientific theory cannot simply be developed on the basis of experiences and observations. By constantly appealing to experiences, one ends up in an infinite regress.[128] The observed phenomena have to be generalized in a general claim (the inductum), but they cannot in themselves claim the validity of the universality of the proposition according to Popper.[129] Scientific theories are not the summaries of observations; they are subjected to trial and error, Popper says. Finally, observations are subjective. This is not a disqualification of the empirical method. Even theories that are deductive have to be tested empirically, if not by the normative principles.

To perhaps clarify a few things for the reader, some conclusions will now be drawn, after which we will continue with a specific discussion of essentialism in Islam.

1. A phenomenon, a thing, or a worldview consists of an essence or is comprised of essences that form integral constructions.
2. Essences do not need to be eternal or unchangeable. The same is true of ideas, of worldviews that are realized in the world; they too could,

---

126 Ibid., p. 381.
127 Karl Popper, *The Logic of Scientific Discovery*, London, New York: Routledge 1999, pp. 27–33; pp. 14–214.
128 Ibid., p. 30.
129 "From a logical point of view, whenever we make an induction, we (tacitly or explicitly) make certain assumptions that are not justified by the observation material on which the generalization is directly based." See: Karl Popper, *The Two Fundamental Problems of the Theory of Knowledge*, London, New York: Routledge 2009, p. 37.

in interaction with other ideas or the real-world circumstances, change into new essences and constructions.

3. Essences are core characteristics of things, phenomena, or ideas.
4. Essences can be part of a theory or general proposition. When we say that all humans are mortal, we are adding an essence, namely mortality, to all humans. The testability and falsifiability of this then become the essence of a scientific theory.
5. Any notion of the absolute and unchanging essences of cultures is foolish. The idea that everything is formless, fluid, and relative is just as foolish.
6. Religions and worldviews have their own essences that can be deductively and empirically studied. However, the creator of these essences is not nature, but mankind, and mankind can destroy, change, enhance, or diminish his own creation.[130]
7. Historicism attributes absolute determinants to history. History in its totality is presented as a deterministic play. Not only the totalitarian regimes of the twentieth century, but also the political religions, such as political Islam, are steeped in historicism.[131]

In conclusion

In conclusion, some final and summarizing remarks:

1. Essences in another reality or ideal reality—if they even exist—fall outside the purview of science and philosophy. Science cannot say anything about them. In the words of Kant: this is about the sources of knowledge and the ways of knowing. The essences do not represent the whole truth. Structures and constructions are the foundations of a reality that is constantly in flux: a game of connection and separation.
2. Popper's critique of essentialism is justified when it comes to idealistic essentialism. However, what we might call empirical essentialism is no problem at all. Better yet, it is indispensable. Science is impossible

---

130 In this light, we cannot only interpret the texts of holy scriptures (like the Quran or the Bible) as independent wholes, but we can also interpret the official story of the birth of Islam or Christianity and their development in order to penetrate the essential structure of religion in different forms: the spiritual domain, the political-ethical domain, or the theological domain. Here, we are concerned with the political-ethical domain. Can these core characteristics (essences) of the original Islam or Christianity never change? No. At least, they cannot do so themselves: they are a part of history, after all. What believers choose to do with these essences, however, is entirely up to them. They do not have to blindly follow history. The believers can reinterpret their faith, or even change it. That is not something that will preoccupy any scientist!
131 See: Popper, *The Open Universe*, 2007.

without empirical essentialism. At the same time, science is always focused on the universal, on generalization. He who claims not to want to generalize says in effect that he does not wish to have science. The philosopher of science Hans Reichenbach rightly notes: "The essence of knowledge is *generalisation*."[132] He also says: "The art of discovery is therefore the art of correct generalisation."[133]

Popper posited that the essentialists deny "that we first bring a group of individual things together and then label them 'white.'" This is certainly true of certain thinkers in the Middle Ages, and, in a certain sense, of Plato as well. However, contrary to Popper's claim that we "[do not need to] believe in the existence of universal terms," we have to also acknowledge that there are universal terms in the form of theories, which were formed through language. Popper's critical rationalism is centered on theory formation: deduction and falsifiability. Universal concepts are necessary. How they came into being is not only an epistemological, philosophical, linguistic, or even theological question, but it is also an anthropological issue, dealing with the development and background of various peoples and languages. Dutch philosopher Ger Groot rightly notes that no manner of thought can function without the use of concepts.[134] Wrongly, Popper turns against Aristotle's methodological essentialism entirely and without nuance, because Aristotle is said to have asked what-questions (like: what is matter?) in his methodology. Earlier, we have demonstrated that, besides the how-questions, the what-questions are also of crucial importance to the methodological issues surrounding the theory of knowledge. We have also shown that Popper is inconsistent in his battle against Plato.

3. Historicism should not be confused with methodological essentialism. Historicism is concerned with set determinants in history that, through a kind of providence, cause history to move inexorably toward a certain point or circumstance. This cannot only be found in the theories of Karl Marx and Friedrich Engels, but also in political Islam. However, the historicism of political Islam is, contrary to Marx's optimistic historicism, apocalyptic and thus pessimistic for this earthly existence: true life begins in the hereafter.

4. The critique of historicism does not imply that we cannot form theories, make deductions, or identify significant aspects and instances (foundational moments) when we study history. In his *Introduction to*

---

132 Hans Reichenbach, *The Rise of Scientific Philosophy*, Los Angeles, London: University of California Press 1951, p. 5.

133 Ibid., p. 5.

134 Ger Groot, "Inleiding: dolende ridders en de roep van de rand" [Introduction: Wandering Knights and the Call of the Edge], in: Jacques Derrida, *Marges van de filosofie* [Margins of Philosophy], Kampen: Kok Agor 1995, p. 14.

the Human Sciences and *The Formation of the Historical World in the Human Sciences*, Wilhelm Dilthey (1833–1911) offers a logical, realistic framework, and also a method for the study of history.

Dilthey posited that all science is the science of experience. Rightly, an important "but" was added to this Kantian perspective: "but the original connectedness of all experience, which is thereby validated, is conditioned by our consciousness."[135] So, the convergence of observations comprises the logical validity of general propositions, or theories. As such, there are three classes of propositions in the humanities: (1) observational statements (the historical element of knowledge); (2) abstractions, the theoretical element; and (3) value judgments.[136] In the logical phase, something extraordinary happens: "every specific science only emerges through the artificial detachment of a part of the historical-societal reality."[137] For Hannah Arendt (1906–1975) or Claude Lefort (1924–2010), this artificial act is a requirement for uncovering the essence (the essence of totalitarianism) from all sorts of facts and tidbits of information. This is a normative philosophical methodology without which ideas, worldviews, religions, and regimes cannot be studied. What remains are the facts. An induction of these facts will not be able to produce a logical theory. This is exactly what Popper did when he analyzed totalitarianism.

5. It was Dilthey who, in contrast to the positivist, empirical, or idealist understanding of the history of the nineteenth century, posited that the historical world does not know any natural-science-type causality (causality as necessary regularity). However, the logic of the situation (Popper) could spark a causal chain. Dilthey summarizes the method of the natural sciences in two terms: self-reflection and understanding (*verstehen*).[138] This brings us to hermeneutics as the method

---

135 Wilhelm Dilthey, "Voorwoord bij het Eerste Boek van de inleiding tot de geesteswetenschappen" [Foreword to the First Book of the Introduction to the Human Sciences], in: Wilhelm Dilthey, ed., *Kritiek van de historische rede. Inleiding en redactie Jozef Keulartz* [Critique of Historical Reason. Introduction and Editing Jozef Keulartz], Amsterdam: Boom 1994, p. 68; Willem Dilthey, "Einleitung in die Geisteswissenschaften. Versuch einer Grundlegung für das Studium der Gesellschaft und der der Geschichte" (Erste Band) [Introduction to the Human Sciences: An Attempt to Lay a Foundation for the Study of Society and History], in: *Wilhelm Dilthey Gesammelte Schriften (Bd. 1)*[Wilhelm Dilthey Collected Works], Göttingen: Vandenhoeck & Ruprecht 1979, pp. 3–120.
136 Dilthey, "Voorwoord bij het Eerste Boek van de inleiding tot de geesteswetenschappen", p. 85.
137 Ibid., p. 86.
138 Wilhelm Dilthey, "Grundlegung der Wissenschaften vom Menschen, der Gesellschaft und der Geschichte: Ausarbeitungen und Entwürfe zum zweiten Band der Einleitung in die Geisteswissenschaften," in: *Wilhelm Dilthey Gesammelte Schriften (Bd. 19)*, Göttingen: Vandenhoeck & Ruprecht 1992, pp. 276–277.

of the humanities, which Dilthey believes is "understanding and interpreting."[139] The interpretation of the text on which ideas and religions are based can be arrived at in different ways.[140] For instance, Spinoza's critique of the Bible offers a technique for various forms of interpretation, Gadamer (1900–2002) says. In a reinterpretation of Schleiermacher (1768–1834) and hermeneutics, Gadamer writes that, in a principled sense, understanding always moves in a circle, making it "essential (*wesentlich*)[141] to repeatedly move back and forth between the whole and its constituent parts."[142] Circularity takes us from the whole to the parts and vice versa, causing the circle to keep expanding, Gadamer says. Scientists' only job is to understand objects, human beings, history, religions, and so on, and to explain their essences.[143] A realistic approach to the term *essence* is a part of critical rationalism that studies the structures of various constructions (however temporary or changeable they may be) in order to use these terms to formulate theories and hypotheses, which are, naturally, subject to a falsification procedure.

139 Dilthey, "Voorwoord bij het Eerste Boek van de inleiding tot de geesteswetenschappen", p. 155.

140 Wilhelm Dilthey, *Introduction to the Human Sciences* (Wilhelm Dilthey Selected Works Volume I), Princeton: Princeton University Press 1989, p. 439.

141 Hans-Georg Gadamer, *Wahrheit und Methode. Grundzüge einer philosophischen Hermeneutik* [Truth and Method. Foundations of Philosophical Hermeneutics], Tübingen: Mohr Siebeck 2010, p. 194.

142 Gadamer, *Wahrheit und Methode. Grundzüge einer philosophischen Hermeneutik*, p. 194.

143 Heidegger puts it in terms of objectivity: "The historiographical disclosure of the 'past' is grounded in fateful repetition and is so far from being 'subjective' that it alone guarantees the 'objectivity' of historiography." See: Martin Heidegger, *Being and Time*, p. 375.

Chapter 5

Three types of legal interpretation

Introduction

In the previous four chapters, we commented on the method of legal science and scholarship. In the first chapter, we have seen that Classical Legal Doctrine is not the only approach to legal matters and that new techniques (ELS) have come to the fore. In Chapter 2, we have shown that the forerunner of contemporary empirical approaches to the law can be found in a movement known as American realism. Chapters 3 and 4 have given us an idea of one of the most well-known philosophers on the scientific method, viz. Karl Popper. And the fourth chapter ended with the method of hermeneutics. In the fifth and final chapter of *A New Introduction to Legal Method*, we will continue with a reflection on hermeneutics, particularly with some authors that have made a great impression on the Dutch legal and scholarly community.

Legal methodology is not only important for the question of the scientific character of legal science, but it also plays a direct role in legal practice. What do jurists, and especially the final arbiters: *judges*, do when they *apply*, *interpret*, or *shape* the law?

The acts of "applying," "interpreting," or "shaping" the law represent three visions of the practice of the administration of justice by the courts—visions that have serious constitutional implications. Do judges merely apply the law? Do they sometimes have to interpret it (and make choices when doing so)? Or do they actually go so far as to shape the law—*creating* law? This chapter analyzes the development thinking on the administration of justice has gone through in the Netherlands *and* what (normative) state-theory positions can be taken with regard to this development. The chapter does this by reflecting on one of the most influential Dutch works on this subject: *Three Types of Legal Method* (1963) by G.J. Wiarda, a work in which both aspects—developments in the theory of legal interpretation and an evaluation of them—come together in a strongly characteristic way, perhaps especially of the Dutch tradition of thought.

DOI: 10.4324/9781003282570-6

The Netherlands is an interesting case study when it comes to legal interpretation and the role of the judge in the system of government. The prohibition against judicial review in article 120 of the Constitution prevents
Dutch courts from subjecting the legislature's most important products,
laws (in a formal sense), to judicial review. At the same time, articles 93 and
94 of the Constitution do enable courts to review laws against "provisions
binding on all" in treaties. This produces a specific dynamic in the development of legal interpretation in which openness to norms that are not primarily nationally conceived—in other words, Europeanization (through the
ECHR) and internationalization (through treaties)—is a clear motive. There
is no such motive in other countries, or its presence is much less significant.
The Netherlands is one of the very few countries with a prohibition against
judicial review in their constitution: in practice, only Finland comes close,
and only in Ethiopia is it specifically included in the constitution.[1] Not only
that, but the Netherlands is the *only* country that has judicial review against
international norms but not against its own constitution.

In the Netherlands, the discussion about the nature and scope of the judge's
work is much less polarized than in the American tradition. In fact, there is
hardly any polarization at all in the Netherlands. Starting in the 1950s, a
basic consensus developed around the relationship between the courts and
the legislative branch that might be best described as "the prevailing paradigm about legal interpretation." This paradigm is characterized by a high
degree of trust in the judiciary and few concerns about—let alone protest
against—a further increase in judicial interference in the steering of society.
The consensus manifests not only in opinion-forming among legal scholars
but also in the high degree of confidence the public has in the legitimacy
of judicial decisions. Calling verdicts into question usually only happens in
smaller circles and among colleagues, for instance, in an annotation a legal
scholar might make to a judicial decision. The Netherlands does not have a
tradition of great political debates about verdicts like the United States does
about cases such as *Roe v. Wade* (1973, about abortion),[2] *Brown v. Board of
Education* (1954, about segregation),[3] or *Dred Scott* (1856, about slavery).[4]

1 Leonard Besselink, "Constitutionele toetsing in vergelijkend perspectief," *Ars Aequi*, 52
  (2003), pp. 89–95; of course, relativization is possible: as Besselink notes, in countries without a written constitution, there is less opportunity for review, and if there is no explicit
  prohibition against review in a country, the review can still be very limited in practice.
2 Lawrence M. Friedman, *American Law in the 20th Century*, New Haven, London: Yale
  University Press, 2002, pp. 236–237, pp. 328–330, pp. 530–532. Bernard Schwartz, *A History of the Supreme Court*, New York, Oxford: Oxford University Press 1993, pp. 337–61.
  Edward Lazarus, *Closed Chambers: The Rise, Fall, and Future of the Modern Supreme
  Court*, New York: Penguin Books 1999 (1998), pp. 350–355, pp. 378–381.
3 Friedman, *American Law in the 20th Century*, pp. 288–297. Schwartz, *A History of the Supreme
  Court*, pp. 167–168, 286–310. Lazarus, *Closed Chambers*, pp. 298–299, pp. 376–377.
4 Friedman, *American Law in the 20th Century*, p. 532. Schwartz, *A History of the Supreme
  Court*, pp. 105–125. Lazarus, *Closed Chambers*, pp. 246–247.

Of course, the Netherlands also has important judicial rulings in which the Supreme Court "turns"; the *Lindenbaum-Cohen* case (1919)[5] being one of the most famous, but that appears to be something different than the American cases mentioned earlier.

And yet, the Netherlands does also have a practice of judicial review of laws against higher law (human rights). From the early 1950s onwards, the Dutch courts have been granted the power to test laws against provisions applicable to all in treaties (articles 93 and 94 of the Constitution), analogous to the American judicial review against the Constitution that was made possible in 1803 (*Marbury v. Madison*).[6] But the debate about judicial review of laws against treaties that is so characteristic of the American tradition when it comes to review against the Constitution has remained absent.[7] The Supreme Court's ruling in *Marbury v. Madison* led to a gradual increase in influence for the judiciary in the constitutional system relative to the legislative bodies.

Dutch authors about legal interpretation

Although the process of the gradual increase of judicial influence on the steering of society in the Netherlands has been acknowledged by authors like the legal scholar and judge G.J. Wiarda (1906–1988), the professor Paul Scholten (1875–1946), and others, it was viewed as a more or less natural result of societal developments that gave no reason for alarm.

In this chapter, we will describe and analyze the Dutch view of legal interpretation, focusing mostly on one of the most influential works on this subject: the book *Three Types of Legal Method* (1963) by G.J. Wiarda.[8]

Acquainting ourselves with Wiarda's theory of legal interpretation teaches us a great deal, not even so much about legal interpretation, but especially about how the central claim of the role of the judiciary in the Netherlands has been accepted more or less without question. This unproblematic acceptance of judicial supremacy can also be found in the work of earlier authors, such as Paul Scholten, particularly his *General Method of Private Law* (1931),[9] to whom Wiarda also refers, but we will focus on

---

5 In this case, the question was whether illegitimate ought to be identical to unlawful. The Supreme Court believed that it should not, which meant that unwritten law was acknowledged in the context of the unlawful act.

6 James M. O'Fallon, "Marbury," in: *Stanford Law Review*, 44 (1992), pp. 219–260.

7 See about this: Antonin Scalia, *Scalia Speaks: Reflections on Law, Faith, and Life Well Lived*, Christopher J. Scalia and Edward Whelan, eds., New York: Crown Forum 2017; Arie-Jan Kwak, ed., *Holy Writ: Interpretation in Law and Religion*, Farnham, Burlington: Ashgate 2009.

8 G.J. Wiarda, *Drie typen van rechtsvinding* [Three Types of Legal Method], first edition, Zwolle: W.E.J. Tjeenk Willink 1963.

9 P. Scholten, *Algemeen Deel* [General Method of Private Law], third edition, Zwolle: W.E.J. Tjeen Willink 1974 (1931).

Wiarda's work here, because his book is more recent, and because, in the form of a fourth edition (1999) edited by T. Koopmans (1929–2015), it influenced generations of post-War Dutch jurists and judges.[10]

In addition, the way in which judicial supremacy was realized in the Netherlands has acquired a specifically Dutch *couleur locale*. This is related to the fact that the Netherlands has had a prohibition against judicial review against the Constitution since 1848 (in article 120), but since the early 1950s, there has been judicial review of laws against provisions binding on all in treaties.[11] In that way, a vigorous practice of judicial review has also contributed to "Europeanization," in the sense of the transfer of sovereignty from the Netherlands to European supranational institutions.

This chapter will deal with the relationship between the legislature and the judiciary, primarily by focusing on Wiarda's theory of legal interpretation. Legal interpretation is an important part of the methodology of legal science. For this chapter's conclusions, we refer to the section "in conclusion" on its final pages. The reader who wishes to see beforehand where this line of argument will lead can also read these final pages first. The chapter consists of two parts. The first part deals with state theory, the separation of powers and the relationship between the legislative and judicial branches, and reflects on some key moments in Western state development. The second part focuses primarily on Wiarda's book.

Part I: General introduction to the separation of powers

1648: the nation-state

The nation-state as a political organizing principle emerged in 1648 with the "Westphalian system," which was born out of the Peace of Westphalia (1648).[12] From that moment on, nation-states were recognized as unified

10 G.J. Wiarda, *Drie typen van rechtsvinding* [Three Types of Legal Method], fourth edition, edited and annotated by Mr. T. Koopmans, Zwolle: W.E.J. Tjeenk Willink 1999 (1963).

11 E.C.M. Jurgens, "Over de illusie dat rechterlijke toetsing van de wet aan onze huidige Grondwet zinvol is," in: Paul Cliteur, Hans Franken, Wim Voermans, eds., *Naar een Europese Grondwet*, The Hague: Boom Juridische Uitgevers 2004, pp. 117–123; Erik Jurgens, "Nogmaals toetsing van wet aan Grondwet," in: *Namens*, November 1989, p. 37; G. van den Bergh, "Beschouwingen over het toetsingsrecht," in *Nederlands Juristenblad*, 26 May 1951, pp. 417–425; P.B. Cliteur, "Argumenten voor en tegen constitutionele toetsing," in: *Nederlands Juristenblad*, 1989, pp. 1369–1375; P.B., Cliteur, ed., *Constitutionele toetsing*, with commentary from R.A.V. van Haersolte, J.M. Polak, and T. Zwart, The Hague: Prof. mr. B.M. Teldersstichting 1991; Lucas Prakke, *Toetsing in het publiekrecht*, Assen: Van Gorcum & Comp. N.V. 1972; M.R. Wijnholt, "Toetsing aan rechtsbeginselen: de klok kan niet meer terug," in: *Namens*, 4(8) (1989) pp. 18–19.

12 G. Molier, *De (on)rechtmatigheid van humanitaire interventie: respect voor staatssoevereiniteit versus bescherming van mensenrechten?* The Hague: Boom Juridische Uitgevers 2003; Gelijn Molier and Timo Slootweg, eds., *Soevereiniteit en recht*, The Hague: Boom

territorial entities with their own sovereignty that other states should, in principle, respect (non-intervention).[13] Characteristic of these nation-states was that a sovereign was able to exercise effective control over the territory.[14] As Voltaire said: "The first king was a successful soldier."[15]

The nation-state has turned out to be a huge success. And, contrary to what is sometimes claimed, it has proven to be the most useful model of political organization until this very day.[16] The current United Nations should really be called the *United Nation States*. The United Nations Charter (1945) sets out the foundations of the organization: it lays out the rights and obligations of member states and establishes the bodies and procedures of the United Nations. The basis of the Charter is the sovereign equality of states and the prohibition against violence in international relations, as well as the basic human rights of all people. In article 2, paragraph 1, we read the following: "The Organization is based on the principle of the sovereign equality of all its Members." The key phrase here is *sovereign equality*. Paragraph 4 of the same article lays out what this means for the territorial integrity of the states: "All Members shall refrain in their international relations from the threat or use of force against the territorial integrity or political independence of any state, or in any other manner inconsistent with the Purposes of the United Nations." The key term here is *political independence*. Paragraph 7 refers to the national sovereignty of states in the following terms:

> Nothing contained in the present Charter shall authorize the United Nations to intervene in matters which are essentially within the domestic jurisdiction of any state or shall require the Members to submit such matters to settlement under the present Charter.

The key phrase is *domestic jurisdiction*.

This is a system the world has operated under since 1648, which is the year of the *establishment of state power*.

Juridische Uitgevers 2009; Benjamin Straumann, "The Peace of Westphalia as a Secular Constitution," in: *Constellations*, 15 (2) (2008), pp. 173–188.

13 Bastiaan Rijpkema, "Over soevereiniteit. Het belang van zuiver definiëren," in: *Nederlands Juristenblad*, Blog, 14 August 2014.

14 See about this: Henry Kissinger, *World Order: Reflections on the Character of Nations and the Course of History*, London: Penguin Books 2014.

15 Cited in: R. Kranenburg, *Algemeene Staatsleer*, Haarlem: H.D. Tjeenk Willink & Zoon 1937, p. 12. See also: *Encyclopédie ou Dictionnaire universel raisonné des connoissances humaines*, vol. 2, art. "Amour," Yverdon, MDCCLXX, p. 416: "Le premier qui fut Roi, fut un soldat heureux."

16 Thierry Baudet, *The Significance of Borders: Why Representative Government and the Rule of Law Require Nation States*, Leiden: E.J. Brill 2012; Jean-Claude Barreau, *Sans la nation, le chaos*, Paris: Éditions du Toucan 2011; Roger Scruton, *England and the Need for Nations*, London: Civitas: The Institute for the Study of Civil Society 2004.

1748: constitutionalism ("Rechtsstaat")

A hundred years later, the nation-state underwent an important trans-formation. In 1748, Charles-Louis de Secondat, Baron de La Brède et de Montesquieu (1689–1755), "Montesquieu" for short, published the book *The Spirit of Laws* (1748).[17] The book is not about the establishment of state power, but about its restriction. Why? Because, even in the hands of the state, power can corrupt. "Power corrupts, absolute power corrupts absolutely," as it was later phrased.[18] This familiar, by now almost clichéd expression by Lord Acton (1834–1902) remains true today. It also reflects Montesquieu's central concern. In wielding power, which it must by neces-sity, the state must be constrained by certain norms. For a start, it must be constrained by its own laws. This is called the *legality principle*. But in order to prevent abuse of power, the power of the state also needs to be *divided* among three separate bodies: a legislative body (the legislature), an execu-tive body (the government), and a judiciary body (the courts). This is the separation of powers, also known as the *trias politica*.[19]

These three bodies (or "powers") also need to be given *equal weight*: they should balance one another out.[20] Only then is state power acceptable. A state that limits its own power through the law and the separation of powers (the three branches doctrine) is legitimate. We call such a state a *constitu-tional* state (*"Rechtsstaat,"* as opposed to a police state or a dictatorship).[21] A good description of a constitutional state is a state that has constrained its own power by the law.[22] This gives us a clear contrast between 1648 and 1748: the first establishes state power and the second restricts it.

---

17 Montesquieu, *Oeuvres completes,* II, text presented and annotated by Roger Caillois, Paris: Gallimard 1951 (*De l'Esprit des lois,* 1748, Chapter VI, De la Constitution d'Angleterre), pp. 396–407; A.A.M. Kinneging, "Montesquieu," in: P.B. Cliteur, A.A.M. Kinneging, and G.A. van der List, eds., *Filosofen van het klassiek liberalism,* Kampen: Kok/Agora and Prof. mr. B.M. Teldersstichting 1993, pp. 89–113. See also: Louis Desgraves, *Montesquieu,* Paris: Éditions Mazarine 1986.

18 Lord Acton (John Emerich Edward Dalberg-Acton), "Letter to Bishop Mandell Creighton," 5 April 1887, in: J.N. Figgis and R.V. Laurence, eds., *Historical Essays and Studies,* Lon-don: Macmillan 1907.

19 See: Montesquieu, *Oeuvres completes,* pp. 396–407.

20 W.J. Witteveen, *Evenwicht van machten,* Zwolle: W.E.J. Tjeenk Willink 1991.

21 See more extensively about this: Paul Cliteur and Afshin Ellian, "Constitutional Democ-racy as a Legitimate Form of Government," in: Paul Cliteur and Afshin Ellian, eds., *A New Introduction to Jurisprudence,* London, New York: Routledge, 2019, pp. 36–75; J.P.A. Mekkes, *Proeve eener critische beschouwing van de ontwikkeling der humanistische rechtsstaatstheorieën,* Utrecht, Rotterdam: Libertas drukkerijen 1940; C.M. Zoethout, "De democratische rechtsstaat als publieke moraal," in: A.J. Nieuwenhuis and C.M. Zoethout, eds., *Rechtsstaat en religie,* Nijmegen: Wolf Legal Publishers 2009, pp. 141–162; Jacques Chevallier, *L'État de droit,* fourth edition, Paris: Montchrestien 2003.

22 According to: C.M. Zoethout, *Constitutionalisme: Een vergelijkend onderzoek naar het beperken van overheidsmacht door het recht,* Arnhem: Gouda Quint 1995.

1848: democracy

Yet another century later, in 1848, Johan Rudolph Thorbecke (1798–1872) introduced democracy. Or the start of a democracy.[23] What is democracy? Democracy means that you can decide by whom you wish to be ruled, but also that the government steps down when the citizens, or the citizens' representatives, believe it is time for a political changing of the guard.

This handover of power is made possible by the system of "ministerial responsibility" (article 42, paragraph 2 of the Dutch Constitution), which means that ministers, those with whom the responsibility for governance rests, resign their posts when the people's representatives indicate that they should. A first incarnation of ministerial responsibility was implemented by Thorbecke in 1848, and this system was developed further in the nineteenth century (1866/1868).

When it comes to ministerial responsibility, we can observe a transformation from "royal governments to parliamentary governments," the Dutch Council of State rightly writes in its *Unsolicited Recommendations Regarding Ministerial Responsibility* (2020).[24] In 1848, the emphasis in the Dutch system of government was on the position of the king, but in the twentieth century, the focus increasingly shifted toward the government's accountability to the people's representatives, especially the House of Representatives. "The democratic control of the government by the parliament has gradually intensified through ministerial responsibility."[25]

This concludes our overview of the three most important building blocks of the constitutional state: the establishment of state power in 1648, the restriction of state power in 1748, and the democratic control of state power in 1848.

1948: human rights

And yet, there was still something missing. An ancient tradition of "natural law thinking" had pointed out the meaning of some individual human (and civilian) rights that should never be violated.[26] Not even by a demo-

---

23 For all the dates mentioned here (1648, 1748, 1848) as pegs for certain ideas, other dates can of course be suggested. For every historical event, another event that preceded it can be pinpointed as its relevant precursor. Nevertheless, we consider the dates named here to be watershed moments in the historical continuum by which the described developments can be aptly illustrated.

24 Raad van State, *Ongevraagd advies over ministeriële verantwoordelijkheid* [Unsolicited Recommendations regarding Ministerial Responsibility], 15 June 2020, The Hague 2020, p. 10.

25 Ibid.

26 P.B. Cliteur, *De filosofie van mensenrechten*, second edition, Nijmegen: Ars Aequi Libri 1999 (1997); H.G. Wells, *The Rights of Man, or What are We Fighting For?* London: Penguin Books 2015 (1940); Dirk Verhofstadt, *De vier vrijheden van Franklin Delano*

cratic majority. Should a democratic majority be allowed to decide that all children with blue eyes must be thrown to the lions in a colosseum built especially for that purpose? No? Why not? If it is a democratic decision, it should be possible, right?

No, because these individual rights, human rights or fundamental rights, forbid it. You cannot just strip a person of their rights. Not even by majority vote. Not even when you can find a legal basis for doing so in 50 percent plus one. That idea led to a list of "human rights" that were universal (valid everywhere), in the form of the *Universal Declaration of Human Rights* (1948) that was adopted by the United Nations (as said, the United Nation States).[27] Just like the separation of powers, these rights constitute a restriction to the state's power (even that of the democratic state), and they are therefore also a part of the idea of the constitutional state. The human right to free expression, for instance, holds that no law can be created that takes away right-wing populists' right to vote or express their views. Although this would be possible if a majority of the legislature wished to pass such a law, at least if the majority principle were not subject to any restrictions. But in the system we have devised, such a restriction is certainly present. A judicial restriction. A judge is meant to rule such a law inapplicable because, although it is "democratic," the law is still unjust.[28] In the Netherlands, however, judicial review does not occur against the Constitution (this review is even explicitly prohibited), but against provisions applicable to all in treaties.

The Americans and judicial review

The French philosopher Montesquieu made a considerable impression on the American Enlightenment thinkers.[29] On the people who created the

---

Roosevelt, Gent: Liberaal Archief 2016; Willy Laes, *Mensenrechten in de Verenigde Naties: een verhaal over manipulatie, censuur en hypocrisie*, Antwerp-Apeldoorn: Garant 2011; Bastiaan Rijpkema, "Alsjeblieft niet nóg meer mensenrechten," in: *De Volkskrant*, 11 December 2013; Bastiaan Rijpkema, "Niet nog meer mensenrechten s.v.p.," in: *Nederlands Dagblad*, 16 December 2013.

27 *La Déclaration universelle des droits de l'homme, Textes rassemblés par Mario Bettati, Olivier Duhamel et Laurent Greilsamer pour Le Monde, nouvelle édition mise à jour et augmentée*, Paris: Gallimard 2008 (1998); Jean-Louis Harouel, *Les droits de l'homme contre le people*, Paris: Desclée de Brouwer 2016; Guy Haarscher, *Philosophie des droits de l'homme*, new revised and expanded edition, Paris: Les Éditions du Cerf 2015 (1993); Georg Jellinek, *Die Erklärung der Menschen- und Bürgerrechte*, fourth edition, edited by Walter Jellinek in the third edition, Munich, Leipzig: Duncker & Humblot 1927.

28 We have put the word *democratic* in quotation marks because we are referring merely to majority decision-making. It is possible, of course, to have a different interpretation of *democratic*, only using the term for systems in which constitutional restriction of majority decisions is the norm.

29 See: Clark in Charles-Louis de Secondat, Baron de La Brède and of Montesquieu, *Mes Pensées* [My Thoughts], translated, edited, and with an introduction by Henry C. Clark,

American Constitution in 1787. The Americans had declared themselves independent from Great Britain in 1776 and were contemplating the creation of a constitution of their own.[30] For that constitution, they also reflected extensively on the separation of powers. Their contribution to that discourse eventually constituted an important strengthening of the position of the judiciary in the separation doctrine and the balance of state powers. Because, what did the Americans believe? The Constitution, adopted in 1787, did not contain a right to judicial review. But in the line of argument presented in *Marbury v. Madison* (1803), it was noted that the judiciary was actually the least powerful of the three branches. The legislature controlled the purse. The executive controlled the police and the army. But the judiciary, in the end, controlled nothing. It only formed "judgments." That was why it was thought that the judiciary ought to be given the power to judge whether the laws created by the legislature were in accordance with the Constitution. This is called *judicial review*.[31] Judicial review was introduced in the United States in 1803. So if the American legislature creates a law that the judge, who has to apply this law in an individual case, considers inconsistent with the Constitution, the judge can declare it inapplicable. In that case, the law is null and void.

This is, of course, a considerable power granted to the judge, which is also why American constitutional history is characterized by a discussion about judicial review. Some consider judicial review to be an indispensable element of constitutionalism (the idea of the "*Rechtsstaat*").[32] It enables the protection of fundamental rights, after all. Others bemoan the "undemocratic" nature of judicial review because it places the judge above the legislator, which some oppose. This also led to a long-running discussion about how the judge ought to use the power of judicial review. With a great deal of restraint, the American justice Antonin Scalia (1936–2016) said.[33]

Indianapolis: Liberty Fund 2012, p. ix: "According to one study, the American founders turned to Montesquieu more often than any other source—four times as frequently as the second-most-cited figure (John Locke)."

30 Carl L. Becker, *The Declaration of Independence: A Study in the History of Ideas*, New York: Vintage Books, Random House 1970 (1922).

31 P.B. Cliteur, "Traditionalism, Democracy, and Judicial Review," in: B. van Roermund, ed., *Constitutional Review, Verfassungsgerichtbarkeit, Constitutionele toetsing*, Deventer, Zwolle: Kluwer/W.E.J. Tjeenk Willink 1993, pp. 55–77.

32 Joachim Hruschka, *Kant und der Rechtsstaat: und andere Essays zu Kants Rechtslehre und Ethik*, Freiburg: Verlag Karl Alber 2015; Gottfried Dietze, *Kant und der Rechtsstaat*, Tübingen: J.C.B. Mohr, 1982.

33 Antonin Scalia, "Modernity and the Constitution," in: E. Smith, ed., *Constitutional Justice under Old Constitutions*, The Hague, London, Boston: Kluwer Law International 1995, pp. 313–318; Antonin Scalia, *A Matter of Interpretation. Federal Courts and the Law, An Essay by Antonin Scalia with commentary by Amy Gutmann, Gordon S. Wood, Laurence H. Tribe, Mary Ann Glendon, and Ronald Dworkin*, Princeton: Princeton University Press

Boldly, said another justice, William Brennan (1906–1997).[34] Of course, court rulings are also brought up in this discussion, especially those of the US Supreme Court. Did the judge trespass onto the terrain of politics here? Did he follow the letter of the law closely enough?[35] Is the wording of the law not too vague? Does it not contain too many open norms, leaving the judge too much room for interpretation?

The debate about the power of the judiciary is old, and it is particularly vibrant in the United States. There is nothing wrong with this kind of discussion, also if it were to take place in the Netherlands. We will return to this at the end of this chapter.

What is a good balance of powers?

Merely identifying the four dates and the principles we have introduced in connection to those dates (the establishment of state power in 1648, constitutionalism in 1748, democratic control in 1848, and the introduction of individual rights in 1948) still leaves many questions unanswered.

For instance: *how many* of these individual rights can be recognized? And which ones? A naïve answer would be: as many as we want. This answer is enticing because there is much to be said in favor of all of these rights. The right to free expression, to religious freedom, to clean drinking water, a right to a roof over your head, to life, to admittance to another country when you have a fear of prosecution in your own, a right to retain the cultural identity of your group, to enjoy art, to not face discrimination, a right to not be offended—the list of claims that could be granted the status of "human right" is endless. There are uncountable "ordinary rights" that could be given the status of "higher law." This unchecked growth of human rights could be called *proliferation*.[36]

1997; Herman Philipse, "Antonin Scalia's Textualism in Philosophy, Theology and Judicial Interpretation of the Constitution," in: Arie-Jan Kwak, ed., *Holy Writ: Interpretation in Law and Religion*, Farnham/Burlington: Ashgate 2009, pp. 15–47.

34 W.J. Brennan, Jr., "Why Have a Bill of Rights?," in: *Oxford Journal of Legal Studies*, 9 (4) (1989) pp. 425–440.

35 Although we are, of course, aware that there are also many female judges, we will use masculine pronouns here for simplicity's sake.

36 Paul Cliteur, "De dreigende proliferatie van mensenrechten," in: N.J.H. Huls, ed., *Grenzen aan mensenrechten*, Leiden: Stichting NJCM-boekerij 1995, pp. 7–33; P.B. Cliteur and A. Ellian, "Kan men teveel rechten creëren?," in: P.B. Cliteur and A. Ellian, *Capita encyclopedie en rechtsfilosofie*, Nijmegen: Ars Aequi 2005, pp. 137–158; Paul Cliteur, "Waardoor worden de rechten van de mens het meest bedreigd: door utopisme of door cynisme," in: K. Groenveld, ed., *Proliferatie van mensenrechten*, The Hague: Prof. Mr. B.M. Teldersstichting, 1996, pp. 17–35; Rijpkema, "Alsjeblieft niet nóg meer mensenrechten"; Carl Wellman, *The Proliferation of Rights. Moral Progress or Empty Rhetoric?* Boulder, Oxford: Westview Press 1999; Mary Ann Glendon, *A Nation under Lawyers, How the Crisis in the*

But why is this proliferation a problem? Because the recognition of every human right also constitutes a restriction on the democratically legitimized legislature. In other words: the constitutional instrument of a human right also limits democracy as a system of majority rule. A human right says: "On this terrain, legislature, you are not to tread." And also: "If you, the legislature, decide something that conflicts with a human right, the judiciary will overrule you by declaring your law null and void." It is clear, therefore, that 1748 (constitutionalism) can come into conflict with 1848 (democracy). Potentially, at least. In some things, democracy and constitutionalism point in the same direction, but not always. There is also a tension. In this chapter, we will shed more light on this tension.

For Montesquieu, this was a reason to impress upon judges that they should strictly adhere to the law. They ought to act as "soulless beings." Judges should not—in our own words—start "ruling." When judges start to rule, thereby assuming power that is better left in the hands of the legislature, we give it the scholarly name *kritarchy* (a government of judges). This term does not originate with Montesquieu, but the concept does. A judiciary that accrues too many powers that are best left to the legislature or the executive could be called a *kritarchy*. That is how the term was used by the constitutional scholar and former social-democratic politician from Amsterdam Erik Jurgens. Jurgens is one of the few critics of judicial review in the Netherlands. He opposes laws being reviewed against general policy aims, because that

> would have the judge utterly usurp the position of the legislative and executive powers, causing a true kritarchy. The complaints that already exist about the juridification of public administration through administrative law would increase exponentially; we will have juridification of politics. And with it, due to impossible demands made of the law and the judiciary, an undermining of the role of the law in society.[37]

Another critic of judicial review against the Constitution was also a constitutional scholar from Amsterdam, and Jurgens' mentor: George van den Bergh (1890–1960).[38] And another prominent character in this discussion is the American legal philosopher Jeremy Waldron, who, after the passing of Ronald Dworkin, is the most prominent thinker of our time.[39]

Legal Profession Is Transforming American Society, New York: Farrar, Strauss and Giroux 1994; Mary Ann Glendon, *Rights Talk: The Impoverishment of Political Discourse*, New York: The Free Press, 1991.

37 See: Jurgens, "Over de illusie dat rechterlijke toetsing van de wet aan onze huidige Grondwet zinvol is," pp. 117–123, p. 121.

38 Bergh, "Beschouwingen over het toetsingsrecht," pp. 417–425.

39 Dworkin defended constitutional review. See: Ronald Dworkin, *A Bill of Rights for Britain*,

The primary discourse of the Dutch tradition, however, was very receptive to not just judicial review (at least insofar as it related to review against treaties), but also to bold judicial interpretation, making judicial supremacy a fact in the post-War period. This main thrust of the Dutch tradition, the prevailing paradigm, is also where we can place the work of G.J. Wiarda. Now, in the second part of this chapter, we will further analyze his *Three Types of Legal Method*.

Part II: G.J. Wiarda's presentation of the prevailing paradigm in legal interpretation theory

In the introduction to the first edition (1963)[40] of *Three Types of Legal Method*, Wiarda shares who had an influence on his thinking. First, this is Paul Scholten, who "was never far from his mind" and whom he calls his "mentor." There are more than 40 years between *Three Types* and Scholten's *General Method of Private Law* (1931).[41] It is good to realize that, as such, judicial review's rise to primacy dates from *before* the time that review against treaties was codified in the Dutch system.[42] The judicial review of laws against treaties from the post-War period solidified a process that was already underway, but it began earlier. In Scholten. "On the liberalization of the process of legal interpretation, it [*General Method*] has had an influence that is difficult to overstate."[43] In addition, Wiarda points out that this liberalization of the process of legal interpretation is not only a result of the judge's stance but that the legislature itself also made this development possible. How? By introducing vague norms into the law. Or open norms. These began to play an ever-greater role in the process of legal interpretation, Wiarda writes. And he continues: "It is particularly the reflection on the problems associated with this that has led to the writing of *Three Types of Legal Method*."[44]

In the foreword to the first edition of *Three Types*, we are already confronted with the methodology that is so characteristic of Wiarda. Crucially, he says about these vague norms: "they have started to play an ever more

---

London: Chatto & Windus 1990. Waldron is critical about it: Jeremy Waldron, "The Core of the Case Against Judicial Review," in: *The Yale Law Journal*, 115(6) (April 2006), pp. 1346–1406, also in: Jeremy Waldron, *Political Theory: Essays on Institutions*, Cambridge, MA: Harvard University Press 2016, pp. 195–246.

40 Wiarda, *Drie typen van rechtsvinding*, p. 5.
41 Scholten, *Algemeen Deel [General Method of Private Law]*.
42 In 1953, the following was included in the Dutch Constitution: "Provisions of treaties and of resolutions by international institutions which may be binding on all persons by virtue of their contents shall become binding after they have been published."
43 Wiarda, *Drie typen van rechtsvinding*, p. 5.
44 Ibid., p. 6.

significant role." He does not say that these norms *ought to* play an ever more significant role, but that they do. Perhaps he believes the former, but he does not say it. Wiarda presents his "reflection" as a *description*. He does not posit that, on the basis of certain arguments (for instance: the judge is more trustworthy than the legislator), these vague norms *ought to* play a bigger role. He could also have argued that this development is justified, because the judge, for whatever reason, is better equipped than the legislator to take the lead in the process of legal interpretation. Wiarda's primary goal seems to be to describe a *process*.

His primary goal, but not his only one. Because we will see that in Wiarda's contribution, in between the descriptive elements, normative choices are made, but they are not explicitly justified or presented as normative choices. They are presented as a more or less self-evident consequence of certain autonomous processes to which, admittedly, the judge made a significant contribution, but only with the legislator's approval. After all, the legislator introduced these vague norms.

In the foreword to the fourth edition (1999), written by the book's editor, T. Koopmans, this methodology is not substantially justified. Koopmans also takes Wiarda's approach in the sense that developments are described under the implied presupposition that what is happening is good. The development toward an increasing liberalization of the legal-interpretation process is not met with opposition from Koopmans either. On the contrary. He has tried, Koopmans writes, "to leave Wiarda's line of argument completely intact." In this, it is safe to say, he has succeeded.[45]

Wiarda died in 1988, and so there were 11 years between his death and the publication of the fourth edition of *Three Types* (1999). In those 11 years, institutional changes have naturally occurred in the world of legal science, but new case law has also emerged. Koopmans incorporated this into *Three Types*, and he also furnished the book with commentary.[46] This creates a line of thought that runs from Scholten (1931), to Wiarda (1963), to Koopmans (1999), a line that could be considered the "prevailing paradigm" in legal interpretation theory in the Netherlands. The prevailing paradigm is based on the following implicit conviction: liberalization of the legal-interpretation process is a good thing. And this "good" requires little argumentation; it is the result of a more or less self-evident development in the course of history. We are almost speaking of an implicitly Hegelian vision of legal history. *Whatever is, is right*.[47] The "historically developed" is accepted more or less without question as inevitable.

---

45 Ibid., p. 6.
46 Ibid., p. 7.
47 Clark Butler, *G.W.F. Hegel*, Boston: Twayne Publishers 1977; W.T. Stace, *The Philosophy of Hegel: A Systematic Exposition*, New York: Dover Publications 1955 (1924).

Away from Montesquieu

In the previous paragraphs, we have characterized 1748 as an important moment in Western state development. We have presented 1748 as the moment at which, 100 years after the Peace of Westphalia (1648), the birthing chamber of the national state, the idea of a constitutional state began to take shape. Why a constitutional state? Because Montesquieu had pointed out the need to constrain the power of the state by the law, more specifically by a legal or constitutional principle, namely the separation of powers. Of course, it is possible to use different historical dates as starting points for central elements of the contemporary constitutional state. Similarly, the idea of individual rights that are meant to constitute a constraint on state power can also be chosen as the defining moment. In that case, John Locke (1632–1704) or one of his predecessors ought to be the object of focus.[48] Or one could shine a light on 1803, the moment at which the American Supreme Court, in the voice of John Marshall (1755–1835) declares legislation that conflicts with the higher law of the Constitution to be null and void.[49] But it is also possible to use 1748, as we do here, because the concept of the separation of powers brings together several ideas. The moment the judiciary is marked as a separate institution that exists alongside the executive and legislative powers, it makes sense to stimulate further reflection on what exactly the responsibilities and powers of this judiciary are. That way, one automatically arrives at reflections about the nature and scope of judicial activity. That is also how it was interpreted by the writers of a first commentary on the American Constitution, the American *Federalist Papers* (1788).[50] As early as 1788, an argument is made in favor of judicial review of laws against the Constitution, an appeal that, as we have seen, will be realized in 1803 by means of judicial intervention.

Wiarda's *Three Types* contains nothing about this history of the judicial-review question, or about the long-running discussion in the United States on how this power ought to be used.[51] With restraint (or "conservatively"),

---

48 John Locke, *Two Treatises of Government*, edited with an introduction and notes by Peter Laslett, New York: Cambridge University Press 1988 (1690). With as a very distant ancestor, Sophocles's *Antigone*. See: Sophocles, *Antigone*, Cambridge: Cambridge University Press 2011; Jean Anouilh, *Antigone*, Paris: La Table Ronde 1946 (2008); Cliteur and Ellian, *A New Introduction to Jurisprudence*, p. 4.

49 James, M. O'Fallon, "Marbury," in: *Stanford Law Review*, 44 (1992), pp. 219–260.

50 James Madison, Alexander Hamilton, and John Jay, *The Federalist Papers*, Harmondsworth: Penguin Books 1987 (1788).

51 See on this: Philip Bobbitt, *Constitutional Interpretation*, Oxford, Cambridge, MA: Blackwell 1991; Kwak, ed., *Holy Writ*; Antonin Scalia and Bryan A. Garner, *Reading the Law: The Interpretation of Legal Texts*, Eagan: Thomson/West 2016.

as some favor?[52] Or more boldly, as the "liberal approach" advocates?[53] Wiarda begins his book with Montesquieu, whose views on the separation of powers and the role of the judiciary he briefly summarizes before qualifying them as out of step with the times. Montesquieu offers an overview of three systems of government that correspond with three types of legal interpretation (hence the title of Wiarda's book). So, for Montesquieu, this is central: form of government → legal interpretation.

Montesquieu distinguishes three combinations of government systems and types of legal interpretation that correspond with them.

Montesquieu's three forms of government

First and foremost: the republic (*"république"*). Montesquieu views this government system as ideal because it has (a) clearly defined laws and (b) judges that follow them. This creates great legal certainty. Wiarda quotes: *"plus le gouvernement approche de la république plus la manière de juger devient fixe."* Translation: "The nearer a government approaches toward a republic, the more the manner of judging becomes settled and fixed." Wiarda paraphrases this as: "The judge applies the law and does this to the letter."[54] This interpretation "to the letter" has a negative connotation for Wiarda. It does not to Montesquieu, because this makes judicial rulings in a republic determinable (*"fixe"*). But words being taken "literally" has a very negative connotation to the proponents of the liberalization of the process of legal interpretation, among whom Wiarda counts himself.

The word *letter* is then often contrasted negatively with the word *spirit*, interpreting based not on the letter of the law but on its spirit, in which the second is considered superior to the first. The notion that interpretation based on the spirit of the law creates a risk to the ideal of the constitutional state, the ideal that the government (and therefore also the judge) is bound to the law, Wiarda does not hold up for closer scrutiny. The entire ideal of constitutionalism seems to play hardly any role in his reflections on the forms of legal interpretation.

The literal approach (Montesquieu: *"les juges suivent la lettre de la loi"*) Wiarda associates with yet another negative image, namely with "automatism." In Montesquieu, judicial activity is "automated," Wiarda writes.[55] He relates the automaton metaphor to another infamous quotation by Montesquieu in which the French philosopher characterizes judges as

---

52 The classic work that is representative of this approach is: *Reading the Law: The Interpretation of Legal Texts* (ibid).
53 Ronald Dworkin, *Law's Empire*, Cambridge, MA, London: The Belknap Press of Harvard University Press 1986.
54 Wiarda, *Drie typen van rechtsvinding*, p. 13.
55 Ibid.

"soulless beings" who only function as mouthpieces of the law (*"Les juges de la nation ne sont que les bouches qui prononcent les paroles de la loi; des êtres inanimés qui n'en peuvent modérer ni la force ni la rigueur"*).[56]

Now that we have discussed the republic and its attendant legal interpretation—Montesquieu's ideal system—we will turn to the second form of government. Here, Montesquieu identifies despotism (*"l'état despotique"*). He uses Turkey as an example. This is a country, Wiarda writes, that was viewed in Montesquieu's time as an ideological antipode to the republic. As such, it played roughly the same role as "Stalinist Russia" in our own time, Wiarda notes.[57] Ironically, however, Montesquieu's example, Turkey, is more apt in *our time* than in Wiarda's. A year after Wiarda's passing, the Berlin wall fell, and Turkey has recently seen the development of another true *état despotique*, as was the case in Montesquieu's time.

What does Montesquieu see as characteristic of despotism? No laws exist there. The judge rules on the basis of his personal view of each individual case, on his own and arbitrarily. After all, the judge is a rule unto himself (*"le juge est lui-même sa règle"*).[58] Wiarda does not ask whether the liberalization of the legal-interpretation process he proposes constitutes a return to Montesquieu's despotic state. Apparently, he considers this hypothesis too unlikely to reflect on as a challenge to his own vision. He continues with Montesquieu's pairs of systems, moving on to that of the monarchy in combination with an intermediary view between freedom and constraint when it comes to legal interpretation.

Montesquieu's monarchy

The monarchy has the following position when it comes to legal interpretation: where the law is precise, the judge follows it to the letter; where it is not precise, the judge tries to find the spirit of the law (*"Dans les états monarchiques il y a une loi; là où elle est précise le juge la suit; là où elle ne l'est pas, il en cherche l'esprit"*).[59] So the monarchy constitutes a middle ground between the extremes of the republic and despotism. In the republic, verdicts are entirely bound by something external: the law. In a despotic state, verdicts are entirely free, unbound to anything else.

We will now take a closer look at the background of Montesquieu's work. As Arnold Heumakers makes clear in his examination of Montesquieu, Montesquieu's typology of systems of government ties in with an old tradition that goes back to Plato and Aristotle. Nevertheless, he calls Montesquieu's

56 Ibid.
57 Ibid., p. 13.
58 Ibid., p. 14.
59 Ibid.

distinction between republic (subdivided into democracy and aristocracy), monarchy, and despotism "original."[60] Montesquieu tries to understand the "nature" or "principle" of each form of government.[61]

Despotism is said to be about the principle of *fear*, which is meant to guarantee unconditional obedience to the ruler. The democratic republic is supposedly about *virtue*. The republican republic is meant to have *moderation* as its inspiring principle. And monarchy is said to be about *honor*.

It is often said that Montesquieu works empirically, that he does not seek to moralize about the forms of government but rather wants to empirically describe how they function. Isaiah Berlin challenges this, however. In a long chapter about Montesquieu in *Against the Current* (1981),[62] he writes that Montesquieu's typologies are often not empirical but deeply metaphysical. In that sense, he was indebted to Aristotle.[63] He says about Montesquieu: "According to him each type of society possesses an inner structure, an inner dynamic principle or force, which makes it function as it does—and this 'inner' force from type to type."[64]

The latter strikes us as correct. Many of Montesquieu's comments about the constructs he developed are hard to grasp; at least they seem fairly random. It is also difficult to determine where he merely makes distinctions and where he includes normative viewpoints. The latter is something he does only with the greatest reluctance, which makes interpretation of his work notoriously difficult. It also explains why he is often accused of being a relativist author. The only thing Montesquieu clearly appears to detest is extreme positions, although he does acknowledge forms of extremism in the prevailing institutions of his time, which does give his work a more or less revolutionary character that made him influential with later revolutionaries. In the *Lettres Persanes* (1721),[65] characterized by Isaiah Berlin as an "entertaining satire on French society and the church of Rome,"[66] two Persian travelers discuss the peculiarities of their country, also revealing a veiled critique of French mores and customs. Heumakers characterizes the tenor of the book as follows: "The absolute monarchy, the Catholic Church, the state's finances, literary life, libertine mores, the adherence to fashion,

---

60 Arnold Heumakers, "Montesquieu (1689–1755)," in: Thierry Baudet and Michiel Visser, eds., *Revolutionair verval en de conservatieve vooruitgang in de achttiende en negentiende eeuw*, Amsterdam: Uitgeverij Bert Bakker 2012, pp. 15–37, p. 25.
61 Ibid., p. 25.
62 Isaiah Berlin, "Montesquieu," in: Isaiah Berlin, *Against the Current. Essays in the History of Ideas*, Oxford, Toronto, Melbourne: Oxford University Press 1981, pp. 130–162.
63 Ibid., p. 140.
64 Ibid.
65 Montesquieu, *Lettres Persanes*, Édition présentée établie et annotée par Jean Starobinski, Paris: Gallimard 1973 (1721).
66 Berlin, "Montesquieu," p. 132.

how the Parisians are always in a hurry—it is all described and judged with mild ridicule."[67] Although it is not so easy to pinpoint where Montesquieu stands in the contrast between monarchy and republic generally, he is clear about despotism—it must be rejected. And it is in relation to despotism that Wiarda, reflecting on Montesquieu's work, introduces a new pair of terms that is of great importance to legal interpretation theory: *heteronomy* and *autonomy*.

Heteronomy and autonomy of the judicial verdict

Wiarda calls complete dependence on something outside of the judge *heteronomy*. Complete independence of judicial rulings he calls *autonomy*. And here, the republic comes out as clearly superior. After all, in the republic, legal interpretation is completely heteronomous, Wiarda says. In a despotic state, legal interpretation is completely autonomous.

Monarchy sits in between these two extremes. Wiarda believes that it can be said about monarchy that it is "the state of reality in which Montesquieu lived and in which he also worked as a judge."[68] This "state of reality" is a legal system that contains both heteronomous and autonomous elements.

Wiarda believes, therefore, that Montesquieu's description of the situation in his own time and his views about the most desirable situation are entirely consistent with one another. And Wiarda also recognizes in himself Montesquieu's positive judgment about his own time and its dominant form of legal interpretation: Wiarda too is very pleased with the situation of legal interpretation in his own Netherlands in the 1960s and 1970s of the twentieth century. And that situation is: sometimes judges can just be the mouthpieces of the law, and sometimes, when there is a lack of concrete legal standards, they must rely on their own sense of justice. Wiarda says that each of the types described by Montesquieu reflects a certain aspect of the judge's role. This is followed by a somewhat cryptic line with which Wiarda characterizes his own position: "The way in which these aspects occur in relation to one another, in which heteronomous and autonomous elements are always combined in the role of the judiciary, is dependent on time and place."[69]

Assessment of Wiarda's adoption of the monarchy

The interpretation Wiarda gives here of Montesquieu's true intentions deserves some scrutiny. He makes it seem as if Montesquieu is completely

---

67 Heumakers, "Montesquieu (1689–1755)," p. 18.
68 Wiarda, *Drie typen van rechtsvinding*, p. 14.
69 Ibid.

happy with the time in which he lived and the model of legal interpretation that was dominant then. In Wiarda, Montesquieu comes across as a somewhat colorless defender of the status quo. Is this warranted? Not all commentators on Montesquieu's work would say so. Isaiah Berlin points out some more revolutionary sides to Montesquieu's work. Berlin writes:

> He believed in justice and the rule of law; defended freedom of opinion and association; detested all forms of extremism and fanaticism; put his faith in the balance of power and the division of authority as a weapon against despotic rule by individuals or groups or majorities and approved of social equality, but no to the point at which it threatened individual liberty; and of liberty, but not to the point where it threatened to disrupt orderly government.[70]

A century after his death, these ideals were shared by most civilized states and citizens of Europe, Berlin writes. But that was not yet the case in his own time.[71] Berlin places Montesquieu's work in the liberal tradition ("the essentials of Montesquieu's teaching formed the heart of the liberal creed everywhere").[72] But there were also "conservative aspects of his teaching," Berlin writes. These were his emphasis on the necessity of evolutionary instead of revolutionary change. He also pointed out the unique character of civilizations. In addition, we find a certain respect for long-held traditions in Montesquieu's work. He points out that proscribing uniform methods of societal change is impossible.

Is this very likely? Two questions could be asked about this: a question about Wiarda's description and a more normative question.

First is the matter of description. Is it likely that the type of legal interpretation that was dominant in Montesquieu's time was truly a model in which autonomy and heteronomy were joined in a happy combination? If that were true, then eighteenth-century France would be an ideal model of legal interpretation for us. But how do we know if it was? We would have to do empirical research into how judges operated back then, into how often they followed the law to the letter and how often they deviated from it. We would have to, in other words, have access to material of which neither Wiarda nor Montesquieu give us examples. That is not an especially convincing foundation for generalizations on this subject.

Another question that arises is this one: if Montesquieu were really so positive about the form of legal interpretation of his time, a form that is linked to what he calls "monarchy," then why does he also say such positive

---

70 Berlin, "Montesquieu," p. 130.
71 Ibid.
72 Ibid., p. 131.

things about the republic? Does he view this as the ideal, but unattainable? As too ambitious? Or is there something else going on here?

What Wiarda does not address at all is the question of whether, with an author like Montesquieu, we should not be reading between the lines more. Was he really free to write what he truly believed? Is it likely that Montesquieu would have committed what he truly thought to paper?

In *Persecution and the Art of Writing* (1952), the political philosopher Leo Strauss (1899–1973) shined a light on the hidden dimension of books that are written under severely constrained conditions.[73] He illustrates his views primarily by focusing on three great books and thinkers: *Guide to the Perplexed* (1204) by Maimonides, Halevi's *Kuzari* (1140), and the *Tractatus Theologico-Politicus* (1670) by Spinoza. These were all writers who faced censorship, who were severely limited in what they could say openly without facing persecution by the governments of their time or a violent reaction to their writings from the intolerant masses.

J.B. Bury's *A History of the Freedom of Thought* (1913) in effect teaches us the same thing, namely that, throughout most of human history, the great thinkers labored under the yoke of censorship.[74] How did they deal with this? Sometimes by not publishing books at all. Sometimes by publishing under a pseudonym. Strauss believes this means we should always read between the lines. Expecting a writer to nonchalantly put all his cards on the table under conditions of censorship is fairly naïve. It is claimed that there are no atheists in Saudi Arabia. Is that likely to be true?[75] Or do they simply stay silent because open atheism can cost a person his head on the square in Riyadh after Friday prayer?[76]

This brings us back to Montesquieu. Would honesty not have had negative consequences for Montesquieu as well? He too wrote in a time of censorship,

73 Leo Strauss, "Persecution and the Art of Writing," 1941, republished in: Leo Strauss, *Persecution and the Art of Writing*, Chicago, London: The University of Chicago Press 1988 (1952), pp. 22–38.

74 J.B. Bury, *A History of the Freedom of Thought*, London: Thornton Butterworth 1932 (1913).

75 Brian Whitaker, *Arabs without God: Atheism and Freedom of Belief in the Middle East*, Charleston: CreateSpace Independent Publishing Platform 2014.

76 Deera Square (Arabic: ساحة الديرة), a public space in Riyadh, Saudi Arabia, is where the executions take place, often by beheading. It is colloquially called Chop Chop Square. Perhaps the situation in Saudi Arabia is extreme. See: Raif Badawi, *1000 Peitschenhiebe weil ich sage, was ich denke, Aus dem Arabischen von Sandra Hetzl, Herausgegeben, eingeleitet und kommentiert von Constantin Schreiber*, Berlin: Ullstein 2015; Ensaf Haider and Andrea C. Hoffmann, *Raif Badawi: The Voice of Freedom, My Husband, Our Story*, translated from the German by Shaun Hiteside, New York: Other Press 2015. But freedom of expression when it comes to criticism of religion is also impossible under the Palestinian National Authority. See: Waleed Al-Husseini, *Une trahison française: les collaborationnistes de l'islam radical dévoilés*, Paris: Éditions Ring 2017.

a time in which crimes like lese-majesty and blasphemy could incur draconian punishments for a writer. Isaiah Berlin discusses Montesquieu's views on religion. Montesquieu views religion as a "natural phenomenon." So, according to him, the Christian theologians were wrong. The nature of religions is determined by natural causes. This led to a more or less tolerant Protestantism in the Northern states, to prosecution in the Catholic South, to stagnation under Islam, and so on.[77] But stylistically, Montesquieu always remains polite and modest in giving offense. His strong suit as a stylist, in Berlin's words, was "to afford the reader the pleasure of watching grave and dignified theologians not thrown roughly on the ground, but sliding gently into the abyss."[78] Montesquieu did not write like (the anonymously published) d'Holbach in his *Le Christianisme Dévoilé ou Examen des Principes et des Effets de la Religion Chrétienne* (1761).[79] Montesquieu wrote carefully in order to stay under the censor's radar. This is true in any case of everything having to do with the existence of God or atheism. But criticism of the king and the monarchy was also a tricky business. Should we therefore not look upon Montesquieu's ode to the monarchy with a critical eye? The rationalists in France were faced with "ecclesiastical censorship," Berlin writes.[80] This limited them in their freedom to critique.

What Montesquieu made public and what he did not

If we take the question Leo Strauss posed seriously, it is self-evident that, for every philosophical work we read, we have to ask ourselves whether it was published under the author's own name or anonymously (or under a pseudonym, which comes down to the same thing). A category in the middle are works of fiction, which might be published under the author's own name, but in which the author can leave the reader guessing about his own views because he puts words that might offend the censor or the general reading public in the mouths of his characters.

The *Persian Letters* appeared under the author's own name, but because it was a work of fiction, Montesquieu succeeded in evading his censors. Henry Clark says the following about the letters:

> The spectacular success of this work—it went through several printing in its first year—made its author a sought-after companion in the salons of Paris, where he spent much time in the 1720s. He had the unusual

---

77 Berlin, "Montesquieu," p. 141.
78 Ibid., p. 142.
79 Pierre Henri Dietrich baron d'Holbach, *Le Christianisme Dévoilé ou Examen des Principes et des Effets de la Religion Chrétienne*, 1761, in: d'Holbach, *Premieres Œuvres*, Préface et notes Paulette Charbonnel, Paris: Éditions Sociales 1971, pp. 94–138.
80 Berlin, "Montesquieu," p. 133.

experience of being elected to the French Academy (1727) mainly on the strength of a work that many found both light and of dubious orthodoxy.[81]

Here, therefore, it is the fictional character of the publication that affords the author freedoms that would have gotten him into trouble if the book had been non-fiction instead.

A second category is the non-fiction that Montesquieu also published. This was the case with his *Considérations sur les causes de la grandeur des Romains et de leur decadence* (1734).[82] This was published anonymously in Amsterdam. Clark characterized it as "one of the most influential interpretative studies in Roman history."[83] It was while writing this book that Montesquieu began to think about how he could praise the English Constitution in writing without encountering the censorship problems that Voltaire had faced over his *Lettres Philosophiques* (1733).[84]

Third, there is the *L'Esprit des lois* (1748), which, as Clark writes, turned Montesquieu from a "moderately important figure" into "one of the founders of modern thought."[85] In this work, a work of non-fiction published under the author's own name, Montesquieu had to impose perhaps the heaviest restrictions of all on himself, according to what Leo Strauss writes. In Wiarda's analyses, this issue receives no attention at all.

Interestingly, Montesquieu also committed a great many "thoughts"[86] to writing during his lifetime, very few of which were published. It was not until the twentieth century that these were made public in their entirety. As Clark says: "they directly illuminate the meaning of his published texts."[87] It is especially in these thoughts that Montesquieu did not share openly that we can sometimes read things that reflect his more radical side. As Clark writes:

> Montesquieu had his own encounters with the French censorship apparatus, and one value of the pensées is the opportunity to sample some of the author's more unvarnished thinking, especially on topics such

81 Clark in Montesquieu, *Mes Pensées* [My Thoughts], p. viii.
82 Montesquieu, *Considérations sur les causes de la grandeur des Romains et de leur decadence*, Paris: Folio 2008 (1734).
83 Clark in Montesquieu, *Mes Pensées* [My Thoughts], p. viii.
84 Voltaire, "Lettres Philosophiques," 1733 (Eng.), 1734 (Fr.), in: Voltaire, *Mélanges, Préface par Emmanuel Berl, Texte établi et annoté par Jacques van den Heuvel*, Paris: Gallimard 1961, pp. 2–133.
85 Clark in Montesquieu, *Mes Pensées* [My Thoughts], p. ix.
86 Just like Pascal, with whose thinking he was also familiar. See: Blaise Pascal, *Pensées*, 1669, in: *Oeuvres complètes*, texte établi, présenté et annoté par Jacques Chevalier, Paris: Gallimard 1954, pp. 1081–1358.
87 Clark in Montesquieu, *Mes Pensées* [My Thoughts], p. x.

a religion and the current politics where the censors would have been particularly vigilant.[88]

For instance, he writes in the *Pensées*: "It is surprising that the people so strongly cherish republican government, but that so few nations have it; that men so strongly hate violence, but that so many nations are governed by violence" (1796).[89] The following thought is also one that would have gotten Montesquieu into trouble if he had shared it openly during his lifetime:

Reasons why republics become more flourishing than countries governed by a single person:

1. More security for what one has acquired;
2. More love of the public good and of Country, which belongs to us, not to another;
3. More equality of conditions, and consequently, more equality of fortunes;
4. More means of succeeding by personal merit, and consequently, fewer means by servility

To fashion a monarchical state, a rich nobility with authority and privileges over a poor people is necessary – luxury and expense in the Nobility; misery in the People. In a republic, where conditions are equal, each person shares or can share the common riches. Each person, having honest subsistence, enjoys the substance of the Nation's goods and seeks to enlarge it. (1760)[90]

Elsewhere, Montesquieu writes: "To prove that morals comport better with the good republic than with the good monarchy: it is because in good republics, one says *We*, but in good monarchies, one says *Me*" (1891).[91]

In the context of such quotations, it seems justified to ask: is it possible that the republic, with its attendant heteronomy, was actually his true ideal? But an ideal that he did not want to loudly proclaim in order to avoid censorship problems?

If that were true, Montesquieu's true preference could be much more in line with that of later writers, the Enlightenment authors who sought to scale back the influence of the judge in favor of legislation. Of course, it must be said that there is no hard evidence for this. Any presumption about views an author did not explicitly entrust to paper will always carry an element of speculation.

88 Ibid., p. xi.
89 Ibid., p. 228.
90 Ibid., p. 525.
91 Ibid., p. 566.

In the work published during his lifetime, Montesquieu meanders back and forth between positive comments about the monarchy and about the republic. And, of course, what Montesquieu says is true: the role of the judge depends on the time and place in which he acts. In one time, he is more autonomous, in another, he is more heteronomous, as Wiarda also points out. This is, of course, undeniable. But is that not still a descriptive point that tells us nothing about how the judge *should* function? We are left with the question: what type of judicial method is desirable? And why? What criteria should we use by which to judge the courts' work? Its compatibility with democracy? With constitutionalism? These are all questions that Wiarda does not answer. What he does, what Scholten did before him, and what Koopmans further develops after him seem to be giving a *description* of the change from heteronomy to autonomy, one with a strongly sympathetic tone. He says that he wants to "paint a picture," a moving picture, "in which it is clear that the factors that determine the judge's legal interpretation are undergoing a transformation from more heteronomous to more autonomous."[92] From this picture, it emerges that the judge is acting "ever more freely." His job description is similar to that of a "referee deciding on the basis of fairness."[93] That this seems to draw the judge closer to what Montesquieu qualified as "*état despotique*," to the judge being a rule unto himself ("*lui-même sa règle*"), Wiarda does not seem to consider a problem. He simply does not address it.

Robespierre and Portalis

So far, we have focused on the views of a twentieth-century author, Wiarda, in relation to an author from the eighteenth century, Montesquieu. But Wiarda does not only write about Montesquieu. He provides further support for his ideas by discussing two figures as more or less representative of certain viewpoints in legal interpretation: Robespierre and Portalis. As representative of Montesquieu's belief that judges ought to function as soulless beings ("*êtres in inanimés*"), he refers to Robespierre's famous adage: "Le mot de jurisprudence doit être effacé de notre langue; dans un pays qui a une constitution, une législation, la jurisprudence ce n'est autre chose que la loi."[94] Translated: "The word *jurisprudence* must be erased from our language. In a State with a constitution [and] legislation, the jurisprudence of the courts is nothing other than the law."[95] He references this quotation

---

92 Wiarda, *Drie typen van rechtsvinding*, p. 15.
93 Ibid., p. 15.
94 Ibid., p. 16.
95 The French word "jurisprudence" usually means "case law" (as in the quotation here), but also "legal science." In English, "jurisprudence" usually refers to legal science, as in: John Austin, *The Province of Jurisprudence Determined and The Uses of the Study of Jurisprudence*, with an introduction by H.L.A. Hart, London: Weidenfeld and Nicolson 1954 (1832/1863).

from Scholten's *General Method*.[96] And it is indeed a nice and thought-provoking quotation, partly because of the hyperbole contained in it. It is a quotation that would go down well in a collection of aphorisms by Vauvenargues (1715–1747)[97] or La Rochefoucauld (1613–1680),[98] or that might have come from the *Pensées* by Pascal (1623–1662)[99] or the *Parerga und Paralipomena* (1851)[100] by Arthur Schopenhauer (1788–1860). But quoting Robespierre also has a rhetorical effect, of course. Robespierre is associated with terror, with the degeneration of the ideals of the French Revolution. No one, when they see a quotation by Robespierre, will expect to agree with its contents. The source guarantees suspicion. It is like quoting Stalin or Pol Pot as a proponent of a particular legal method: it would immediately shed a negative light on any analysis of that model. Such a thing has an impact on the reader.

Robespierre's view—the "wrong view," to put it bluntly—is then contrasted by Wiarda with the position many will read as the "sympathetic view." We find this in a scholar who is likely no more than a name to most readers: Portalis. On 24 Thermidor an 8 (12 August 1800) Jean-Étienne-Marie Portalis (1746–1807) gave a speech on the occasion of the presentation of the concept of the Code Civil. Unlike Robespierre, Portalis realizes that the law is inevitably incomplete. The legislator cannot foresee every circumstance, after all.

> Un code, quelque complet qu'il puisse paraître, n'est pas plus tôt achevé que mille questions inattendues viennent s'offrir au magistrat. Car les lois, une fois rédigées demeurent telles qu'elles ont été écrites. Les hommes, au contraire, ne se reposent jamais.[101]

This is the view Wiarda holds up as correct, because, as Portalis writes, many things (*"une foule de choses"*) have to be left to the free judgment of the courts (*"l'arbitraire des juges"*).[102]

---

96 Scholten, *Algemeen Deel [General Method of Private Law]*, third edition, chapter 1, paragraph 1.

97 Luc de Clapiers de Vauvenargues, *Introduction à la connaissance de l'esprit humain*, Paris: Garnier Flammarion 1993 (1747).

98 François de la Rochefoucauld, *Maximes et Réflexions diverses*, Paris: Garnier Flammarion 1999 (1665).

99 Blaise Pascal, *Pensées*, 1669, in: *Oeuvres complètes, texte établi, présenté et annoté par Jacques Chevalier*, Paris: Gallimard 1954, pp. 1081–1358.

100 Arthur Schopenhauer, *Parerga und Paralipomena*, Kleine Philosophische Schriften II, in: *Sämtliche Werke*, Band V, Frankfurt am Main: Cotta-Verlag/Insel-Verlag 1965 (1851).

101 Wiarda, *Drie typen van rechtsvinding*, p. 17: "A code, however complete it may appear, is no sooner completed than a thousand unexpected questions arise for the magistrate. For laws, once written, remain as they were written. Men, on the contrary, never rest."

102 Ibid., p. 17.

It has been discussed before: what makes this representation of matters somewhat unsatisfactory is the fact that Wiarda does not distinguish
between facts and norms, between Sein and Sollen. It would have been more
fitting if Wiarda had said that what Robespierre proposes, despite the repre-
hensibility of his terrorist beliefs,[103] nevertheless corresponds with a certain
view about legal interpretation that also aligns with that of Montesquieu.
The reader may agree or disagree with this view, but whatever the case may
be, it is a perspective that deserves serious discussion. Merely noting that
this view no longer garners much support in judicial circles can hardly be
regarded as an argument. Incidentally, arguments can be made in favor of
Robespierre's belief, arguments, in fact, that are derived from an important
ideal: democracy. Namely that the legislature, preferably the democratic
legislature, establishes the rules by which the community of citizens wishes
to live. On the basis of that ideal, democracy truly is government by the people. In one of the most famous speeches from American history, Abraham
Lincoln reminded his audience of the fact that the country's founders sought
to establish a state "conceived in Liberty, and dedicated to the proposition
that all men are created equal."[104] We have become accustomed to calling
a system of government based on the freedom and equality of all citizens
a *democracy*. The word *democracy* does not appear in Lincoln's *Address
at Gettysburg* (1863), but he does give one of the most often quoted characterizations of it when he speaks of a "government of the people, by the
people, for the people."[105] It has become so self-evident that a state exists
for its citizens that people are hardly able nowadays to imagine that this was
not always the prevailing line of thought. Yet, that is the case. For centuries, people viewed the state as a construct that existed for the greater glory
of God.[106] Or as the private property of a monarch (whether he ruled by
divine right or not).[107] It is the democratic revolutions of the Enlightenment
period that have changed our thinking on this.[108] Why do people obey the

103 See: Michael Burleigh, *Blood & Rage: A Cultural History of Terrorism*, London: Harper
    Press 2008, p. 67; Glenn Gough, "The Terror in the French Revolution," in: Brett Bowden
    and Michael Davies T. Davis, eds., *Terror: from Tyrannicide to Terrorism*, foreword by Geof-
    frey Robertson, St. Lucia: University of Queensland Press 2008, pp. 77–92; Jonathan Israel,
    *Revolutionary Ideas: An Intellectual History of the French Revolution from The Rights
    of Man to Robespierre*, Oxford, Princeton: Princeton University Press 2014, pp. 503–574.
104 Abraham Lincoln, *Address at Gettysburg, Pennsylvania* (1863), in: Abraham Lincoln,
    ed., *Selected Speeches and Writings*, New York: The Library of America, Vintage Books
    1992, p. 405.
105 Ibid., p. 405.
106 Jean Prieur, *Déclaration universelle des droits de Dieu*, Agnières: Éditions Le Temps
    Présent 2012.
107 John Neville Figgis, *The Divine Right of Kings*, second edition, Cambridge: Cambridge
    University Press 1934.
108 A.C. Grayling, *Towards the Light: The Story of the Struggles for Liberty & Rights
    That Made the Modern West*, London: Bloomsbury Publishing 2007; Jonathan Israel, *A*

law, Canadian philosopher Michael Ignatieff asks? At least partly, he says, due to this "Lincolnian tradition," because people recognize the law as something of themselves, as a product of "democratic suffrage."[109] But, so Wiarda could have retorted, that is impossible, unfortunately. It is impossible because, as Portalis very realistically describes, there are always things the legislature cannot foresee. In other words, Wiarda could have upheld Robespierre's *ideal*, while at the same time praising Portalis's *realism*. What Wiarda does, however, is heap praise on Portalis because Portalis puts the work of the judge in such a central position. This is done by means of the construct of interpretation. The legislature can only establish general laws; the judge has to interpret them. Wiarda believes the legislature has to stay far removed from this interpretative work. Expecting the judge to look to the legislator from time to time in order to determine what he might have intended is viewed as unnecessary by Portalis (and by Wiarda too): "*forcer le magistrat de recourir au législateur, ce serait admettre le plus funeste des principes.*"[110] Detrimental even. Uncompromising language. But Wiarda embraces it all. In Wiarda, Portalis is clearly the hero of the story. He is a pioneer in the liberalization of the legal-interpretation process, as Wiarda approvingly describes it. Employing the image of the automaton, which has such a negative connotation to Wiarda, he writes that the court's judgment ("*science du magistrat*") does not exist in the automatic application of what the law instructs him to do. The judge's job is to orient himself toward the spirit of the law, not its letter. The key is to study the spirit of the law, while the letter kills ("*d'étudier l'esprit de la loi quand la lettre tue*").[111]

Letter and spirit

Letter and spirit. These are extremely important images: the letter kills, the spirit frees. Here, we are leaving the terrain of sober scientific analysis and stepping onto the terrain of religious rhetoric: "Because the letters kills, but the spirit gives life" (2 Cor. 3:6). This religious dimension, and the promise it contains, hums along in tune beneath Wiarda's comments.[112] The free-thinking interpretation is favored by many as freeing, as emancipating. Not

---

Revolution of the Mind: Radical Enlightenment and the Intellectual Origins of Modern Democracy, Princeton, Oxford: Princeton University Press 2010; Jonathan Israel, *Democratic Enlightenment: Philosophy, Revolution, and Human Rights 1750–1790*, Oxford: Oxford University Press 2011.

109 Michael Ignatieff, *The Lesser Evil: Political Ethics in an Age of Terror*, Princeton, Oxford: The Gifford Lectures 2004, p. 35.

110 Wiarda, *Drie typen van rechtsvinding*, p. 17.

111 Ibid.

112 See in the field of theology: "Armstrong's Plea for Liberal Interpretation," in: Paul Cliteur, *The Secular Outlook: In Defense of Moral and Political Secularism*, Chichester: Wiley-Blackwell 2010, p. 248.

what the text literally says, what the author of the text intended must be leading, but what the interpreting body can make of it. Portalis is lauded by Wiarda as one of these liberators.

It is remarkable that Wiarda pays no attention at all to what can be said against this liberal legal doctrine. Nowhere does he offer names and arguments of thinkers who, in line with Montesquieu, point out the need for adherence to the law as a foundational element of both the democratic and the constitutional ideal. A judge freeing himself from the ties that bind him to the law: are there no objections to be raised to this? In Wiarda, at least, we do not hear any. He does, however, explicitly connect Portalis's position to Paul Scholten's legal doctrine. Scholten spoke of an "open system of law," and Portalis essentially does the same thing. An open system, in Wiarda's words, is a system to which "every legal verdict, in effect, adds something new as a separate element."[113] *Every* verdict? It must be a sad state of affairs for legal certainty if *every* verdict brings something new. Of course, in Wiarda's defense, one could say: Wiarda says that "something" new is being added, not that *everything* about that verdict is new. Still, the impression remains that Wiarda seeks to erect very few roadblocks to constrain the judge's ambition to develop the law further. About Portalis, he says:

> Rarely, I feel, have such happy phrasings been seen about the relationship between the judge's subjection to the law and his freedom in regard to it, between the heteronomous and autonomous tendencies in the role of the judiciary. They express views that are strongly related to those prevalent today.[114]

Two things stand out. First, that Portalis, like Wiarda, never spoke about the judge's subjection to the law and what the ideals are behind that norm. Second, that Wiarda again speaks of views that are "prevalent today" without explaining in any way why these views *should* be prevalent. It is somewhat surprising that Wiarda does posit, however, that the point of departure in all judicial work is that "the law is by far the most important heteronomous factor"[115] and that most legal provisions "are still clear enough that their application poses no difficulty whatsoever." And that means that the thought process as described by Montesquieu often still conforms to "what Montesquieu thought was ideal."[116]

These are confusing statements because surely Montesquieu and Portalis cannot *both* be right? If Portalis phrased it all so well, then Montesquieu

---

113 Wiarda, *Drie typen van rechtsvinding*, p. 18.
114 Ibid.
115 Ibid., p. 19.
116 Ibid.

must clear the field as a source of inspiration. If, on the other hand, Montesquieu is right, then the judicial freedom Portalis claims for the judge must be rejected. So who is right here? Portalis or Montesquieu?

Although Wiarda mainly supports Portalis and is critical of Montesquieu, he sometimes confuses the reader with small concessions to Montesquieu's thinking. Such as here: "Legal questions for which the law provides no handhold at all are rare. But especially when it comes to a legal dispute, these handholds are often not so clear and compelling that they can lead directly to the verdict."[117] On the one hand, therefore, heteronomous legal interpretation is possible, Wiarda seems to say. After all, the law offers a solution in the majority of cases. On the other hand, however, it does not, because the handholds in the law are "not so clear" as to be decisive.

The techniques known to legal science to bind judicial discretion to certain norms,[118] such as an orientation toward the everyday language meaning of the words of the law, Wiarda mentions only in passing. He says that legal interpretation is a largely heteronomously determined affair in certain cases. Which ones?

> This is the case both when the judge tries to determine what the text means through grammatical interpretation and when he tries to track down what the author meant through an examination of the relevant legislative history. Systematic interpretation, too, can be viewed as a method that, by placing the legal provision in the context of other provisions, can lead to a better understanding of the text, to a better idea of its intent.[119]

Autonomy remains the main feature of Wiarda's argument

But despite these factors, which limit autonomous legal interpretation, Wiarda still believes that that the autonomous factor will continue to play

---

117 Ibid., p. 21.
118 F. Bydlinksi, *Juristische Methodenlehre und Rechtsbegriff*, Vienna, New York: Springer Verlag 1982, pp. 428–472; R.W.M. Dias, *Jurisprudence*, fifth edition, London: Butterworths 1985, pp. 166–187; William Lucy, "Adiudication," in: Jules Coleman and Scott Shapiro, eds., *The Oxford Handbook of Jurisprudence and Philosophy of Law*, Oxford: Oxford University Press 2002, pp. 206–268; Manfred Rehbinder, *Einführung in die Rechtswissenschaft, Fünfte Auflage*, Berlin, New York: Walter Gruyter 1983, pp. 71–84; Karl Larenz, *Methodenlehre der Rechtswissenschaft*, Studienausgabe, Berlin: Springer Verlag 1983, pp. 188–241; Richard A. Posner, *The Problems of Jurisprudence*, Cambridge, MA: Harvard University Press 1990, pp. 247–313; Fritjof Haft, *Einführung in das juristische Lernen: Unternehmen Jurastudium*, Bielefeld: Verlag Ernst und Werner Gieseking 1997, pp. 56–57; Karl Engisch, *Einführung in das juristische Denken*, Stuttgart: Verlag W. Kohlhammer 1977 (1956), p. 85ff.
119 Wiarda, *Drie typen van rechtsvinding*, p. 22.

an important role. In his discussion of the factors that can play a role in the process of legal interpretation, Wiarda also points to a number of important theories that have come to international prominence. For instance, he posits that, in choosing the arguments that can lead to a fair interpretation of the law, it matters "what has a socially favorable effect."[120] This could be called the *utilitarian approach* to legal interpretation.[121] Wiarda also points to the meaning of "the principles that are the foundation of the law."[122] As an example he offers: he who, without legal grounds, enriches himself at the expense of another is obligated to compensate the other in the amount by which he enriched himself. This principle was invoked in the case of Quint/Te Poel (HR 30 January 1959, NJ 1959, 548). Although the appeal to a principle was not recognized in this case, it is important that the Supreme Court rejected the claim that any obligation must rest directly on a legal provision. If certain circumstances are not settled by law, the solution that "aligns with the system of laws and with the circumstances the law *does* settle,"[123] ought to be accepted.

One case in particular, one in the field of private law, illustrates the growing autonomy of the judicial verdict well: the developments surrounding the unlawful act. According to article 6:162 of the Dutch Civil Code, an unlawful act is "what according to unwritten law has to be regarded as proper social conduct."[124] This means the legislator has given the judge "additional norm-setting authority that spans all the goings on of society."[125] And in exercising this authority, the judge "has nothing to turn to but his own sense of justice."[126]

What should we conclude from this? Wiarda says that it is understandable that, in this context, the judge's role has been described as that of a "substitute legislator."[127]

What Wiarda means by "in this context" is not very clear. Does he mean "in connection with the unlawful act"? Or does he view the substitute-legislator role more broadly, meaning it can also be applied to all sorts of other legal concepts? The latter seems likely. This means that, in the entire legal field, developments point to increased vague or open norms, as Wiarda describes it.[128] And this has the following implication, as Wiarda summarizes it in the fourth chapter of his book:

120 Ibid., p. 23.
121 Richard A. Posner, *The Problems of Jurisprudence*, Cambridge, MA: Harvard University Press 1990.
122 Wiarda, *Drie typen van rechtsvinding*, p. 25.
123 Ibid., p. 26.
124 Ibid., p. 27.
125 Ibid.
126 Ibid.
127 Ibid., p. 28. The term originates with M.J.P. Verburgh, NJB 1977, p. 508.
128 Ibid.

The image of judges who, as "les bouches qui prononcent les paroles de la loi," are automatically led to their decision through subsumption of the established facts and by a rule handed to them by the legislator, we have slowly drifted away from in the overview given above.[129]

It is once again a telling sentence for Wiarda's way of arguing. It is not a line of reasoning consisting of normative argumentation as to how a judge in a democratic constitutional system *ought* to function. Instead, Wiarda "paints a picture." That is to say, he descriptively establishes that judges have (factually) distanced themselves from what Montesquieu had held up as the ideal. In so doing, he also uses a word that has a negative connotation for him: *subsumption*. The idea that the judge can practice legal interpretation by categorizing ("subsuming") facts as falling under a particular legal provision, Wiarda believes is incorrect. Legal interpretation cannot take place "automatically." And he uses an overview in order to lend support to this claim. That way, Wiarda thinks, we will gain an understanding of a "role" the judge plays, which is best compared to that of "arbiters" (article 1054 of the Dutch Code of Civil Procedure).[130] Parties have given these arbiters "the authority, as 'good men,' to judge 'what is fair.'"[131]

So, the picture Wiarda paints of legal interpretation and the role of judges is very harmonious. Without conflict, one could say. He observes that judges have been given more and more authority, and he thinks everyone is perfectly happy with this. After he has presented the image of arbiters as "good men," who judge "what is fair," Wiarda even concludes that this strongly resembles what Montesquieu described as the judge sometimes being *"lui-même sa règle."*[132] But the difference is that Montesquieu is concerned about this, while Wiarda welcomes it.

It is entirely in line with the thrust of Wiarda's argument that he also has great sympathy for the Roman *jus in causa positum*. This means legal interpretation not oriented toward a generally phrased or abstract rule, but legal interpretation of a more abstract nature. Or, as it is called in the German literature, a shift from *Normgerechtigheid* to *Einzelfallgerechtigkeit*. Wiarda then relates this to Pascal's contrast between *"l'esprit de géométrie"* and *"l'esprit de finesse."*[133]

Wiarda also quotes the existentialist Georg Cohn (1887–1956): *"Die richterliche Entscheidung braucht keine Norm, weder eine alte noch eine neue. Sie ist auf sich selbst gegründet, und hat ihre Voraussetzungen, so wie*

---

129 Ibid., p. 30.
130 Ibid.
131 Ibid., p. 40.
132 Ibid., p. 30.
133 Ibid., p. 31.

ihren Endzweck in sich selbst."[134] Or: "The judicial decision needs no norm, neither an old nor a new one. It is founded on itself, and has its preconditions, as well as its final purpose, in itself." Although Wiarda does say of this position that it seems highly exaggerated. Wiarda agrees with Scholten, who had noted that every judicial decision requires generalization about the nature of the case:

> In principle, I believe, the judge will be required, even in cases where the legislator offers him no handholds other than references to reasonableness, fairness, or good faith, to align his decision with general viewpoints, and to offer a justification of this in his motivation that is not focused entirely on the concrete case in question.[135]

And, again, Wiarda concludes by saying:

> it seems hard to argue with the fact that, in the relationship between the different forms of legal interpretation that have existed in our justice system in the 20th century, developments have occurred that brought with them a shift from more heteronomous to more autonomous forms.[136]

Here, Wiarda also lists the factors that have contributed to the liberalization of the legal-interpretation process:

1. The *doctrine* (a factor Wiarda views as the "ringleader" of the liberalization process)
2. The *judiciary* (which pointed to an orientation toward societal needs, reasonableness, and fairness)
3. The *legislature* (because it left more and more up to the judge).[137]

European and international law

The fifth chapter of *Three Types* again opens with Wiarda's characterization of "the shift from more heteronomous to more autonomous forms of

---

134 Ibid., p. 32. See: Georg Cohn, *Existentialismus und Rechtswissenschaft*, Basel: Kommissionsverlag Helbig & Lichtenhahn 1955. And also: Alfred Verdross, *Abendländische Rechtsphilosophie: ihre Grundlagen und Hauptprobleme in geschichtlicher Schau, Zweite erweiterte und neubearbeitete Auflage*, Wien: Springer Verlag 1963 (1958), p. 234: "*Georg Cohn versucht aus dem Existentialismus auch praktische Folgerungen für den Einzelfall abzuleiten, da er meint, dass die gerichtlichen Entscheidungen nicht auf allgemeinen Normen beruhen, sondern sich nur aus existentiellen Entscheidung im Einzelfall ergeben.*"
135 Wiarda, *Drie typen van rechtsvinding*, p. 32.
136 Ibid., p. 34.
137 Ibid.

legal interpretation," in which he once again describes the "influence of doctrine, the judiciary, the legislature, and European law."[138] Wiarda uses the same descriptive approach with a sympathetic undertone, only this time the emphasis is on the developments in European and international law. "The development of European law," Wiarda believes, has "had a profound influence."[139]

This is indeed an important issue, and it is also a point on which the legal-interpretation discussion in the United States and that in the Netherlands and the rest of Europe differ. The United States is an important point of comparison with Europe because the United States also has a Supreme Court that can review laws against the Constitution. In the United States, however, the discussion only relates to *national* constitutional review. This national review of laws against the national Constitution is impossible in the Netherlands due to the prohibition against judicial review against the Constitution. Since, on the basis of articles 93 and 94 of the Constitution, review *is* possible against treaty provisions binding on all, it is important to include the international and European dimensions in this discussion. This, Wiarda does. He writes:

> Here, I am thinking particularly of European Community law, of the treaties that relate to fundamental rights—and of these, particularly of the ECHR [European Convention on Human Rights]—and, more generally, of the task of shaping the law the judge derives from the effect of articles 93 and 94 of the Constitution.[140]

This passage contains a number of ambiguities, suggestive ambiguities in fact, that deserve some closer attention. Of course, Wiarda is entirely correct in saying that articles 93 and 94 made it possible for national laws to be reviewed against, among other provisions, the fundamental rights of the ECHR. But some apparently believe that articles 93 and 94 legitimize the judge not only to *apply* the law but also to *shape* it. Wiarda is one of these people. This reading, however, is tendentious, or more carefully put, not self-evident. Articles 93 and 94 say no more than that the judge can review laws, including laws in the formal sense, against treaty provisions that are binding on all. These articles contain no encouragement to do this in an "activist" way, meaning to get ahead of a consensus for which the legislature and society were not yet ready.

Wiarda joins a consensus with regard to the literature as well. He observes that, when it comes to doctrine, the twentieth century has seen an increasing

---

138 Ibid.
139 Ibid.
140 Ibid., p. 35.

flow of publications dedicated to the relationship between the judge and the law. "The main trend of this literature, of which I will only highlight a few salient points here, essentially comes down to a plea for more judicial freedom, at least in private law, on which this literature was primarily focused."[141]

So, yet another reference to consensus. But Wiarda makes a second point, one that, once again, does not tempt him to further reflection: this literature about legal interpretation was related to private law. And the views about legal interpretation that developed in relation to private law were consequently extensively applied to other areas of law as well, such as public law in general and criminal law too. But is that a good thing? Is, for instance, "a plea for more judicial freedom" in *criminal law* compatible with the constitutional ideal of the principle of legality?[142] Is it not problematic to convict someone on the basis of legal provisions whose content cannot be clearly established beforehand? Should criminal law scholars not have been warier about the "private-lawification" of the legal domain?

Interpretation methods

The discussion about less or more judicial freedom is, of course, closely related to the discussion about desirable methods in the process of legal interpretation. Wiarda touches on that discussion, but he does not really engage with it. He again observes a "clear shift."[143] This is a shift

> from interpretation methods in which only the linguistic meaning of the law's wording or the intention of the legislator is sought to methods in which the quest for the spirit of the law and its underlying reasons and principles are held up as the basis for extensive interpretation, analogy, and legal refinement, or supplementation or legal gaps.[144]

The word "only" as an introduction to linguistic meaning and the legislator's intent speaks volumes. Wiarda does not believe in it. But he does not offer arguments for this. Interpretation methods that favor the "spirit of the law" and its "underlying reasons" have his preference, just like interpretation methods that focus primarily on "principles." How judges can prevent the projection of their own views into the law, he also does not fully address.

---

141 Ibid.
142 Volker Krey, *Keine Strafe ohne Gesetz. Einführung in die Dogmengeschichte des Satzes "nullum crimen, nulla poena sine lege"*, Berlin, New York: Walter de Gruyter 1983.
143 Wiarda, *Drie typen van rechtsvinding*, p. 36.
144 Ibid.

Another important element in the liberalization of the legal-interpretation process were the developments in European law, according to Wiarda:

> As a result of articles 93 and 94 of the Constitution, the Dutch judge is meant to include not only domestic law in his decisions, but also treaty provisions and the decisions of international bodies whose content is applicable to all, giving them priority over the provisions of Dutch law where necessary.[145]

The result of this is: "The international provisions have a direct effect on the Dutch legal system, and they have priority within it."[146] In the case of European Community law, this is even truer. "European Community law must be assumed to possess this effect in and of itself."[147] Why? Because the Court of Justice of the European Communities has always been of the opinion, Wiarda says

> that provisions of the EC treaty and the regulations and guidelines based on them that are suited to it by their nature must be applied directly by the national courts, and that they have priority over national legal rules in the case of conflict.[148]

For legal interpretation, this means that a Dutch judge will apply European Community law regulations and provisions from the ECHR as they are applied by the Court of Justice of the EC and the European Court of Human Rights. The consequences of this for the methods of legal interpretation are threefold, Wiarda says:

1. The diminished significance of the law as a source of justice
2. A more frequent appeal to general legal principles
3. A growing confidence in the judge's own creativity.[149]

What Wiarda means by this last point, the "growing confidence in the judge's own creativity [his own words]," his book does not make clear. Does Wiarda mean:

1. That he personally (i.e., Wiarda) is of the opinion that confidence in the creativity of the judge is warranted?
2. Or that he thinks that many others have confidence in the judge's own creativity?

145 Ibid., p. 51.
146 Ibid.
147 Ibid.
148 Ibid.
149 Ibid., p. 53.

Also intriguing is the word "growing." This seems to imply that this confidence in the judge's own creativity was lacking before, and this has now changed. It begs the question: *why* was there less confidence in the judge before? Did people in the past have arguments for this? If so, what were they? Can Wiarda and those who agree with him that the judge is given confidence defeat these arguments?

The word "creativity" also deserves some attention. Why creativity? Is this meant to convey that those who take a critical view of the liberalization of the legal-interpretation process do this on the basis of their lack of confidence in the judge's creativity? This would mean that the critics of judicial autonomy are drawing on a *psychological theory*: the judge is not creative enough. If only judges were more creative, legal-interpretation theory would be fine. In that case, the revolution that has taken place in legal-interpretation theory (presented by Wiarda largely as an *evolution*) is a revolution of changing insights about the role of the psyche of the most important actors in this process: judges. Is this convincing?

Doubts are not unreasonable on this score, especially because other factors that have contributed to judicial liberalization are perhaps more convincing as the main causes of this process. The movement toward a liberalization of constraint by the law was mostly started by the "European courts," Wiarda says.[150] They "have set the tone for a method of legal interpretation in which an appeal to general legal principles has come to occupy an important place."[151] The ECHR also played a significant role in this. After all, the Convention contains very general provisions that must be interpreted. This interpretation is the job of the judge.[152] But the role of the judge has come even more to the fore in EC law. Why?

> Because there, the Court (i.e., European Court of Justice in Luxembourg, PC, AE, BR) was faced with the necessity of developing a legal system ("the law" of article 164), when there were few handholds for this in the European treaties themselves.[153]

Judicial activism[154] (a term Wiarda does not use, incidentally) is not something Wiarda opposes. This can be deduced from the fact that, when he

---

150 See for a monograph in which this process is described: Karen Alter, *Establishing the Supremacy of European Law: The Making of an International Rule of Law in Europe*, Oxford: Oxford University Press 2001.
151 Wiarda, *Drie typen van rechtsvinding*, p. 54.
152 Ibid.
153 Ibid., p. 55.
154 M. Scheltema, "Wie stelt de wet: de wetgever of de rechter?," in: P. van Dijk, ed., *De relatie tussen wetgever en rechter in een tijd van rechterlijk activisme*, Amsterdam: Koninklijke Nederlandse Akademie van Wetenschappen 1989, pp. 85–94; C.M. Zoethout,

discusses the explanation of the ECHR, he posits that the terms in the ECHR "can acquire a different meaning" over time. As an example, he points to the Marckx case (1979), named for Paula Marckx (1925–2020), which dealt with the application of the equality principle to the distinction between legitimate and illegitimate children in Belgian inheritance law.[155] The European Court in Strasbourg reasoned that this distinction had been generally accepted when the treaty was signed, but that it no longer was today. What should today's judges do? This is interpretation "in the light of present-day conditions."[156]

So, does Wiarda have no problem at all with the development toward more and more liberalization? It seems not, although he does also object to the "Einzelfallgerechtigkeit" of authors like Georg Cohn. Nevertheless, his descriptions constantly summon the image of the liberalization of the legal-interpretation process, and every time Wiarda's accommodating attitude toward this shines through.

Wiarda's cautious reservations about the liberalization process

Nevertheless, in chapter 8 of *Three Types*, Wiarda shares "some reservations" about the liberalizations. He begins this chapter with the claim that the "development" he has described has "taken us far away from Montesquieu's 'république,' in which judges are merely mouthpieces of the law."[157] It is a telling passage due to the vagueness of what the author is trying to say. What does it mean to say that a description has taken us "far away" from a certain model (in this case Montesquieu's)? Is it a good thing that we have moved away from a particular model? Or not? We know, on the basis of everything previously discussed, that Wiarda considers it a good thing. At least, he seems to think it out of touch to resist it. Is it perhaps the case that he thinks it does not matter how we feel about it because the liberalization is an unstoppable process in any case? One to which all resistance is futile? It is all possible, but the author does not provide any clarity on this score.

To the observation that we have moved "far away" from Montesquieu's model, Wiarda then attaches the remarkable addition that we sometimes think ourselves to be "on the edge of 'la Turquie', de 'état despotique'," a

---

"Rethinking Adjudication under the European Convention," in: Jeroen Temperman, ed., *The Lautsi Papers: Multidisciplinary Reflections on Religious Symbols in the Public School Classroom*, Leiden: Martinus Nijhoff Publishers 2012, pp. 413–427.

155 See about the case's backstory: Elisabeth Matthys, "Paula Marckx," in: Dirk Verhofstadt, ed., *Beroemde feministes: de strijd voor vrouwenrechten*, Antwerp/Amsterdam: Houtekiet 2019, pp. 199–211.

156 Wiarda, *Drie typen van rechtsvinding*, p. 57.

157 Ibid., p. 77.

state in which there were no laws, and in which the judge was "lui-même sa règle."[158] Here, it suddenly turns out that Wiarda does seem to be aware of the objections that can be made against his tolerant description of the liberalization process of legal interpretation. He even says: "Of course, the described—possibly inescapable—development has its downsides, and so it does not seem inappropriate to place a warning sign before passage across this 'Turkish' border."[159] This is a remarkable passage because it reveals a number of things.

First, it shows that even Wiarda realizes that he is describing a development. Strictly speaking, this says nothing about the desirability of this development.

A second remarkable point here is that Wiarda posits that this development is "possibly inescapable." Why would that be the case? If a development is bad, could it not be averted? Could we not reflect on a relationship between the legislator and the judge that is better suited to the model of the democratic constitutional state (G. *Demokratische Rechtsstaat*)? Why would the developments Wiarda describes be "inescapable"? This skepticism seems all the more justified because Wiarda himself brings up Turkey, in front of which we ought to put up a warning sign. At least, in his very careful wording, it would not be inappropriate to put up such a sign. Are we to take from this that he considers it *appropriate* to put up the sign? That, perhaps, it is imperative that we do so? Then why does Wiarda not do this? He was one of the most important jurists of his time. Why does he jump on the developments' bandwagon for no other reason than that they seem "inescapable"? Were they perhaps inescapable merely because the best jurists of the post-War generation neglected to take action? Inadvertently, the words of Edmund Burke come to mind: "The only thing necessary for the triumph of evil is for good men to do nothing."[160]

Whatever the case may be, Wiarda feels obligated, despite his tolerant description of the liberalization, to formulate some objections to the development he has discussed.

As a first reservation about a "free judiciary," Wiarda points to the "dangers of arbitrariness and legal uncertainty resulting from the unpredictability of what the judge who is not bound to fixed and generally knowable norms will decide."[161]

As a second reservation, he brings up that, in his role as "substitute legislator," the judge does not have the tools the real legislator has access to

158 Ibid.
159 Ibid.
160 In a letter addressed to Thomas Mercer, www.openculture.com/2016/03/edmund-burke-on-in-action.html.
161 Wiarda, *Drie typen van rechtsvinding*, p. 77.

when preparing the legislative proposal. For instance, the legislator can consult with experts and examine the problem from every angle. A civil judge, however, is restricted to what the parties to the case bring to bear.[162]

As a third reservation, Wiarda asks (a question he characterizes as falling within in the "constitutional domain") if the judge derives his authority "especially from the law."[163] The risk factor being that, if the judge no longer follows that law, his authority might diminish. Wiarda formulates it like this: "Does the judge not derive his authority particularly from the law, and will this authority not wane if he increasingly detaches himself from the legal system?"[164]

Although this shows that Wiarda is not entirely blind to the objections that can be made to the liberalization of the legal-interpretation process, his reservations are not very impressively formulated.

Let us take a somewhat closer look at three of Wiarda's points here than Wiarda does himself.

The unpredictability of the judicial verdict

The first point is about something that has come up before in this book when we discussed American realism. They were critical of the fact that the judge's verdict was unpredictable because it left so much room for judicial discretion that no one can predict how it will turn out. Jerome Frank phrased this critique very sharply when he said that a "right" is nothing more than a "law-suit won."[165]

As the American jurist and legal philosopher Lon Fuller understood well, such a thing can never be accepted. Characteristic of the law is an "inner ethic," in which predictability plays a significant role. That is why the law cannot apply retroactively. It should not make impossible demands of us. The law must be sufficiently clear so that its subjects understand the demands that are made of them.[166]

Not a real legislator

A second point is that Wiarda addresses *en passant* is the fact that the judge may have been called a "substitute legislator" by Van den Burg, but he is a

162 Ibid., p. 78.
163 Ibid., p. 79.
164 Ibid.
165 O.W. Holmes, "The Path of the Law," in: *Harvard Law Review*, 1897, also in: Oliver Wendell Holmes, *Collected Legal Papers*, New York: Peter Smith 1952, pp. 167–202; Jerome Frank, *Law and the Modern Mind*, Gloucester, MA: Peter Smith 1970 (1930).
166 Lon L. Fuller, *The Morality of Law*, revised edition, New Haven, London: Yale University Press 1978 (1964).

legislator who does not possess the required tools to function as a *real* legislator. Anyone familiar with the working of the Dutch Senate and House of Representatives can confirm that, before a law is finalized, there are all sorts of opportunities to consult experts and have in-depth discussions about the standards that are elevated to legal status, and that an army of civil servants is involved in the preparation of the law. Should a small group of judges— however dedicated and educated they may be—be free to ignore all this because they have different ideas about what the contents of the law ought to be than the democratically legitimized legislature?

Proponents of judicial review against treaty provisions binding on all and fundamental rights from the Constitution often make it seem as if the incompatibility of a law with higher law can be established more or less unproblematically. As if it is like a mathematical equation that can simply be checked again. First, the House of Representatives solves the equation. That is check 1. Then the Senate works out the equation again. That is check 2. What could be wrong with letting the judge have a third pass at doing the math? That is check 3. What objection could there be against doing the math one final time?

The objection is that a judicial verdict cannot be compared to a mathematical equation. Those without any legal education, people who do not know how the legal-interpretation process works, often base their judgment on the assumption that incompatibility between a law and higher law can be established the way an empirical fact can be established in everyday life. They think a judge can conclude something that previous institutions involved in the matter have apparently "overlooked." But often that is not the case at all. Often, it involves issues that political institutions were also fully aware of, but about which they consciously made a different decision. The question then becomes: can the judge make an entirely different choice simply because he believes the political institutions *should have chosen differently*?

This brings us to a third point Wiarda raises. This is again an important issue that he touches on very briefly, without providing the careful analysis it requires.

The constitutional problem

As a third reservation, Wiarda asks, in an almost Montesquieu-like fashion, if the judge derives his authority "particularly from the law."[167] This is a good question. Wiarda characterizes it as falling within the "constitutional domain," which reveals an important truth. After all, it is constitutional law that deals with the question of what, ultimately, gives the legal system

---

167 Wiarda, *Drie typen van rechtsvinding*, p. 79.

its legitimacy. The way in which Wiarda further develops this question, however, is less convincing, because Wiarda goes on to present this constitutional problem as a risk to the judge: the risk that a judge who does not restrict himself to the law might lose his authority. This is true, of course, but it should not be our main concern. As if the greatest misfortune that can befall us is judges losing their authority. Our greatest problem, perhaps, would be judges not applying the law but more or less retaining their authority because the citizenry does not recognize that they are not doing what Montesquieu's model says they *should do*: apply the law. The central problem is that (a) the judge retains his authority while (b) violating the trust on which that authority is based. It can be phrased as follows: the wider public still believes that the courts are applying the law. The law is the expression of the will of the people. By upholding the rule of law, the people rule over themselves, maintaining a democracy in the true sense of the word (think of the Lincoln quotation shared earlier). But if, contrary to what is claimed, the judge is not actually applying the laws at all, but is prioritizing other standards ("reasonableness," "fairness," or others, but not the law) *the judge deserves* to lose authority. The judge deserves to be evaluated the way we evaluate politicians. In that case, the judge deserves to lose his *a priori* authority, to have it replaced with critical mistrust, skepticism: the kind of skepticism politicians have to deal with.

Perhaps it can also be phrased like this: there is a broadly held skepticism of politicians. This might be partly justified. And it might even not be an entirely bad thing, because a healthy suspicion is essential to a democracy. It keeps politicians and citizens on their toes, which is good for democracy. Such a critical attitude about judges does not yet exist among most of the writers dealing with legal interpretation. Most of them, we ought to repeat. This cannot be said about authors like Antonin Scalia,[168] Raoul Berger,[169] Robert Bork,[170] and Jeremy Waldron[171] to name a few. But they are an exception to the rule. How can this be explained? Do the legal scholars who write about this topic not understand what judges are actually doing? Or do they understand it, but they are not alarmed by it for some reason

---

168 Scalia and Garner, *Reading the Law*; Scalia, "Modernity and the Constitution," pp. 313–318; Scalia, *Scalia Speaks*.
169 Raoul Berger, *Government by Judiciary, The Transformation of the Fourteenth Amendment*, Cambridge, MA, London: Harvard University Press 1977.
170 Robert H. Bork, *Coercing Virtue: The Worldwide Rule of Judges*, Washington, DC: The AEI Press 2003; Robert H. Bork, *Slouching towards Gomorrah: Modern Liberalism and American Decline*, New York: HarperCollins 1996; Robert H. Bork, *The Tempting of America: The Political Seduction of the Law*, London: Sinclair-Stevenson 1990.
171 Jeremy Waldron, "The Core of the Case Against Judicial Review," in: *The Yale Law Journal*, 115(6) (April 2006), pp. 1346–1406, also in: Waldron, *Political Theory*, pp. 195–246.

or other? If so, why not? Do legal scholars identify themselves more with judges than with politicians? Do they think "it is better to entrust judges with decision-making power because they are people like us"? And do they perhaps think: "politicians ought to get as little power as possible because they are the 'others'"?

The citizens, in any case, believe that the judges are, in accordance with Montesquieu's model, applying the laws. On the basis of this belief, judges deserve authority, and they get it. Their authority derives from the authority of the law. And the law has authority because it is of the people's own making. A democracy is also about government "by the people," as Lincoln said. But reading *Three Types of Legal Method* should shatter the citizens' illusion, making clear to them that leading jurists have very different opinions about this legal-interpretation process. This apology for judicial freedom from proponents of an ever-increasing liberalization of the legal-interpretation process ought to worry democratically minded citizens. Citizens who take what the book says seriously ought to think: "so judges are apparently not doing what they were trained to do." According to Wiarda, this is the case because there is an inescapable development in legal interpretation going on, one that he merely describes without furnishing this inescapability with arguments.

So, the constitutional dimension of this discussion is only addressed indirectly by Wiarda. He does this, for instance, by referring to the discussion in Germany about the power of the Bundesverfassungsbericht. Wiarda refers to the book *Vom Gesetzesstaat zum Richtersstaat* (1957) by René Marcic (1919–1971).[172] Wiarda phrases it as follows:

> In Germany, the constitutional court made a profound intervention in the formation of law by measuring the constitutionality of laws against its own views on fairly vague constitutional phrases like "Würde des Menschen," "freie Entfaltung der Persönlichkeit," "freiheitliche demokratische Grundordnung," and "Sozialstaat."[173]

Wiarda does not explore this point further, but it is worth taking a moment to consider the terms presented here. "Human dignity" is a good starting point for the preamble to a constitution.[174] But it is not something against which laws ought to be reviewed.[175] The "free development of personality"

---

172 René Marcic, *Vom Gesetzesstaat zum Richterstaat: Recht als Maß der Macht*, Vienna: Springer Verlag 2012 (1957).
173 Wiarda, *Drie typen van rechtsvinding*, p. 80.
174 P.B. Cliteur and W.J.M. Voermans, *Preambules*, Alphen aan den Rijn: Kluwer 2009.
175 See on the concept of value: Ferdinand von Schirach, *Die Würde ist antastbar: Essays*, Munich: Verlagsgruppe Random House 2017; Bernhard Giese, *Das Würde-Konzept*, Berlin: Duncker & Humblot 1975.

is a praiseworthy moral ideal, but if we allowed the laws that—in the Dutch case—150 members of parliament and 75 senators passed to be invalidated because a court of a few judges believes that the "free development of personality" is not optimally protected, it would mean the end of the democracy and the beginning of an oligarchy. The objections shared here are *a fortiori* true with regard to "Sozialstaat." A social state or a social constitutional state is a political concept.

But, of course, Wiarda does not phrase it as pointedly as it is done here. In his commentary on the title of Marcic's book, Wiarda notes that he believes it will not come to that in the Netherlands. He writes that he thinks it an "exaggeration" to characterize the Dutch developments as a shift from "Gesetzesstaat" to "Richtersstaat."[176] After all, the German situation "is not entirely comparable to ours." This is true in the sense that the German Bundesverfassungsgericht has powers the Dutch Supreme Court does not. The Bundesverfassungsgericht has the ability to review laws against the German Constitution. But what Wiarda neglects to mention is that we should not be making a comparison between the Bundesverfassungsgericht and the Dutch Supreme Court, but between the Bundesverfassungsgericht and the European Court of Justice in Luxembourg or the European Court of Human Rights in Strasbourg. And of these courts, Wiarda had argued that they have far-reaching authority to review national legislation (Dutch legislation, therefore) against fairly vague provisions in international treaties. This gives judges in Strasbourg and Brussels decision-making powers that are equal to that of the American Supreme Court or the German Bundesverfassungsgericht. Perhaps, therefore, Marcic made a sharper analysis of the case than Wiarda. Wiarda's comforting words that the Dutch situation cannot be compared with what Marcic describes are therefore hardly convincing.

Equally unconvincing is what Wiarda writes about the position of the Dutch judge in Dutch constitutional law. Wiarda writes: "In Dutch constitutional law, the judge has a politically neutral and fully independent position; he is not accountable to any other organ of state, including the Parliament, about how he fulfils his role." He continues with: "This independence is necessary as a safeguard to the complete impartiality inherent to the judicial function."[177] In a footnote, Wiarda adds that the judge does not have a "political agenda," as Royer argued at his retirement as president of the Dutch Supreme Court.[178]

These are, again, confusing considerations Wiarda offers, and not very convincing proof of the claim he wishes to make. The fact that a president

---

176 Wiarda, *Drie typen van rechtsvinding*, p. 80.
177 Ibid., p. 81.
178 Ibid. See on Royer, NJB 1996, p. 1574.

of the Supreme Court *said* at his retirement that the Supreme Court has no political agenda tells us nothing more than that at least one Dutch judge is apparently unaware of political *bias*.[179] The statement that the judge has a completely independent position is only reassuring to those who are also convinced that he judges in a politically neutral way. In fact, it is particularly the combination of complete independence with an attitude that is not politically neutral that poses a problem. Here, Wiarda seems captivated by an assumption that is common among participants in the debate about the independence and impartiality of the judiciary: that impartiality will naturally follow if only the judge is independent. Independence is viewed as a *sufficient condition* for impartiality. This is a fragile assumption. It is better to view independence as a *necessary condition*. This means that in order to maximize the likelihood of the impartiality of judicial verdicts, it is best to make the judge independent in the constitutional-organizational sense. But doing so does not absolutely guarantee impartiality. This impartiality also depends on the way in which the judge perceives his own role. A judge will have to be conscious of his job in the constitutional system, and that is that he *applies the laws*. Not that he judges them.

This final element does not receive enough attention from Wiarda. And in this, his work is representative of the main thrust of Dutch legal-interpretation theory. These writers trust that the judicial verdict will be impartial as long as constitutional independence is optimally realized. In combination with this, there is a plea for more and more judicial freedom (irrespective of whether it is presented as inescapable), thereby in effect undermining the safeguards for judicial independence. In the case of an activist judiciary, more judicial independence only lends support to the view that the judge is "lui-même sa règle."[180] On very rare occasions, even Wiarda seems to realize this, such as in this passage: "This independence is necessary as a safeguard for the complete impartiality that is inherent to the judicial role, although it would grant the judge too much power if he were also free to truly be 'lui-même sa règle.'"[181] Apparently, Wiarda also sees that this completely independent position the judiciary has in our legal system can only be entrusted to the judge "especially because, in the state, he represents the legal order, which is objective in principle."[182] The judge's job is not to indulge certain political, social, or economic preferences, but to play his part "in accordance with the, in principle, so objectively determined standards of the law."[183]

---

179 Research into prejudices and predispositions has received a boost lately with the publication of: Daniel Kahneman, *Thinking Fast and Slow*, London: Penguin Books 2012 (2011).
180 Wiarda, *Drie typen van rechtsvinding*, p. 81.
181 Ibid.
182 Ibid.
183 Ibid.

This brings us back to the beginning of *Three Types*, in which the three forms of legal interpretation were discussed in combination with Montesquieu's forms of government. Is Montesquieu's model not a much better basis for independence and impartiality than the picture painted by Wiarda? Wiarda wants to uphold independence and impartiality, but all the developments he describes, developments he believes are inescapable, seem to point in the opposite direction. Wiarda even goes so far as to *acknowledge* that the democratic legitimation of the judicial verdict is weak. But he thinks he can compensate for this with a "gain" in constitutionality. He writes: "In that sense, it is possible to say that judges' action might lack a democratic legitimation, but it is legitimized by the constitutional idea."[184] Wiarda does not fully explain what he means by this, but for those who have closely tracked the path of his argument, it is clear nonetheless. As a result of the developments Wiarda has extensively described, the judicial verdict is not democratically legitimized. What he does not mention, however, is that it could have been. A judge who orients himself toward the law makes democratically legitimized decisions. At least if the law came about through a democratic process. But there is probably no point in speculating about this for Wiarda because he considers the process of liberalization, the development from heteronomy to autonomy, to be inescapable. It *is simply the case* that the Court of Justice created an entirely new legal order. It *is simply the case* that articles 93 and 94 of the Constitution give the European judge in Strasbourg the authority to act as a substitute legislator. As such, Wiarda considers this a starting point of his reflections that does not need to be further debated. It is only possible, perhaps, to minimize the consequences of this democratic deficit, to compensate them with something else. And that is how we arrive at the *compensation factor*. The judge might not be able to deliver when it comes to democracy, but he might be able to do so in the area of constitutionalism. Judges' decisions are constitutional, not democratic. But Wiarda also tries to minimize the democratic deficit by insisting that, although judges are allowed to go along with the legal-interpretation liberalization process, they should not go too far in this. This can be seen in the fourth reservation he offers in his description of the development from heteronomy to autonomy.

This fourth reservation is remarkable because, although it takes the same descriptive form that characterizes *Three Types*, it nevertheless contains a norm. Wiarda says that a fourth objection can be made against free legal interpretation. He phrases it as follows:

As a politically independent and strictly impartial body, one that has no interest but to uphold the legal order, the judge is expected to disregard

184 Ibid.

as much as possible not only his own interests, but also his politically, socially, and economically determined preferences in deciding his verdict.[185]

Wiarda phrases it descriptively: "the judge is expected to." But it is clear that he expects this as well. He encourages the judge to disregard his political, social, and economic preferences as much as possible.[186] It is unclear how this is possible in the context of the development toward autonomy Wiarda describes so approvingly, but he nevertheless holds up this ideal as a norm.

In a subsequent chapter, he also tries to advise the legislator to constrain the judge's autonomy. The legislator has to be as concrete as possible about the norms he sets. The legislator should not be "too quick" to resort to vague norm descriptions.[187] But Wiarda does not seem too confident about his own advice, because it "is foreseeable that the circumstances that caused the increase in vague norm descriptions will remain operable in the same direction in the future."[188] So here we again find the general sanguinity that characterizes the entire book. Wiarda describes a process, considers it to be inevitable, and then makes the leap to the normative: the way things are going is good.

This brings us to an important issue. Is *Three Types of Legal Method* not based on what is called the "naturalistic fallacy"? Is its author not guilty of mixing up "Sein" and "Sollen"? This brings us to another important Enlightenment philosopher (besides Montesquieu): David Hume.

Hume's warning that we cannot deduce norms from facts

These are the notorious passages from Hume. The volume of what has been written about them could fill whole libraries. The question is whether norms can be deduced from facts. This is also the basis for a centuries-long feud between two schools of legal philosophy: natural law thinking and legal positivism.[189] The proponent of natural law thinking posits that facts and

185 Ibid.
186 Ibid.
187 Ibid., p. 83.
188 Ibid.
189 Paul Cliteur and Afshin Ellian, "Legality and Legitimacy in Natural Law and Legal Positivism," in: Paul Cliteur and Afshin Ellian, *A New Introduction to Jurisprudence: Legality, Legitimacy, and the Foundations of the Law*, London, New York: Routledge 2019, pp. 1–36; P.B. Cliteur, "The American Conservatives, Edmund Burke and Natural Law," in: *Archiv für Rechts- und Sozialphilosophie*, 1988 (LXXIV)/Heft 4, 4. Quartal, pp. 452–460; Robert P. George, "Natural Law and Civil Rights," in: Robert P. George, *The Clash of Orthodoxies. Law, Religion, and Morality in Crisis*, Wilmington, DE: ISI Books 2001, pp. 153–169; Charles Grove Haines, *The Revival of Natural Law Concepts: A Study of*

norms, *is* and *ought*, cannot be so easily separated.[190] To the legal positivist, a clear distinction between these two things is the ABC of legal-scientific rigor. Never confuse the facts with the norm, a legal positivist would say.[191] Hume is the father of the legal-positivist methodology, as the following quotations from his work will demonstrate.

> In every system of morality, which I have hitherto met with, I have always remarked, that the author proceeds for some time in the ordinary ways of reasoning, and establishes the being of a God, or makes observations concerning human affairs; when all of a sudden I am surprised to find, that instead of the usual copulations of propositions, is, and is not, I meet with no proposition that is not connected with an ought, or an ought not. This change is imperceptible; but is however, of the last consequence ...
>
> For as this ought, or ought not, expresses some new relation or affirmation, 'tis necessary that it should be observed and explained; and at the same time that a reason should be given, for what seems altogether inconceivable, how this new relation can be a deduction from others, which are entirely different from it ...
>
> But as authors do not commonly use this precaution, I shall presume to recommend it to the readers; and am persuaded, that this small attention would subvert all the vulgar systems of morality, and let us see, that the distinction of vice and virtue is not founded merely on the relations of objects, nor is perceived by reason.[192]

It is a relief, after the bureaucratic and—let us be honest—fairly dry prose that characterizes many legal writings in the Netherlands (not in Great Britain!), to read a great stylist. Hume begins by expressing his surprise at seeing a particular transition in books that goes unnoticed. These authors Hume subtly criticizes start with the facts of a situation ("establishes," "observations"), only to transition "all of a sudden" to what "ought" to or "ought not" happen. It occurs subtly ("this change is imperceptible"), Hume says. But it has big consequences.

---

the Establishment and the Interpretation of Limits on Legislatures with Special Reference to the Development of Certain Phases of American Constitutional Law, New York: Russell & Russell Inc. 1965 (1958).

190 H.L.A. Hart, "Positivism and the Separation of Law and Morals," in: *Harvard Law Review*, 71 (1958), pp. 593–629.

191 Hans Kelsen, *Reine Rechtslehre, Mit einem Anhang: Das Problem der Gerechtigkeit, Zweite vollständig neu bearbeitete und erweiterte Auflage 1960, Unveränderter Nachdruck 1976*, Vienna: Verlag Franz Deuticke 1976.

192 David Hume, *A Treatise of Human Nature*, London: John Noon 1739, p. 335.

This is a sharp observation. It was this passage, therefore, that inspired our discussion of Wiarda's argument. And it is also why we spent so much time analyzing Wiarda's wording. After all, Wiarda too silently moves from description to the setting of norms. Oftentimes, also, it is hard to *determine* whether he is describing or proscribing something. Perhaps the author does not always know this himself, or maybe he sometimes has doubts about it.

Hume, however, has no patience for ambiguity on this score. Every writer ought to be clear about what he is doing: is he describing or is he prescribing? Someone who seeks to argue for a normative claim cannot simply establish that something is the case.

This sounds obvious at first glance. It seems almost unbelievable that a great philosopher such as Hume would say it, it sounds so trivial. But Hume points out that the consequences of acknowledging the distinction are far-reaching because applying the distinction would change the very nature of many moral systems ("subvert all the vulgar systems of morality").

A counterweight to Wiarda's views on legal interpretation

We do seem to find some resistance to the increasing autonomy of legal judgment in an article by the criminal-law scholar Klaas Rozemond. Rozemond writes about the "linguistic interpretation method," also known as "grammatical interpretation." When we translate this to terminology commonly used in the Anglo-Saxon world, we could call it "textualism." A focus on the text ought to take precedence.

"The linguistic interpretation method prescribes that all terms in a legal provision ought to be given meaning in relation to the cases in which the provision is applied," Rozemond writes.[193] He points out that one of the basic principles of criminal law is that "people have to be in a position to know beforehand which behaviors are illegal and what punitive measures the government may apply."[194] The outcome of criminal procedures must also be unambiguously established. After all is said and done, suspects have to know "what they're facing."[195]

In addition, a legal provision has to be explained before it can be applied. Rozemond concludes, however, that judges have a tendency to reach for interpretation methods other than the grammatical. But that is a trend about which he gives warning. The literal meaning of a legal provision ought to be given a little more consideration, he believes. It is important to decide what the literal meaning of a legal provision is "before other legal-interpretation

---

193 Klaas Rozemond, "De betekenis van taal in het strafrecht," in: *Ars Aequi*, July/August 2015, pp. 624–631.
194 Ibid., p. 624.
195 Ibid.

methods are applied."[196] In practical terms, what he suggests comes down to the judge going through the components of a legal provision and "discerning the meaning of those components in and of themselves and in connection with one another before applying other methods."[197]

To illustrate his views on interpretation, Rozemond refers to a famous Dutch case, the so-called "Electricity Case" (1921) already mentioned in Chapter 1 in the context of a discussion of the views of Oliver Wendell Holmes.[198] The case involves the dentist who rigged the electricity meter in order to tap electricity without paying for it. Is this "theft?" Dutch law states that in order for a theft to have occurred, a "good" has to have been "appropriated." But is electricity a "good"? And can the rigging of a meter be seen as "appropriating"?

Rozemond argues—in line with legal philosopher C.E. Smith—that in such a case, the judge ought first to look at the literal meaning of the words "good" and "appropriate," so to make a grammatical interpretation, before seeking refuge in other interpretation methods. The approach of a judge who violates this principle is at odds with the *legality principle*.[199] And the legality principle is another prominent tenet of criminal law—it is the principle, in fact, that the Dutch Criminal Code lists first, in Article 1.

In the historic Electricity Case (1921), Rozemond demonstrates, this grammatical interpretation was not applied, and therefore the legality principle was violated. So what did the Dutch Supreme Court do?

> It is notable that the Supreme Court skips the step of linguistic interpretation, moving straight to the teleological method. The linguistic step could consist of the judge discerning the meaning of the provision's wording in the light of ordinary cases from legal practice that anyone can recognize as clear instances of theft.[200]

But that is not what the Court did.

When the Supreme Court decided that electricity could be designated a "good" and the rigging of the meter as "appropriation," it was not able to base this on a literal reading of the legal provision. Is this a problem?

Here we have two opposing views. The first is that of the Advocate General (Besier), who argued that abandoning a literal reading of the text was incorrect in this case. He opposed the "broad interpretation" of art.

---

196 Ibid., p. 625.
197 Ibid.
198 HR 23 May 1921, NJ 1921, 564 (Elektriciteit).
199 Rozemond, "De betekenis van taal in het strafrecht," p. 626.
200 Ibid.

310 Sr., because such an interpretation would be incompatible with art. 1 Sr., in which the legality principle is established.[201]

> In Besier's view, the literal meaning of the wording of the law establishes the perimeters within which the judge must remain, and the meaning of the law cannot be decided "in a figurative sense."[202]

An entirely different view of abandoning a literal reading of the criminal code was held by annotator B.M. Taverne (1874–1944). Just like Besier, Taverne also concluded that the Dutch Supreme Court had not followed the literal reading, although this actually pleased him. He applauded the broad interpretation. "The judge," Rozemond paraphrases Taverne, "ought not only follow the legal text when interpreting the law, but also rule in concordance with 'the people's broadly shared sense of justice.'"[203]

With the latter, Taverne introduced something that would later become infamous as a part of how the Nazis believed the law ought to be interpreted, which was according to the "*Gesundes Volksempfinden*," the healthy "common sense of the people."

In the Nazi ideology, this common sense of the people became a direct source of law, a source that superseded the legal text. In deciding what was and was not legal, it was no longer the view of the legislator, as captured in the text of the law, but the common-sense view held by the people that would win out. All of this comes at the cost of the legality principle, and with it of legal certainty. The principle of *Nulla poena sine lege* (no penalty without law) is essentially abandoned. A state in which this happens on a large scale is no longer a state "under the rule of law," but a state "under the rule of men." The impersonal authority of the law has been replaced by the authority of *people*.

In conclusion

One of the important themes at the beginning of this chapter was the development of the democratic constitutional state. That development was pegged to four central dates. The first was 1648: the establishment of the nation-state as the new form of political organization. Then came 1748: the advent of the separation and balance of powers as an important constitutional principle. Next was 1848: the first rudimentary formulation of the principle of ministerial responsibility, and with it of democracy. Finally, there was 1948: the adoption of the Universal Declaration of Human Rights.

---

201 Ibid., p. 627.
202 Ibid.
203 Ibid.

These four key moments in the development of the democratic constitutional state describe what we "want to be": (1) a state; (2) that is also a constitutional state; (3) and a democracy; (4) in which human rights or fundamental rights are respected.

But balancing these four things correctly is not easy. This chapter focuses mainly on the judiciary's relationship to the legislature, and with it, on two important elements of the separation of powers. Which should have primacy? The democratically legitimized legislator? Or the judge, who is expected to realize the constitutional element of the democratic constitutional state?

In legal-science doctrine, the discussion about the role of the judge mostly emerges in theories about legal interpretation, which form the heart of legal-science methodology. Legal interpretation is about the way in which the judge applies the law (*is*) and about how he should apply it (*ought*).

An important theory is the model that is ascribed to Montesquieu. Montesquieu not only developed the separation of powers, but he also had a view about how the judge ought to fulfill his role: with restraint. He ought to apply the law, but he should adopt a reluctant attitude when it comes to evaluating it.

Although Montesquieu's views about judicial restraint played a role throughout the history of legal-interpretation theory, they came under particular pressure after the Second World War. An influential book on the context and reasons for this is *Three Types of Legal Method* (1963) by G.J. Wiarda. *Three Types* was the central text of Dutch post-War legal-interpretation theory.

But Wiarda did not only summarize for subsequent generations how the legal-interpretation process factually functioned; he also shared how, in his view, it ought to function. Wiarda *described* how the legal-interpretation process was increasingly liberalized, with judges accruing more and more powers, more and more room for discretion, and more and more autonomy. Less and less did they consider themselves bound to the external factor of "the law" (and with it, heteronomy).

We have shown in this chapter that the process Wiarda describes is based on few methodological principles. Wiarda presupposes that the march toward ever-greater judicial discretion is inevitable, but he provides almost no arguments to support this. The development from heteronomy to autonomy is a product of evolution, not of conscious choices.

We have also seen how this development is closely related to Europeanization, in the sense of the gradual transfer of more and more national powers to supranational bodies and organizations.

As Wiarda shows, this also had to do with the power of judicial review of laws against higher law, which meant that the liberalization of the legal-interpretation process went hand in hand with the Europeanization of legal interpretation. By the latter, we mean that supranational bodies such as the

European Court of Human Rights in Strasbourg and the European Court of Justice in Luxembourg began to exert ever-greater influence over legal development, influence which came at the expense of the national parliaments. The legislative power lost ground to the judiciary. Wiarda described this process, but in a sympathetic way. He did not object. He seemed to regard the development from heteronomy to autonomy as inevitable, but perhaps also as desirable. He did touch upon a few objections to this process, but he only barely engaged with them. This makes him representative of the attitude of the post-War generation of jurists in favor of an increasing emphasis on the meaning of the unfettered judicial verdict.

Of course, the question is whether the fairly uncritical acceptance of judicial supremacy will also be continued in the future. An increasing number of critical questions are posed on that score. A relevant name here is the Dutch constitutional scholar E.C. Jurgens, one of the few critics of constitutional review in the Netherlands.[204] Another more or less critical voice was that of the Dutch legal philosopher and constitutional scholar R.A.V. van Haersolte (1919–2002).[205] So critical voices do exist, the critics of judicial review are also present in the Netherlands, but they are in the minority. Jurgens warns against more and more judicial review on the basis of "general policy aims."[206] He gives the following reason: it "would have the judge utterly usurp the position of the legislative and executive powers, causing a true kritarchy."[207] Jurgens uses the term *"dikastocracy"* (government by judges, "gouvernement des juges").[208]

The complaints that already exist about the juridification of public administration through administrative law would increase exponentially, Jurgens writes; we will have the juridification of politics. That will make impossible demands of the judge, Jurgens believes. He warns against the "undermining of the role of the law in society."[209]

Another critic of judicial review against the Constitution was also a constitutional scholar from Amsterdam, and Jurgens' mentor: G. van den Bergh (1890–1966). Van den Bergh made great contributions to the field of "militant democracy."[210] He believed that democracy ought to be protected

204 Jurgens, "Over de illusie dat rechterlijke toetsing van de wet aan onze huidige Grondwet zinvol is," pp. 117–123, p. 121.
205 Cliteur, *Constitutionele toetsing.*
206 Jurgens, "Over de illusie dat rechterlijke toetsing."
207 Ibid.
208 Édouard Lambert, *Le gouvernement des juges et la lutte contre la législation sociale aux États-Unis*, Paris: Giard 1921.
209 Jurgens, "Over de illusie dat rechterlijke toetsing."
210 George van den Bergh, "The Democratic State and the Non-Democratic Parties," in: Paul Cliteur and Amos N. Guiora, *Populist and Islamist Challenges for International Law*, Chicago: American Bar Association 2019, pp. 367–391. See on the concept of militant democracy: A. Ellian and B.R. Rijpkema, eds., *Militant Democracy—Law, Political Sci-*

against parties that seek to abolish it, such as (in his time) the Nazist movements that openly admitted that the only reason they were participating in the democratic process was to win a majority with which they could abolish democracy. Can a consequence of democracy be that such a process is enabled? Van den Bergh thought not.

But van den Bergh was not only critical of political *parties* that might abolish democracy: he was also critical of *judicial bodies* that—due to a misinterpretation of the nature of their role—could undermine democracy. Just like Jurgens, as described earlier, he was critical of constitutional review. After all, constitutional review would enable the judiciary to hollow out the role of the legislature.

It does not need to be pointed out that this line of argumentation, highly relevant to the doctrine of legal methodology, differs fundamentally from Wiarda's. Van den Bergh, who died in 1966, would have seriously objected to the line of argument about legal interpretation that Wiarda would so successfully introduce into the Dutch legal-scholars community in 1963.

ence and Philosophy, Berlin, Heidelberg, New York: Springer Verlag 2018; Paul Cliteur and Bastiaan Rijpkema, "The Foundations of Militant Democracy," in: Afshin Ellian and Gelijn Molier, eds., *The State of Exception and Militant Democracy in a Time of Terror*, Dordrecht: Republic of Letters Publishing 2012, pp. 227–273; Bastiaan Rijpkema, *Militant Democracy*, London, New York: Routledge 2018.

Index

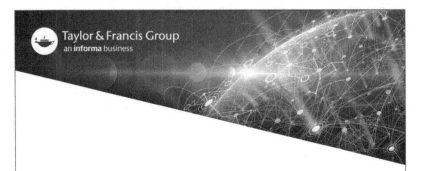